Elisabeth Huber
**Tri-Constituent Compounds**

# Topics in English Linguistics

Editors
Susan M. Fitzmaurice
Bernd Kortmann

## Volume 114

Elisabeth Huber

# Tri-Constituent Compounds

A Usage-Based Account of
Complex Nominal Compounding

**DE GRUYTER**
MOUTON

Zugleich Dissertation an der LMU München im Jahr 2021

ISBN 978-3-11-162920-9
e-ISBN (PDF) 978-3-11-108169-4
e-ISBN (EPUB) 978-3-11-108211-0
ISSN 1434-3452

**Library of Congress Control Number: 2023933707**

**Bibliographic information published by the Deutsche Nationalbibliothek**
The Deutsche Nationalbibliothek lists this publication in the Deutsche Nationalbibliografie; detailed bibliographic data are available on the Internet at http://dnb.dnb.de.

© 2024 Walter de Gruyter GmbH, Berlin/Boston
This volume is text- and page-identical with the hardback published in 2023.
Typesetting: Integra Software Services Pvt. Ltd.

www.degruyter.com

# Contents

**List of figures and tables —— IX**

**Abbreviations —— XI**

1        Introduction —— 1

## Part I: Theoretical Prerequisites

2        **Compounds and Compounding —— 5**
2.1        What is a compound? —— 6
2.2        Compound features —— 7
2.3        Delimitation of compounding —— 10

3        **Multi-word compounding —— 12**
3.1        Coverage in literature —— 12
3.2        Research focus and terminology —— 15

## Part II: Data acquisition and annotation

4        **Compilation of a compound database —— 19**
4.1        Corpus data used in this project —— 19
4.2        Data retrieval —— 20
4.2.1        Recall of noun sequences —— 21
4.2.2        Finding compounds within compounds —— 23
4.2.3        Improving precision with regard to form —— 26
4.2.4        Improving precision with regard to meaning —— 29
4.2.5        Lemmatization —— 31
4.3        Results and discussion —— 32

5        **Annotation of internal structure —— 35**
5.1        Determining the branching pattern —— 36
5.1.1        Criteria suggested in other approaches —— 36
5.1.2        Critical evaluation of the criteria —— 38
5.1.3        Discussion of the value of paraphrasing —— 40
5.1.4        Compounds with unclear internal structure —— 43
5.1.5        Summary and conclusion —— 48
5.2        Automated assignment of branching pattern —— 50

| 5.2.1 | Choice of criteria —— 50 |
| 5.2.2 | Operationalization —— 51 |
| 5.2.3 | Results and discussion —— 53 |

## Part III: Formal and functional description of three-noun compounds

**6  Formal analysis of three-noun compounds —— 59**
6.1  How complex are three-noun compounds formally? —— 60
6.1.1  Length of compounds and constituents —— 60
6.1.2  Morphological complexity —— 63
6.1.3  Conclusion —— 67
6.2  Do left- and right-branching compounds differ formally? —— 67
6.2.1  Length of compounds and constituents —— 68
6.2.2  Morphological complexity —— 70
6.2.3  Conclusion —— 72
6.3  Orthographic aspects of complex compounds —— 72
6.3.1  How could spelling be related to morphological structure? —— 73
6.3.2  Which spelling formats are established in three-noun compounding? —— 76
6.3.3  Is there within-type variation? —— 79
6.4  Stress in complex compounds —— 85
6.4.1  Are complex compounds stressed like simple compounds? —— 85
6.4.2  Does stress differ with regard to morphological structure? —— 88
6.5  Summary and conclusion —— 91

**7  Functional analysis of three-noun compounds —— 93**
7.1  General semantic categorization —— 93
7.2  To what extent are three-noun compounds used? —— 95
7.3  Are left-branching compounds more frequent than right-branching ones? —— 101
7.4  Do right-branching compounds require special kinds of heads? —— 104
7.5  Do simple and complex modifiers differ in quality? —— 106
7.6  Which areas of discourse are three-noun compounds used in? —— 110
7.7  What semantic areas do three-noun compounds come from? —— 114
7.8  How compositional are three-noun compounds? —— 118
7.9  Do compositional three-noun compounds compete with syntactic phrases? —— 125

| 7.9.1 | Which syntactic phrases exist as alternatives to three-noun compounds? —— **126** |
|---|---|
| 7.9.2 | Are the phrases competitors to the compounds? —— **131** |
| 7.9.3 | Is there any systematicity in the usage of compounds and phrases? —— **134** |
| 7.9.4 | Which three-noun compounds show variation? —— **137** |
| 7.9.5 | Conclusion and discussion —— **138** |
| 7.10 | Summary and conclusion —— **139** |

## Part IV: **The formation of tri-constituent compounds**

| 8 | **Productivity in complex compounding** —— **145** |
|---|---|
| 8.1 | The concept of morphological productivity —— **145** |
| 8.2 | Are some compounds more productive than others? —— **148** |
| 8.3 | Are compounds used as heads and modifiers equally? —— **157** |
| 8.4 | Can productivity be specified semantically? —— **167** |
| 8.5 | What distinguishes productive compounds from unproductive ones? —— **177** |
| 8.5.1 | Formal complexity —— **178** |
| 8.5.2 | Frequency —— **181** |
| 8.5.3 | Association strength —— **183** |
| 8.5.4 | Summary and implications —— **192** |
| 8.6 | Why are some compounds used more productively than others? —— **193** |
| 8.6.1 | The idea of entrenchment —— **193** |
| 8.6.2 | Approaching entrenchment through corpus data —— **197** |
| 8.6.3 | Entrenchment processes on complex elements —— **203** |
| 8.6.4 | Relevance of entrenchment for compound productivity —— **210** |
| 8.6.5 | Conclusion and discussion —— **212** |
| 8.7 | How is knowledge of compound productivity stored cognitively? —— **215** |
| 8.7.1 | Schematization over variable patterns —— **216** |
| 8.7.2 | Schematization in the formation of complex compounds —— **219** |
| 8.7.3 | What about more abstract types of representation? —— **227** |
| 8.8 | Which three-noun compounds are likely to be formed? —— **230** |
| 8.9 | Summary and conclusions —— **234** |

## Part V: Synopsis

9 **A portrait of three-noun compounds** —— 239

10 **Summary and conclusions** —— 243

11 **Outlook** —— 247

**References** —— 251

**Subject index** —— 259

# List of figures and tables

## Figures

**Figure 1**  Working mechanism used to identify 3N within 2N —— 24
**Figure 2**  Variants to be found and lemmatized for *credit card company* —— 32
**Figure 3**  Branching patterns in tripartite nominal compounds —— 35
**Figure 4**  Morphological structures for *children's bookstore* —— 41
**Figure 5**  Potential morphological structures for four-constituent compounds —— 49
**Figure 6**  Mapping between orthography and internal structure of 3N —— 75
**Figure 7**  Distribution of stress points in left- and right-branching 3N —— 89
**Figure 8**  Most frequent types of three-noun compounds —— 99
**Figure 9**  Relationship between branching patterns across frequency ranges —— 101
**Figure 10**  Token frequencies of most frequent left- and right-branching 3N —— 103
**Figure 11**  Distribution of 3N tokens among registers —— 111
**Figure 12**  Semantic fields established by the USAS —— 115
**Figure 13**  Categorization of semantic areas denoted by 3N modifiers —— 116
**Figure 14**  Degrees of compositionality in 2N —— 120
**Figure 15**  Degrees of compositionality in 3N —— 122
**Figure 16**  Examples of compounds with different degrees of productivity —— 153
**Figure 17**  Relationship between constituent family sizes —— 158
**Figure 18**  Distribution of compounds on functions in 3N —— 159
**Figure 19**  Semantic map of head nouns in the pattern '*football* + N' —— 169
**Figure 20**  Semantic map of head nouns in the pattern '*weekend* + N' —— 171
**Figure 21**  Semantic map of head nouns in the pattern '*birthday* + N' —— 174
**Figure 22**  Semantic map of head nouns in the pattern '*roadside* + N' —— 175
**Figure 23**  Relationship between productivity and formal complexity —— 179
**Figure 24**  Relationship between productivity and frequency —— 182
**Figure 25**  Relationship between productivity and association strength —— 191
**Figure 26**  Relationship between corpus data and entrenchment —— 198
**Figure 27**  The Entrenchment and Conventionalization Model —— 199
**Figure 28**  Different strengths of syntagmatic associations for '*health care* + N' —— 220
**Figure 29**  Use of exemplary patterns —— 221
**Figure 30**  Potential degrees of schematicity for three-noun compounds —— 227
**Figure 31**  Potential levels of representations in three-noun compounding —— 229
**Figure 32**  More and less typical instances of three-noun compounding —— 240

## Tables

| | | |
|---|---|---|
| Table 1 | Compounds with identical word pair frequencies | 54 |
| Table 2 | Branching patterns assigned to 3N categorized as "unbiased" | 55 |
| Table 3 | Average number of syllables for 3N in different frequency levels | 61 |
| Table 4 | Average number of syllables distributed among constituents | 63 |
| Table 5 | Average number of morphemes for 3N in different frequency levels | 64 |
| Table 6 | Average number of morphemes distributed among constituents | 65 |
| Table 7 | Syllable counts distinguished for frequency levels and BPs | 69 |
| Table 8 | Morpheme counts distinguished for frequency levels and BPs | 71 |
| Table 9 | Use of available spelling formats | 77 |
| Table 10 | Distribution of 3N tokens on spelling formats | 80 |
| Table 11 | Stress assigned to left- and right-branching 3N | 87 |
| Table 12 | Count of 3N types in different token frequency ranges | 96 |
| Table 13 | Distribution of types and tokens among frequency ranges | 98 |
| Table 14 | Type-token relationship distinguished for branching patterns | 103 |
| Table 15 | Most frequent left-branching and right-branching compounds | 107 |
| Table 16 | Distribution of 3N tokens among registers | 112 |
| Table 17 | 3N and corresponding syntactic phrases | 128 |
| Table 18 | 3N and corresponding syntactic phrases with token frequencies | 131 |
| Table 19 | Most productive compounds based on types of 3N | 149 |
| Table 20 | Compounds with lower degrees of productivity | 150 |
| Table 21 | Categorization of 2N based on number of 3N formed | 152 |
| Table 22 | Number of 3N formed by 2N of different productivity categories | 155 |
| Table 23 | Correlation coefficients for different productivity subsets | 160 |
| Table 24 | Head and modifier family sizes for most productive compounds | 161 |
| Table 25 | Head and modifier family sizes for less productive compounds | 162 |
| Table 26 | Most productive modifiers (left) and heads (right) | 164 |
| Table 27 | Comparison of constituent family sizes for embedded compounds | 165 |
| Table 28 | Average number of 3N formed per 2N | 166 |
| Table 29 | Contingency table for *health care* | 186 |
| Table 30 | Association scores for exemplary compounds | 189 |

# Abbreviations

| | |
|---|---|
| N | noun |
| 3N | compound consisting of three nouns |
| 2N | compound consisting of two nouns |
| N1N2 | the sequence of the first and second noun in a three-noun compound |
| N2N3 | the sequence of the second and third noun in a three-noun compound |
| BP | branching pattern |
| LB | left-branching |
| RB | right-branching |

# 1 Introduction

When naming new concepts, speakers commonly utilize the word-formation process of compounding. In English, compounds typically consist of two words, more precisely two nouns, as in the examples of *toilet paper, football, ice-cream, nail polish* or *trade union*. However, there are also sequences consisting of three nouns that have become established as naming units, such as *toilet paper roll, football game, ice-cream van, nail polish remover* or *trade union leader*. These sequences raise a multitude of questions. Can they be categorized as multi-word compounds? Are their formal and semantic features comparable to those of compounds consisting of two nouns or do they show differences on a formal and semantic level? Are, for example, stress and orthography in these multi-word compounds more intricate than in two-word compounds? What does the underlying morphological structure of three-noun compounds look like? And how homogeneous are these complex sequences? Is it possible to identify more and less typical instantiations? Finally, why do language users utilize and produce only particular instances of multi-word compounds even though, theoretically, any number of nouns could be combined to form maximally complex compounds? Are there any elements that are used repeatedly for the formation of multi-word compounds? And is it possible to systematically describe the elements that speakers use as an input for multi-noun compounding?

The work presented in this book advances the field of compounding by exploring one particular sub-type of multi-word compounds, namely English compounds consisting of three nouns, such as *birthday party, food delivery service, bus timetable, guest bedroom* or *speed limit sign*. I will answer several research questions that will help elucidate the phenomenon of multi-word compounding, using both quantitative and qualitative methodology. Employing a usage-based perspective, I will work with a database of almost 60,000 types of three-noun compounds. The basic ambition of this project is to identify recurring patterns within the word-formation process that gives rise to compounds consisting of three lexemes. This will allow retracing the step from two-word compounding to more complex compounding and thus help gain general insights into the process of compounding.

This book is divided into four parts. Part I includes two chapters and provides the theoretical foundation for the field of compounding. Chapter 2 portrays the most important aspects of this word-formation process and defines the term *compound* as used in this book. Chapter 3 presents the state of research on multi-word compounding, which permits outlining the target of the investigations performed in this book.

Part II reports on the generation of a corpus-based database of three-noun compounds for the English language, on which the empirical research that is conducted in the remainder of this work is based. Its two chapters describe how the data was collected with the help of computational methods (Chapter 4) and how it was annotated with regard to morphological structure through an automated tagging system (Chapter 5).

In Part III, various research questions are addressed that aim to provide a detailed description of English three-noun compounds. Its two chapters focus on different aspects. Chapter 6 is dominated by a formal perspective, investigating several structural aspects that are established research areas in two-word compounding. Chapter 7 is dedicated to functional aspects of three-noun compounds. It explores the semantic characteristics of these word-formation products and gives insight into their usage.

Part IV is the most extensive part of this work. It hosts Chapter 8, which is divided into eight sections that answer various research questions concerned with both qualitative and quantitative aspects of productivity. I will identify and describe those elements which occur repeatedly in tri-constituent compounds with the aim to explain why only certain multi-word compounds are formed by native speakers of English. On this basis, I will investigate the cognitive aspects of productivity in compounding, attempting to explain the mental processes involved in the production and processing of multi-word compounds.

Part V provides a summary of the typical features of three-noun compounds in Chapter 9, highlights the central insights gained in this work in Chapter 10, and gives directions for further research in Chapter 11.

# Part I: **Theoretical Prerequisites**

# 2 Compounds and Compounding

Research in the field of compounding is plentiful. In early approaches to this word-formation process, scholars mostly focused on identifying the defining characteristics of compounds (e.g. Ball 1938, 1941; Marchand 1960). Especially the large field of meaning aspects that can be expressed in compounds was an area of interest in early accounts and still is today (cf. Downing 1977; Levi 1978; Jurafsky et al. 2001; Schäfer 2018). More recent approaches to compounding have also dealt with cognitive aspects, investigating the storage and processing of compounds (e.g. Sandra 1994; Libben and Jarema 2006; Baayen et al. 2010) or attempting to explain the phenomenon of compounding in the framework of Cognitive Linguistics (e.g. Benczes 2006; Heyvaert 2011).

Despite the extensive research on various aspects related to compounds, "compounding is [still] a field of study where intricate problems abound, numerous issues remain unresolved, and convincing solutions are generally not so easy to find" (Plag 2003: 132). This starts as early as trying to find a definition for the term *compound*, since what is categorized as a compound by one linguist is not necessarily termed so by another, as has already been pointed out by Faiß four decades ago (1981: 132). Although further research has been carried out, even today many aspects remain controversial. This is nicely illustrated by Lieber and Štekauer (2011a: 3), who compare compounding to the parable of the blind man's elephant, explaining that there are still quite differing images of what a compound is.

This work will not engage in the various discussions that revolve around the phenomenon of compounding; the aim is to instead provide a basis for the exploration of multi-word compounds. Therefore, I will only briefly present those aspects that reach general consensus, fully aware that with this depiction I am not doing justice to the complexity of the topic. For a more in-depth approach that discusses the relevant aspects in detail, the reader is referred to Bauer (2017). The following sections will define the phenomenon of compounding (Section 2.1), summarize the most important aspects related to this word-formation process (Section 2.2) and explain the understanding of compounding in this project (Section 2.3). As this work focusses on compounds consisting of three nouns, the explanations will mostly be limited to noun compounds.

## 2.1 What is a compound?

Compounding describes the formation of a new lexeme by adjoining two or more existing lexemes (Bauer 1983a: 28; Adams 2001: 2). This is presumably the definition that is most concise, with the cost of not being fully precise regarding the input items. It is mostly lexemes that are combined in compounding; however, the elements of compounds can also be blocked morphemes or combining forms (cf. Schmid 2016: 127–130). Although consisting of lexemes, constructions like *jack-in-the-box* are generally not counted under the category of compounds, following the "no-phrase constraint", which determines that complex words are not formed from explicit syntactic phrases (Adams 2001: 3).

The output of the process of compounding is a new lexeme, i.e. a complex word that functions like a single word (Quirk et al. 1985: 1567). Behaving like a single word in a grammatical sense has several implications concerning the modification of a compound, its interruptability, the substitutability of its constituents and its possibilities regarding co-ordination (cf. Bauer 2017: 15–25). A combination of two words is categorized as one word if it is not separable, i.e. it can only be relocated as a whole in a syntactic context and cannot be rearranged or interrupted with other words or inflectional morphemes. This implies that compounds are inflected as a whole, i.e. the plural is formed on the right-most element (e.g. *bus drivers*, *\*busses driver*). If a compound is modified, the modifier refers to the whole combination and not just the first constituent (e.g. in *old bus driver*, the adjective *old* does not describe *bus* but *bus driver*). As opposed to syntactic formations, a compound can usually not be used in a coordinative structure in which the right-most element is replaced by *one* (e.g. *I bought a blue shirt and a green one* vs. *\*I know a cab driver and a bus one*). For a discussion of these aspects including exceptions see Bauer (1998).[1]

Almost all approaches to compounding work with the notion of headedness, a concept that has been taken from syntax. Analogous to syntactic structures, compounded lexemes are assigned a head, which in English compounds is typically the right-most element. This entity determines the grammatical features of the compound, such as its word class and grammatical gender, as well as semantic features (Haspelmath 2010: 143). The left-most constituent is traditionally assigned the role of the modifier, whose function is to specify the head.

---

1 There are, for example, exceptions in the form of compounds whose first constituent appears in the plural form or the possessive, as in the case of *parks commissioner*, *programs coordinator*, *driver's license* or *children's hour* (Lieber and Štekauer 2011b: 13–14).

Considering that compounds constitute a very heterogeneous phenomenon, there are several ways to categorize them. An overview of the various types of compounds based on different criteria can be found in Sanchez-Stockhammer (2018: 43–56). For a description of the formal and semantic types of compounds see Bauer (1983a: 202–215) or Schmid (2016: 122–130). The least controversial categorization of compounds is based on parts of speech. In this context, noun-noun compounds are the most common product of compounding in English (Bauer 1983a: 202; Plag 2003: 145; Schmid 2016: 138). This is due to the fact that the extra-linguistic development mainly gives rise to new products rather than activities, which calls for more instances of nominal compounds than, for example, verbal compounds (Carstairs-McCarthy 2018: 67–68).

## 2.2 Compound features

Besides the grammatical aspects addressed in the previous section, there are further features that are commonly associated with compounds, affecting their orthography, stress pattern and meaning. This section will briefly introduce and discuss each of these features.

As a reflection of their word-status, compounds are sometimes expected to be spelt as an orthographic unit, i.e. an uninterrupted sequence of letters (e.g. *bedroom*, *wheelchair*). In early approaches to compounding, this spelling format was seen as a defining feature. Scholars such as Ball, for example, were quite strict in this respect, rejecting word sequences that are spelt as two orthographic words as instances of compounding (cf. Ball 1951: 3). It is true that many compounds show orthographic unification, as is the case in *deadline*, *football* or *birthday*, for example. However, there are numerous items that are generally accepted as compounds but occur in open spelling, such as *health care*, *trade union* or *passenger seat*. There are even compound types which occur exclusively in this format, such as the pattern [V+*ing*] + N, as in the examples of *nursing home* and *dancing girl* (Schmid 2016: 122). Besides open and solid spelling, another format that is employed in English compound spelling – albeit not as frequently as the former two – is hyphenation, as found in *night-time*, *call-girl* or *long-term* (Plag et al. 2015: 100). In English, open spelt compounds are actually the most frequent format (cf. Sanchez-Stockhammer 2018: Chapter 7.2).

Besides the fact that there are three different spelling formats available for the products of compounding, there are compounds for which several orthographic variants are used and accepted. The example that is popularly cited in this context is that of *girlfriend*, which is attested in all three spelling formats as *girlfriend*, *girl friend* and *girl-friend* (Bauer 1998: 69). The same situation is nicely reflected in the fact that Bauer, an expert in the field of compounding, uses the compound *stress pattern* twice in one paragraph and spells it open in one place and with a hyphen four lines further down (Bauer 2017: 127). Although there seems to be some degree of variation in the spelling of English compounds, this does not mean that it lacks principles: Sanchez-Stockhammer (2018) demonstrates with the help of an empirical study that there are principles that govern the variation in the spelling of English compounds. A compound's number of syllables, for example, is one of the most important predictors that can account for its orthographic realization (Sanchez-Stockhammer 2018: 352).

Another aspect that is relevant for compounds is their stress pattern. According to the *Compound Stress Rule* (CSR) established by Chomsky and Halle (1968: 16–18), compounds show fore-stress, which means that the heavy syllable of the first constituent receives prominent stress (e.g. ˈbus driver, ˈbedroom, ˈwheelchair). This feature used to be one of the defining criteria for compoundhood, which is why fore-stress was soon also referred to as *compound stress*. However, several linguists have demonstrated that stress is not as distinctive as had been claimed, since there are, for example, compounds that are stressed on the right-hand constituent, such as *apple ˈpie, silk ˈshirt* or *full ˈstop* (Lees 1968; Plag 2006b; Plag et al. 2008: 761; Kunter 2011: 9; Huddleston and Pullum 2017: 451). This end-stress is particularly typical of attribute-head compounds (Giegerich 2009: 6). Copulative compounds, by contrast, tend to show stress on both constituents: ˈbitter-ˈsweet (Schmid 2016: 145). Several researchers have busied themselves with explaining the different stress patterns found among compounds, for example by semantic aspects (Plag 2006b, 2010; Plag et al. 2007; Plag et al. 2008; Giegerich 2009; Plag and Bell 2012). Krott et al. (2001; 2007) point out that these works show only tendencies and are not reliable as explicit linguistic rules. What this research still shows, however, is that variation in stress assignment is not random but partly systematic (cf. Bauer 2017: 129–132).

Other scholars have pointed out that stress assignment is not always straightforward: not only is there variation between speakers (Huddleston and Pullum (2017: 1650) claim that there are speakers who stress the second constituent of *hotdog*), but also do individual speakers differ in the way they pronounce a sequence of words at different times (Bauer 1983b: 49, 1998: 70; Kunter 2011: 183–189). Bauer (2017: 127) furthermore points out that the assignment of stress to the front or end of a compound can differ between the varieties of English. Furthermore, it is known that compound stress can be influenced by context (Bauer 1983b: 48; Kunter 2011: 193–196). Despite these restrictions, it is still acknowledged that most compounds show a relatively fixed stress pattern even across different contexts and speakers. It can thus be claimed that typically, even if not exclusively, compounds tend to be stressed on the first syllable. If other stress patterns occur, then this is to some degree predictable.

A further critical aspect concerns the semantic characteristics of compounds. Typically, the meaning of a compound is not fully equivalent to the summed meaning of its constituents (Jespersen 1942: 137). This is commonly demonstrated by the example of *blackbird*, which does not describe any bird that is black but a particular species that has also further specific characteristics (cf. Marchand 1960: 18; Faiß 1981: 134; Langacker 1987a: 457). Schmid (2016: 142–143) illustrates this situation with the example of *barman*, a compound that does not simply denote any man in a bar. Its meaning includes aspects that are absent in the mere combination of the concepts of *bar* and *man*, such as the fact that a barman serves drinks, cashes up, etc. In cognitive linguistic accounts of compounding, these extra attributes can be explained by an additional input space or a blending process that gives rise to the new conceptual structure (cf. Heyvaert 2011: 250; Ungerer and Schmid 2013: 271). Thus, a compound can be semantically more specific than the combination of the meanings of its constituents.

A further relevant aspect regarding the meaning of compounds is the semantic relation between their constituents. Generally, the head in a compound determines the semantic category of the whole compound, while the modifier specifies it. A *bus driver*, for example, is a kind of driver. There are, however, various ways in which the modifier can specify the head, which are neutralised in the compound format.[2] For this reason, compounds – noun compounds in particular – show a high degree of semantic flexibility as the exact relation between the two lexemes can be manifold (cf. Langacker 1987a: 157; Schmid 2016: 123–125). A *cat toy*, for example, can be a 'toy FOR cats' but could just as well be a 'toy HAVING THE FORM OF a cat'. As a consequence, compounds can be ambiguous if they are presented in isolation as there might be more than one possible interpretation (cf., e.g. Ryder 1994). Olsen (2000: 898) demonstrates this with the example of *sun spots*, which can denote 'spots ON the sun', 'spots CAUSED BY the sun' or 'spots IN THE SHAPE OF the sun'.[3]

Many scholars have busied themselves with exploring the semantic relations in compounds, aiming at establishing an inventory of semantic patterns that can connect the elements of a compound (see, for example, Lees 1968; Downing 1977; Levi 1978). A summary of the various semantic categorizations can be found in

---

[2] In this context, it must be pointed out that the traditional descriptions of modifier-head relations, which reduce the role of the modifier to merely specifying the head constituent, are simplified accounts. In an attribute-listing task with compounds, Ungerer and Schmi (1998) report that participants also listed attributes of the modifier, which indicates that the role of the modifier has been underestimated (for an explanation from a cognitive view see Ungerer and Schmid 2013: 94–95). This is also supported by the results of Libben et a. (2003), who show that the first constituents of compounds also show priming effects.

[3] Another semantic factor that can render the interpretation of novel compounds difficult or at least make it ambiguous are polysemous constituents, where speakers need to select the appropriate sense. Schäfer and Bell (2020: 42–43) exemplify this situation with the compound *rubber plant*, where the second constituent could both refer to a living organism and a factory.

Adams (2001). Bauer (2017: 72–73) criticizes these attempts, claiming that classifications of this kind are never exhaustive; moreover, there are items which cannot be assigned clearly and exclusively to one of the categories, and, thirdly, there is no proof for a psycholinguistic reality to these categorizations (Bauer 2017: 106). Bauer suggests the assumption of a quite general relationship between the constituents of a compound, which is described as "the N1 denotes something which pragmatically allows for an appropriate subclassification of the class of N2 and an appropriately mnemonic label for the class" (Bauer 2017: 74).

In view of the fact that semantic aspects are underspecified in the form of a compound, how are speakers able to derive a compound's meaning? Studies of modifier-noun compounds have indicated that compounds generally tend to follow regular semantic patterns (Downing 1977; Bell 2015). For this reason, although the exact relation between the modifier and the head of a compound can be vague, speakers are generally able to derive the appropriate relationship between the components in a compound, making use of world knowledge, contextual clues and problem-solving strategies (cf. Coolen et al. 1991; Ryder 1994; Carstairs-McCarthy 2018: 101–102). Furthermore, psycholinguistic studies have shown that speakers make use of statistical regularities when they interpret novel compounds, which is why compounds based on frequently occurring relationships are easier to interpret (cf. Gagné and Shoben 1997; Gagné and Spalding 2006; Krott 2009). Therefore, despite the loss of semantic information through their condensed format, compounds can generally be claimed to be precise and understandable in the moment of usage through the context shared by the speakers, as Downing (1977: 823) demonstrates with the example of *apple-juice-seat*. This makes compounds an easy and efficient tool for naming.

## 2.3 Delimitation of compounding

As explained in the previous section, compounds are sometimes spelt as an orthographic unit, tend to be stressed on the first constituent and their meaning can be different from the combined meanings of the components. Early linguists such as Ball (1938) and Marchand (1960) strictly applied these features as criteria for compoundhood, allowing only sequences to be categorized as compounds that are orthographically realized as one word, show fore-stress and are lexicalized to some extent. These traditional criteria have been contested, discussed and refined by later linguists as they have turned out to not be fully waterproof (cf. Bauer 1998). Still, they are relevant when distinguishing compounds from syntactic phrases, to which English compounds that are not spelt as an orthographic unit can look similar due to the lack of inflectional morphemes, cf. *blackbird* vs. *black bird*; *greenhouse* vs. *green house* (Lieber and Štekauer 2011b: 5). Noun-noun sequences are notoriously hard to pin down between the interfaces of morphology and syntax, as is addressed explicitly by Bauer (1998): "When is a sequence of two words a compound and when a syntactic construction?" The categorization of noun-noun sequences into compounds and phrases has been a focal point for a long period of time (cf. Olsen 2000: 899–900). Several scholars have tried to use the above-mentioned criteria to assign the status of compounds to some word sequences and that of phrases to others (cf. Ball 1938; Marchand 1969). I do not intend to repeat the compound-phrase debate at this point; it can be followed in detail in Bauer (1998). By now, it is mostly agreed on that the above mentioned criteria are not suitable for distinguishing between a lexical category of complex nominals and a syntactic one (cf. Lieber et al. 2015: 342). In line with current approaches to this question (cf. Olsen 2000: 898), I assume that there is only one type of noun sequences, which I understand as word-formation products and thus categorize as compounds. From this perspective, the traditional compound criteria can be understood as features that allow distinguishing between more and less typical instances of compounding.

Accordingly, in a more liberal understanding of compounding – as supported in this book – a compound is typically, but not exclusively, spelt as one orthographic unit and tends to carry a main stress on its first constituent. It describes a conceptual unit that can (but does not necessarily have to) be different from that of the combination of its components. I will classify all instances as an act of compounding in which speakers combine two or more lexemes to encode a particular meaning to refer to a unified concept, even if this act of naming is only temporary or only shared between a limited number of speakers. Compounds are thus naming units in the sense established by Štekauer (2000: 337) which serve the speech act of reference. This understanding of compounding does not require a compound to be an established expression that is listed in a dictionary and also accepts formations which are compositional. Thus, this definition of compounding does not only comprise complex nominals with a lexical function but also those with a syntactic or deictic function, such as, for example, Downing's *apple-juice seat*. Noun sequences that are excluded from the category of compounding are those including proper names (e.g. *President Obama*) as well as elliptic quantifier-noun combinations (e.g. *one spoon sugar, one kilo apples*). The latter examples are instances of juxtaposed words in which a preposition seems to have been omitted. These formations clearly do not form a naming unit.

# 3 Multi-word compounding

Although the field of compounding has been studied so extensively, researchers in this area have mostly directed their attention at two-word compounds, which constitute the idealized, default case of compounding. The situation for compounds consisting of more than two lexemes is different. There is no systematic account in which those aspects that have been examined for two-word compounds are considered for more complex compounds. Those scholars who have addressed multi-word compounds have mostly done so in side notes of works dedicated to the compounding of two lexemes. The information on multi-word compounding that can be found in the literature will be summarized in Section 3.1, where I will also point out aspects that lack coverage. With this foundation, Section 3.2 will argue why this book focuses on one particular subtype, namely three-noun compounds, and will outline the relevant concepts and terms.

## 3.1 Coverage in literature

In principle, the definitions of compounding that are given in works focusing on two-word compounds implicitly include multi-word compounds. They define compounding as the combination of "at least two" lexemes (Schmid 2016: 142), "two or more potential stems" (Bauer 1983a: 28) or "more than one base" (Quirk et al. 1985: 1567). Accordingly, a compound can theoretically contain any number of lexemes. This aspect is captured through the principle of recursion, which states that each of the constituents in a compound can be a compound itself (Warren 1978: 10; Quirk et al. 1985: 1567; Lieber 2010: 44). Not all languages that employ compounds as a means of word formation also feature recursive compounding (Bauer 2017: 45). English is usually not categorized as a language that makes extensive use of recursion.

The products of recursion are generally referred to as *complex compounds* (Olsen 2000: 904). The German language commonly employs complex compounds such as *Tierarztpraxis* ('veterinary clinic'), *Fahrkartenkontrolle* ('ticket inspection'), *Notarzteinsatz* ('emergency service'), *Prüfungsanmeldebestätigungsformular* ('form for confirmation of exam registration'), *Kopfschmerztabletten* ('headache pill') or *Ticketrückerstattungsprozess* ('process for ticket refunding').

As Plag (2003: 134) points out, from a structural perspective there is no limit to recursivity in compounding; however, the more lexemes are combined in a compound, the more effort it requires for production and processing, which is why compounds composed of a high number of lexemes are rather rare, especially in spoken language (cf. Donalies 2003: 78; Schmid 2016: 208–209). For the English language, this is supported by empirical evidence: Warren (1978: 14) observes that the upper limit in complex compounding is reached at the combination of six lexemes. Schmid (2016: 208) finds only few compounds consisting of more than three lexemes in his database. Nevertheless, Warren (1978: 15) points out that the decline in the use of complex compounds in English starts with compounds consisting of more than three elements, which suggests that compounds consisting of three lexemes still show considerable usage.

There are a few scholars who make explicit reference to multi-word compounds in English, such as Schmid (2016: 205–210), Warren (1978: 10–18), Plag (2003: 133–134), Carstairs-McCarthy (2018: 83–86, 100–102), Lieber (2010: 44–45) and Haspelmath (2010: 143–144). However, they generally only cover selected aspects. Most of these scholars exclusively address multi-word compounds to explain that compounding is recursive and/or to illustrate the principle of binarity in the internal structure of complex compounds. Analogously to multiply-affixed words, whose internal structure is analysed as hierarchically organized pairs of immediate constituents, complex compounds can be analysed as products of a morphological operation that combines two constituents at a time, which is traditionally illustrated in the form of tree diagrams or bracketing (Olsen 2000: 904; Plag 2003: 133–134; Schmid 2016: 206–207). This principle of binarity gives way to different nesting or branching patterns, depending on the position in the multi-word compound where the inner compound(s) is (/are) located. Warren (1978: 13–15) illustrates all available branching patterns for compounds consisting of up to six elements. She shows that the combination of five lexemes adds up to 14 different ways of structuring, while the combination of six lexemes results in 42 options for the internal structure of these compounds. In three-word compounds, there are only two branching patterns (Warren 1978: 12):
- *left-branching*: compounds with a complex modifier
    e.g. *wartime circular*
- *right-branching*: compounds with a complex head
    e.g. *morning newspaper*

Several authors point out that these structural variants differ with regard to the extent to which they are used. More often, the inner compound is located in the position of the modifier than in that of the head, which means that left-branching is the more commonly encountered morphological structure (Warren 1978: 10; Ortner and Ortner 1984: 116; Schmid 2016: 206–208).

Besides the structure within complex compounds, there is little mention of other aspects in the literature. Carstairs-McCarthy (2018: 76) shares his thoughts on the stress pattern of multi-word compounds but lacks a systematic and empirical basis. Giegerich (2009: 9–13) demonstrates that there are eight possible stress patterns for tripartite noun compounds when it comes to the combination of fore- and end-stress. Schmid (2016: 208) assumes that right-branching compounds might be special with regard to the heads they employ.Similarly, Warren (1978: 15) suspects that complex compounds might be easier to process if they "contain combinations whose semantic interpretation and syntactic unity is 'ready-made' (i.e. can be assumed to be memorized)".

Furthermore, none of the works mentioned are representative with regard to the data used. Most researchers who address multi-word compounds content themselves with naming a few hand-collected, striking examples. Carstairs-McCarthy (2018: 76–84), for example, works with a small number of probably self-invented instances such as *Ebola virus vaccine patent lawsuit*, which I consider unnatural and not representative for the phenomenon of complex compounding. Schmid (2016) uses authentic items from a corpus but works with a fairly small sample of 75 items only.

In view of the extensive literature that exists in the area of compounding, the absence of research in the field of multi-word compounding is surprising. Research in this area is not only scarce but also lacks detail. The cited approaches generally do not make any distinction within the group of complex compounds but lump together all compounds consisting of more than two constituents into one large group of complex compounds. None of the existing approaches deliver a systematic and encompassing account of multi-word compounds that addresses the features that have been researched for two-word compounds. Judging from the lack of attention that has been given to multi-word compounds, it seems that this subcategory of compounding is not deemed interesting. This is surprising, considering that compounds are one of the strongest means of expanding the English lexicon.

One reason for the negligence of multi-word compounds in the English language might be that compounds consisting of more than two lexemes are generally not assessed to be a very frequent phenomenon in English (cf. Schmid 2016: 208; Bauer 2017: 44). Another reason that could explain the lack of research might be that the image of these word-formation products is distorted. Scholars who address multi-word compounds often make use of highly complicated, lengthy or barely authentic examples such as *window oven cleaner marketing* (Carstairs-McCarthy 2018: 85) or *paper towel dispenser factory building committee report* (Lieber 2010: 44). These items clearly must be regarded as peripheral instances of the phenomenon of compounding – if they are existent instances in the first place.

A much more practical issue that has certainly contributed to the dearth of research in this area is the lack of material. There are no comprehensive and representative inventories of multi-word compounds that research in this area could draw on. This shortcoming is most likely due to different kinds of methodological hurdles that are involved in detecting compounds in corpora, as will be demonstrated in later sections of this work.

## 3.2 Research focus and terminology

In trying to fill the gap in research on complex compounding in English, it makes sense to start with three-word compounds. Bauer (2017: 46) states that one condition for recursive compounding is a productive pattern of compounding. Considering that Noun+Noun compounding is classified as the most common type of compounding in English (Lieber et al. 2015: 451; Bauer and Huddleston 2017: 1647), it seems reasonable to use compounds consisting of three nouns, i.e. Noun+Noun+Noun (N+N+N). Based on the definition given in Section 2.3, I categorize as N+N+N compounds all combinations of three nouns that speakers of English have formed to refer to a conceptual unit.

With regard to terminology, N+N+N compounds will be referred to as "tri-constituent/tripartite compounds" or "three-noun compounds". By contrast, the notion of "three-noun sequence" is neutral and also encompasses combinations like *spoon olive oil*, which do not serve to name a concept and are thus not considered compounds. I will especially make use of this term in the first part of the project, where I will be dealing with sequences consisting of three nouns, some of which will not actually be compounds. The terms "tri-constituent" and "tripartite" will not refer to compounds with any kind of constituents (e.g. morphemes) but will exclusively mean 'consisting of three lexemes'. Accordingly, a tri-constituent compound can contain complex constituents that show affixation (e.g. *school bus driver*). It has been explained earlier in Section 3.1 that based on the principle of binary branching, complex compounds are always bi-constituent but the constituents themselves can be complex again. The notion of "tri-constituent" will be used in the sense of compounds that formally consist of three lexemes and does not mean to express that these compounds are not based on binary branching.

Another term that has been used to refer to compounds consisting of more than two lexemes is *polymorphemic compounds* (Schmid 2016: 205). This term does not seem fully adequate if it is meant to refer to multi-word compounds, as a polymorphemic compound could also be a two-word compound that carries further (bound) morphemes, such as *bus driver*. Therefore, I will use the term "polylexemic compounds" instead. I will also refer to these compounds as "complex compounds" in contrast to "simple compounds" (i.e. consisting of two lexemes). The notions of "complex compounds", "polylexemic compounds" and "multi-word compounds" will be used interchangeably. The abbreviation "3N" will be used in tables and graphics to refer to three-noun compounds; analogously "2N" will be used to refer to two-noun compounds. Compounds within compounds (e.g. *football* in *football game*) are generally referred to as *inner compounds* or *embedded compounds* (cf. Giegerich 2009).

It is the aim of this book to deliver a systematic account of three-noun compounds in English. I will complement the pieces of information collected so far by addressing those aspects that have not been covered sufficiently. To do so, I intend to answer various research questions, including the following:

- What do typical instances of three-noun compounding look like? Do they tend to be lengthy and morphologically complex sequences which deserve the term "complex"?
- Are formal and semantic aspects in complex compounding more intricate than in simple compounding?
- How homogeneous is the phenomenon of three-noun compounds? Do the two types of three-noun compounds that can be distinguished based on their internal structure (i.e. left- and right-branching compounds) demonstrate differences on a formal and semantic level?
- Can the word-formation process that combines three nouns in English be considered productive?
- In theory, any three nouns could be combined to form a tri-constituent compound, so why do speakers only produce certain examples?

In the endeavour to answer these and several other research questions, this work will provide a starting point for more extensive research in the area of multi-word compounding.

Part II: **Data acquisition and annotation**

# 4 Compilation of a compound database

Unlike scholars like Carstairs-McCarthy (2018: 85), who uses examples that feel remote from linguistic reality (e.g. *holiday car sightseeing trip* or *window oven cleaner marketing*), this work embodies a descriptive, usage-based approach to complex compounding. I intend to gain insights into the different ways in which speakers utilize the resources of the English language to form tri-constituent compounds, which is why I will exclusively work with authentic material, i.e. compounds that have been formed by speakers of the English language.

This project is grounded on a systematically compiled, corpus-based and exhaustive inventory of English three-noun compounds. It contains almost 60,000 instances and can be seen as a representative database of tri-constituent noun compounds for the English language. The data acquisition process will be documented in the following sections: Section 4.1 will introduce the material that was used as a basis; Section 4.2 will describe the data retrieval process in considerable detail to provide an insight into the intricacies that are involved in the search for compounds in corpora. Section 4.3 will present the setup of the database and point out its flaws.

## 4.1 Corpus data used in this project

This project is based on *The Corpus of Contemporary American English* (COCA), a computerized database provided by Marc Davies (2008). This corpus was chosen primarily because the material in COCA covers a broad variety of the English language. It is distributed over various genres such as fiction, magazines, academic texts and newspapers,[4] and contains both written and spoken data. Moreover, COCA is remarkably large: it has been compiled since 1990 and encompasses more than one billion words taken from 485,202 different texts. With this scope, it is significantly bigger than other established corpora such as, for example, the *British National Corpus* (BNC). Due to its size and the variety of the material used, the language in COCA can be considered an authentic and representative sample of American English. The focus on this variety of English was not a choice made with regard to the phenomenon under investigation (i.e. three-noun compounds are not assumed to be more relevant in American English than in other English varieties), but for practical reasons, as COCA is not only large enough to contain sufficient

---

[4] Status: September 2019. The corpus has by now been extended with further categories.

https://doi.org/10.1515/9783111081694-004

instances of complex compounds, but is furthermore available in a downloadable format, which permits the use of computational methodology.

The specific demands posed by the different sorts of investigations performed in this project required working with three sets of material related to COCA, including the online edition of the corpus and two sources of offline material. The latter consist of a downloadable n-gram package and an offline version of the corpus, both available for purchase on the website.[5] The n-gram package contains 2-, 3-, and 4-grams which occur at least three times in that sequence. It comprises a total of 155 million strings, including part-of-speech specification. Its 2-gram and 3-gram sets were used as source material for the compilation of the list of three-noun compounds. The offline version of the corpus was used for counting different kinds of token frequencies that could not be extracted from the n-gram sets. The online source was only used for qualitative, small-scale experiments and was accessed via the web-interface provided by English-Corpora.org. The word frequencies in these three sources do not match as the time periods they cover differ slightly: the online edition is up to date and thus yields higher word frequencies than the n-gram lists, which only date to 2011, while the time coverage of the offline corpus is to 2012. These differences, however, are unlikely to affect the overall results as they are generally relatively small (compare, for example, the occurrences of the three-noun compound *weekend edition* with 3,013 tokens in the offline database, as opposed to 3,033 tokens in the online edition).

## 4.2 Data retrieval

The methodological work with complex compounds entails intricacies that are systematic enough to sketch them in order to allow later approaches to take them into account. It is the aim of this section to point to aspects that complicate and manipulate the access to complex compounds in corpora on the one hand, and, on the other hand, to provide solutions by presenting the steps that were taken to overcome these difficulties.

A major hurdle that impedes the identification of complex compounds in corpora is their spelling. For tri-constituent nominal compounds the possible combinations of hyphens, spaces and solid spelling theoretically add up to nine different formats that need to be taken into account: N-N-N, N N N, NN N, N-N N, N N-N, N NN, NN-N, N-NN and NNN. This has serious implications for the search process, as finding

---

[5] Licensed for the Department of English at LMU, Munich; acquired in June 2016 (n-grams) and February 2017 (corpus).

these compounds cannot be efficiently resolved through a query in the format of "Noun Noun Noun".

Orthography is also the source of a more serious problem which significantly hampers the discovery of a particular type of three-noun compound. There are a high number of tri-constituent compounds in which the embedded two-noun compound forms an orthographic unit, i.e. sequences in the format NN N or N NN, such as *football game, family network, sunflower seeds* or *research database*. In the process of automated tagging in corpora, the embedded compound is generally not recognized as a complex word but tagged holistically as one single noun, e.g. *football$_N$ game$_N$*. Therefore, the relevant tri-constituent compounds are "hiding" in what looks like a bi-constituent compound. This poses a major challenge for finding them in a corpus, as they cannot be identified through a standard search for a sequence of three nouns. Due to the fact that the formats NN N and N NN are extremely common, excluding types of this format from the project was not an option as it would not permit justified generalizations on the phenomenon of tri-constituent compounds to be made. A sighting of two-noun compounds for hidden three-noun compounds is not feasible, as the number of two-noun compounds in English is extremely high. The procedure undertaken to solve this problem and to find three-noun compounds in their different spelling formats in the corpus will be presented in the following sections.

### 4.2.1 Recall of noun sequences

Compiling a database of three-noun compounds clearly requires the use of computer-linguistic work. Using a POS-tagged corpus lends itself to this purpose, which is why the n-gram sets of COCA were chosen as source material. The sets of interest were, obviously, the 3-gram list, but also that of 2-grams, as this is where the above-mentioned problematic type *football game* was expected to be found. The list of 2-grams contains 6.2 million types; the list of 3-grams is even more extensive with 11.9 million types. These lists were uploaded to the online data management software MySQL on the servers of the CIS of LMU Munich to be further searched for the sequences of interest. In order to reduce both n-gram lists to actual noun sequences, the different noun tags were identified with the help of the CQP query syntax. The sequences selected were those where both (2-gram set) or all three nouns (3-gram set) were labelled with a noun tag, only excluding the tag that marks proper names ("np1").

Not surprisingly, the work with large data and automatized tagged corpora delivers results which include instances of noise, which is why the lists of noun sequences needed to be refined thoroughly. In what follows, I will portray the kinds of unwanted items that can be encountered in a search for noun compounds and propose solutions to eliminate them systematically. The following examples are an extract of the supposed noun sequences in the 2-gram data set and are intended to give an impression of the degree of noise that was prevalent in the data. In all of these instances, the constituents had been tagged as nouns:

- -- beef
- /ABC Mr.
- precedent sensori
- dritti riservati
- depositati piu
- Footage-alternates Mr.
- **28;5463;TOOLONG account
- tat violence
- fishery// Roses
- c-Stairs ph
- /Cmp Yds
- -Jon-Sr. -and-
- a-Hoffpauir ph
- A-L-P-H-A dot-com
- ni modo
- -- $
- Photos-of-the-Kenn President

Clearly, some of the constituents do not represent words at all, other combinations contain words in senseless combinations or constitute foreign expressions that are not established in the English language. This kind of noise can be traced back to erroneous tagging, which is why it cannot be avoided by means of a more precise recall. Instead, the respective items must be removed from the list of results. In order to eliminate such entries, phenomena to be searched for explicitly are, for example, the following:

- hyphens
- regular expressions
- numbers
- sequences of two or more vowels
- sequences not containing vowels
- less common letters of the English language (e.g. *x*, umlauts)
- extremely long words
- repetitions of the same word

This procedure will help identify a high amount of noise. In the two n-gram sets this kind of noise proved to be widespread: more than 10,000 instances of unwanted items could be eliminated with the help of this procedure. In a further attempt to reduce noise, the n-gram sets were reduced to sequences where each of the constituents had a minimum length of three letters. This, of course, meant losing compounds containing nouns like *ar*. The number of English nouns containing only two letters, however, is considered low enough to accept this drawback.

Besides non-words, noise in the search for noun compounds can occur in the form of words that are not nouns but have been tagged as such. This affects wrongly tagged words of other word classes (e.g. *max, min*) or words which cannot be considered established expressions in the English language (e.g. *conteste, beaux, ese*). The extent to which this kind of noise can be eliminated is limited, as far fewer systematic searches are possible. Nevertheless, the clean-up process can effectively be done by scrutinizing the data with the help of different sorting mechanisms, for example by frequency, by alphabet, by word-length, etc.

This way, the 2-gram and 3-gram data sets were cleansed systematically and reduced to actual sequences of two and three nouns respectively. In order to provide usage frequencies for each noun sequence, a Python-script was written that counts the number of occurrences for each sequence within the n-gram sets and adds the token frequencies to the entries. Before the two n-gram sets could be further refined, the 2-gram list needed to be reduced to those items that were suspected to be three-noun sequences.

### 4.2.2 Finding compounds within compounds

This section documents the procedure used to identify three-noun compounds within sequences tagged as two nouns. As has been described earlier, compounds of the type *football game* cannot be found in the three-noun set, but are hiding among items classified as two-noun sequences. To find them, a Python-script was designed that searches the components of the noun sequences in the two-noun data set in order to detect whether one of them is itself complex in that it consists of two lexemes.

To achieve this, a list of English nouns was compiled with the help of the online edition of COCA. This noun list, as well, first needed to be refined thoroughly, as it contained noise in the form of sequences that were not nouns or even words (e.g. items containing regular expressions, numbers, non-words, etc.). These were identified through systematic searches and deletions as described in the previous section 4.2.1 (e.g. searching for instances containing numbers, less than three letters, repetitions of the same letters, no vowels, uncommon letters of the English language, etc.). In this way, the list was reduced to 17,988 items that could be considered nouns of the English language. This list was used as an input for the Python-script.

The Python-script searches each individual component of the 2-gram set for whether it contains two nouns. It linearly compares the strings of each component of the two-noun sequences to the items in the noun list and checks for agreement. If the program identifies a matching string, this part of the component is identified as a noun and, in consequence, split off from the rest of the word by breaking the word at the end of the string. In the next step, the code searches the remainder of the word to ascertain whether this fragment, too, is identical to any other word in the noun list. Only those instances where this is the case, i.e. where the code can identify two nouns from the noun list within either the first or the second constituent of a two-noun sequence, are marked as potential three-word compounds. Figure 1 illustrates the working mechanism of the code with the help of examples. The vertical bars illustrate the positions where the code splits off parts of the words after identifying them as potential nouns, in order to check whether the remaining part is a noun as well.

| | | | |
|---|---|---|---|
| *bay area* | → | \| bay$_N$ \| ar$_N$\|ea$_N$ \| | → 2 items from noun list, no hit |
| *sports car* | → | \| sport$_N$ \| s$_N$ \| car$_N$ \| | → 2 items from noun list, no hit |
| *football game* | → | \| foot$_N$ \| ball$_N$ \| game$_N$ \| | → 3 items from noun list, potential hit |
| *football games* | → | \| foot$_N$ \| ball$_N$ \| game$_N$ \| s$_N$ \| | → 3 items from noun list, potential hit |

**Figure 1:** Working mechanism used to identify 3N within 2N.

In the case of *bay area*, for example, the code sequentially compares the strings of the components *bay* and *area* to the items in the noun list. It will not find entries for *b* or *ba* in the noun list. When processing the sequence *bay*, it will find a matching entry and thus mark *bay* as a noun. It will proceed by splitting *bay* off from the rest of the word. As *bay* ends here, there is nothing to be split off, i.e. the "remainder" is not identical to any noun from the noun list, which is why the first component does not qualify as a compound. The code will move on to the second constituent, *area*, and proceed in the manner just described, i.e. first process *a*, not find a match in the noun list, then proceed with *ar*. It might find *ar* as a noun and thus search for the remainder, i.e. *ea*, which it will not identify as a noun and thus reject *area* as complex noun. It will continue with the string *are*, which it will not find in the noun list, and finally proceed to identify the string *area* as a noun from the noun list. Here, too, it will not find that the remainder (which again is empty) is another noun of the English language. As none of the constituents has a noun-remainder, *bay area* is not listed as a potential hit for a three-noun compound.

In the case of *sports car*, the code will approximate the first constituent and after processing the first five letters, i.e. *sport*, it will find a matching noun in the noun list. It will mark *sport* as a noun and split it off from the rest of the word, i.e. the plural *-s*. As this remainder is a potential second noun, the code will check for entries in the noun list. This search will be unsuccessful, as there is obviously no entry for *s*, which is why this fragment will not be categorized as a noun. Consequently, *sports* will be rejected as a sequence of two nouns. For *car*, too, the code will not be able to split off a remainder that is a noun. For this reason, *sports car* will not qualify as a potential three-noun compound either.

In the case of *football game*, by contrast, the code will process *foot* and find a matching entry in the noun list. Splitting off the rest of the word results in the remainder *ball*. A comparison of this remainder with the items in the noun list will yield a positive result, so *ball* will be marked as a noun as well. In the processing of the second constituent, the code will identify *game* as a noun in the noun list. In sum, three strings will be classified as nouns. Accordingly, *football game* is marked as a potential three-noun sequence. In the case of *football games*, however, after identifying *foot*, *ball*, and *game* as nouns each, the code will check for the remainder, i.e. the plural *-s*. It will not be identified as an item from the noun list, which is why despite discovering four fragments in total, only three nouns will be identified, and, as a consequence, the code will mark *football game* as a potential three-noun compound.

Although this proposal seemed a highly promising solution to the task of finding three-noun compounds in the 2-gram data set, its recall rate was not as precise as expected, as it delivered a surprisingly high number of false positives. In fact, the English language proved to have many instances of what I would like to call "fake compounds". These are words that were split into two nouns by the code but are either monomorphemic and happen to contain two string sequences which are each homonymous to actual nouns, or they constitute complex lexemes including a suffix that is homonymous to an English noun. The following list provides a small sample of the fake compounds produced by the Python-script to give an impression of the phenomenon:

- *break age*
- *lab oratory*
- *nap kin*
- *stag nation*
- *sin king*
- *can teen*
- *medal lions*
- *leg end*
- *pal ace*
- *can vases*
- *mans laughter*
- *ball ads*
- *don key*
- *man dates*
- *champ ion*
- *pronoun cement*
- *car pet*
- *account ant*

Reading these erroneously split words as actual compounds is almost a delight, especially when we think about the potential literal meanings (e.g. 'pet for the car', 'nation of stags', 'teens nourished from cans', 'cement made out of pronouns', 'the king of sins', 'ant responsible for accounts'). However, interesting and funny as these results might be, they had to be eliminated. These cases are not malfunctionings of the script as they are a correct implementation of the instructions. Thus, refinements could not be made to the code but had to be carried out either to the source material, i.e. the noun list, or to the result list of potential hits for complex compounds. Here, the considerations were generally practical, based on the balance of expected benefits and costs for precision and recall. If a noun from the noun list was the cause for a high number of fake compounds, it was deleted from the noun list, even though that meant compounds with that noun would be lost. Examples of this category are words like *ion* or *ant*. Taking them off the noun list increased the precision of the results. As the number of real compounds containing these words was considered to be fairly low and the costs in terms of missed recall were therefore low, too, the loss of potential compounds seemed justified in order to prevent noise in the form of fake compounds. A different case was posed by noun strings in fake compounds that were intuitively categorized as potentially recurrent components of compounds, such as *age* or *king*. These were not deleted from the noun list, but the results in which they occurred were searched for and, if necessary, manually deleted from the list of potential three-noun compounds.

Further minor inadequacies produced by the script is the splitting of nouns in the wrong place, e.g. *goats-kin, candles-tick, cars-hare, windows-ills* or *airs-trip*. Here again, in random scrolls through the data some instances of this kind of mistake were detected, which led to a systematic search for the error (e.g. check all instances containing the string *kin*), so that the items concerned could be corrected manually.

It must be noted that due to the proceeding of the code, it does not identify neoclassical compounds (e.g. *biology*) as complex words but passes them as monomorphemic instances, as their constituents (e.g. *bio* and *logy*) are unlikely to be lexemes in the noun list. This drawback, however, had to be taken into account.

Once the error rate within the results had been reduced to less than 2 percent, the process of finding three-noun compounds within two-noun compounds was deemed completed. With the help of this methodology, more than 20,000 three-noun sequences could be detected within the 2-gram data set, which is why – despite the production of fake compounds – this methodology can be rated as highly effective.

### 4.2.3 Improving precision with regard to form

After the 2-gram set had been reduced to items containing three nouns, the two sets of three-noun sequences needed further refinement in order to narrow down the three-noun sequences to actual compounds. For this, sorting on a highly fine-grained level was required to eliminate instances which look similar to noun compounds. As the two data sets were very large, they were not merged into one list of three-noun sequences yet but were first refined each individually.

A large category of form-related problems in this respect goes back to the phenomenon of conversion, giving rise to a large number of words in the English language which have multiple word class memberships. This aspect can contribute to false positives in the case of lexemes which can potentially be nouns but represent verbs in this particular instance and are thus cases of mistagging. In tri-constituent sequences, this is especially prone to appear in the following structures:
(i) verbs followed by an object in the form of a compound
 e.g. *control blood sugar, studies human rights, abuse human rights, study environment management, fight breast cancer*
(ii) compounds followed by a verb
 e.g. *chairman talks, chess game ends, sport games end*

These examples from the 3-gram data set indicate that verbs are highly likely to be mistagged as nouns in corpora, even if they are inflected for third person singular, which can be interpreted as an instance of a plural noun. Automatized tagging in corpora clearly still needs to be improved when it comes to differentiating instances of conversion. In order to identify such instances, the data must be searched for nouns marked as plural, as well as for typical instances of verb-noun conversion in the N1 (i.e. first) or N3 (i.e. third) position of a three-noun sequence, such as, for example *talk, care, hold, change, bomb, plan, state, note, end*, etc. This procedure requires a decision for each sequence containing such constituent, which is not always straightforward without further context. Compare, for example, the sequences *lifestyle changes* or *health care needs*. Both instances could be a three-noun sequence with the last noun in the plural or equally a two-noun compound followed by a verb in third person singular. In such cases, the sequences were explicitly searched for in the online edition of COCA to examine which version was more frequent.

Besides instances of incorrect tagging, there are compound constituents whose multiple word class membership renders its word class in a concrete structure debatable. This was especially found in instances from the former 2-gram set, such as *play* in *playground safety* or *cook* in *cookbook author*. Do the relevant constituents represent nouns or verbs in these compounds? To solve these cases, the *Oxford English Dictionary* (OED) was consulted and compounds in which the respective component was explicitly marked as a verb were excluded. When information on the word class of the compound constituents was not available, the compound was paraphrased. In those cases where paraphrasing suggested that a constituent was a verb rather than a noun, the sequence was excluded from the list.

Nevertheless, to understand how laborious the cleaning process can be for even one single item, consider the formal sequence *back*, which can be a noun but also a verb, adjective or adverb. It occurs quite commonly in established compounds, in which it is not always an easy task to tell whether it is a noun or not. Compare, for example, the instances of *backyard, background, cornerback, paperback, quarterback* and *backbone*. In some of these cases, such as *paperback*, the *back*-constituent can be clearly identified as a noun. In cases like *backbone* or *backyard*, however, it could just as well be an adjective. In the 3-gram data set, there were 1,016 instances of potential complex compounds that contained the form *back* in one of the three positions. For each of these, the *back*-component had to be analysed in order to be able to decide whether the respective sequence should remain in the list or be removed. The decision whether to keep a compound with a *back*-component is even harder if the status of the other constituent in the compound is unclear as well, as it could represent both a noun and a verb, as in the cases of *playback, flashback, cutback* or *drawback*. As above, the OED was consulted in the decision-making process of whether to include or exclude the relevant sequences. If compounds were not listed or no information about the word class of the constituents was provided, those instances in which paraphrasing clearly identified the corresponding constituents as non-nouns were deleted. This led to the deletion of the majority of sequences with *back*-constituents, as most of them are derived from verb-particle constructions.

A similar kind of problem arises through adjectives that can also be used as nouns. If they occur in the N1 position of a tri-constituent sequence, it can be particularly difficult to determine whether they represent a noun or an adjective, cf. <u>plastic bottle disposal</u> or <u>silver</u> earring (cf. Giegerich (2009: 5–8), who argues that these elements are adjectival attributes). Here the decisions were made as follows: in those cases where there are similar constructions in which these constituents have an analogous meaning but are not adjectives, the items were maintained (as for example in the case of <u>silver</u> earring – <u>feather</u> earring and <u>plastic</u> bottle – <u>glass</u> bottle). As this project follows an inclusive approach rather than an exclusive one, in case of continuing doubt about the word class of an element the respective sequences were not deleted. This was the case, for example, in sequences in which the first element is *executive*, e.g. *executive committee member*. This proposal seems justified, considering that other current works on noun compounds seem to proceed similarly (cf. for example, Schmid (2016: 207–208), who lists *household* and *playmate* as instances of N+N compounds).

Another delicate issue involves the status of noun sequences with components ending in *-ing*, as for example in *dancing girl job, gas exporting countries, voting minority members* or *fundraising event*. Such constructions can be different in nature. They can be a noun (sequence) modified by an adjective in participle form, as in [*a*] *moving love story*, or a verb in the progressive form followed by a direct object, as in [*The city was*] *building playgrounds*. These instances are clearly not three-noun sequences and thus need to be excluded, as opposed to sequences where the *-ing* constituent constitutes a noun, e.g. in *building evacuation plan*. These cases, too, require an individual decision for each sequence, as the unwanted instances are too similar in form to three-noun compounds to permit an automated removal (compare *building estate houses* vs. *building security manager*).

### 4.2.4 Improving precision with regard to meaning

Obviously, not all sequences of nouns are compounds, let alone meaningful expressions, but can be other kinds of phenomena in which nouns appear in juxtaposition but do not form a semantic unit. Before addressing the grammatical phenomena that are formally similar to compounds, I will address nonsensical instances that need to be taken into account in working with corpus data.

The latter are found in the data are due to the computerized data sampling technique employed for the compilation of corpora. An automated script also collects juxtaposed words that are not part of utterances that would be found in actual speech production. A source of mistake in this context is text which stems from websites, resulting in noun sequences in the 3-gram data set like *name surname age*, *apple apple apple* or *questions comments feedback*, which are clearly not semantic units. These examples demonstrate that in filtering data, frequency of recurrence (as a reminder, the frequency threshold in the n-gram sets is at a token frequency of 3, cf. Section 4.1) is a good but obviously by no means robust criterion to escape nonsense items. These unwanted matches can barely be detected systematically but their identification requires manual inspection of the data. In the detection of an unwanted item, an onomasiologically oriented search for co-hyponyms can be performed to identify similar instances of this category.

Grammatical phenomena that constitute a formal interference between three-noun compounds and juxtaposed nouns can be of different kinds. One category to be mentioned contains noun sequences that are preceded by a lexeme which only modifies the first of these nouns and not the whole sequence, as in the case of *security trust fund*, or *intelligence authorization act*, which must be assumed to have been preceded by the adjectives *social* and *artificial* respectively. These adjectives modify the first of these nouns only, which is why the three-noun sequence does not constitute a conceptual unit. The same is true for the three-noun sequence *night comedy show*, which is generally preceded by *late*. This adjective modifies the first of these nouns only and thus disqualifies the sequence as a three-noun compound. Instead, *comedy show* is a two-noun compound that is modified by *late night*. Other examples are instances like *percent success rate*, where again the first noun is generally modified by a number that it forms a semantic unit with and thus the lexeme *percent* is not part of the compound. Further instances of this category are those where the three-noun sequence is part of a longer sequence of nouns, as is the case in the instance *treatment research center*, which is generally preceded by the subject of treatment, such as *cancer*, for example. A similar case is provided by the sequence *consumer product safety*, which is normally followed by the word *commission*. The fact that examples like the latter two found their way into the 3-gram list must be attributed to an erroneous tagging of the nouns before or after these sequences in the corpus, as I had explicitly selected sequences of three nouns that are not preceded or followed by another noun. Unfortunately, the search for this kind of false positives cannot be systematized but is left to accidental discovery during scrolls through the data.

Another source of false positives are sequences that do not form a semantic unit but are elliptic variants of syntactic phrases in which the preposition is omitted. This is the case, for example, in the sequences *bag potato chips*, *cup olive oil*, *teaspoon sugar* or *container ricotta cheese*. These instances can at least partly be identified systematically through searches for typical markers of quantification, e.g. *kilo, meter, bag, cup, spoon*, etc.

Further instances that do generally not fall under the scope of compounding are noun phrases containing proper names. Although proper names had been excluded by the selection of the relevant noun tags, the data sets contained many instances in which names had been erroneously tagged as common nouns. This led to entries in the three-noun list in the form of *actress sienna miller*, *secretary caspar weinberger*, *minister keizo obuchi*, *attorney bill ritter* or *friend bill flanagan*, to name just few examples. Obviously, automatized tagging in corpora for proper nouns is still highly erratic. In order to identify and remove instances of this kind, explicit searches for titles or descriptions (e.g. *president, leader, democrat* or *friend*) must be performed. Likewise, the names of places can be identified by searching for sequences containing words like *place, square, resort, valley, bay* or *hotel*.

Once the two lists of noun sequences had been cleansed of phenomena that are clearly outside the scope of compounding, the most frequent items were scrutinized for whether they could be accepted as instances of compounding. The criterion for the decision was whether the sequence potentially referred to a conceivable concept. In this context, it was not important whether I could identify what a compound was meant to denote but whether it is conceivable that a speaker used this form as a naming unit to refer to a particular concept. For example, the sequence *paper bag players* was not removed from the data set, as it is plausible that a speaker had a certain concept in mind at the moment of coinage. By contrast, the sequence *moment deletion end* was deleted, as it seems highly unlikely that it was created to denote a concept but it is probably a non-sensical juxtaposition of nouns. In those cases that did not permit a straightforward decision making (e.g. *association education foundation*), the relevant sequences were searched for in the online edition of

COCA to help decide whether to include or exclude them. In case of continuing doubt, sequences were not deleted.

The kind of screening described in this section helped identify and eliminate approximately 3,000 unwanted noun sequences and thus increased the precision of the two data sets considerably. Having narrowed down the two lists of noun sequences to the actual instances of interest, the data cleansing process was deemed completed.

**4.2.5 Lemmatization**

The procedures described in the previous sections resulted in two lists of three-noun sequences. The list derived from the 3-gram list encompassed 41,750 types of three-noun compounds; that derived from the 2-gram list contained 21,450 types. Uniting them would lead to double entries for those compounds that exist in different spellings and are part of both n-gram lists. Furthermore, even within the two lists, there were noun sequences that occurred repeatedly but in different formats due to variable spellings as well as singular and plural forms. All of these variants needed to be merged under a lemmatized form, just as the respective tokens needed to be added up in order to provide correct type and token counts.

The first step in the lemmatization process was to bring together all orthographic variants of the same type. A Python-script was written which searches for all possible spelling variants of each word, chooses the most frequent format as the lemma form and adds up the respective frequencies. The second step was to combine singular and plural variants within the more frequent form. Plural forms could not simply be identified by the plural ending -s, as there are singular words ending in -s (e.g. *bus*), which is why they were identified through the plural tags of the nouns (i.e. nn2, nnt2). The respective forms were converted into singular bases to see whether they could be matched with a singular form, in which case the frequencies were added up. In those cases where the singular-plural merge was unsuccessful (e.g. *body mass index* and *body mass indices* were not united by the script), this is due to the items not being correctly tagged as plural forms in the corpus.[6] To provide a concrete example of the lemmatization process, Figure 2 shows all the forms of *credit card company* that needed to be searched for and merged as tokens of the same type.

---

[6] The process of singular-plural lemmatization can be done much more effectively with the "Inflect library" provided by Python, which, however, unfortunately I was unaware of at that point.

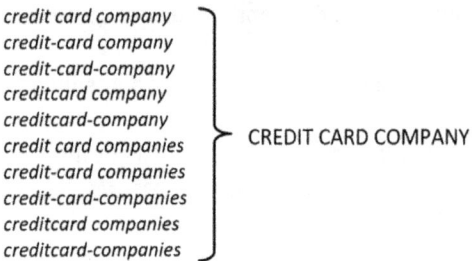

**Figure 2:** Variants to be found and lemmatized for *credit card company*.

The lemmatization process identified almost 6,000 instances of multiple entries which could be subsumed under one base form, with the token frequencies added up accordingly.

## 4.3 Results and discussion

The procedure described in the previous sections produced an inventory of 57,741 tri-constituent noun compounds of the English language, manifested by 678,737 tokens. These numbers already indicate that the word-formation process that combines three nouns is more frequent than is commonly assumed, which underlines the need to explore this phenomenon in more detail. The inventory of three-noun compounds including their token frequencies is available on the servers of the ITG LMU Munich on request and will henceforth be referred to as "3N database". In this database, the three-noun compounds are listed in the format N N N, as this format makes it possible to search not only for complete sequences of three nouns but also for the individual constituents.

All compounds in the 3N database are reported in the form in which they occur most frequently, which is why some are listed in the plural, others in the singular. Therefore, strictly speaking "lemmatization" is not the correct term for the procedure carried out, as what is listed are not lemmas in the sense of lexemes. However, listing actual lemma forms would have been unreasonable for those instances that mainly occur in the plural form (e.g. *airline pilots, season-ticket holders, problem-solving strategies*). Accordingly, in the usage of examples from the 3N database in the remainder of this work, some three-noun compounds will be cited in the singular, others in the plural.

Needless to say, the work with large data sets and an overwhelmingly automatized data retrieval process cannot deliver a perfect list of three-noun compounds. Even though the relevant scripts were designed extremely narrowly with a focus on precision, unwanted matches found their way into the results. This is a common by-product and well-known drawback of working with large data sets and automatized data processing. Accordingly, despite the care taken with the revision and cleansing of the data, there are still instances in the database that are outside the scope of interest of this project, as they constitute nonsensical sequences, such as *butter heat oven* or *summer sea ice*. Not surprisingly, the error rate is highest among low-frequency instances.

Besides clear cases of noise that are found in the 3N database, there are further instances of unwanted items that are worth mentioning, as they can be summarized into different categories and might be useful for future projects that aim to compile their own inventory of multi-word compounds or intend to further refine the 3N database. Firstly, the database contains a certain number of four-noun compounds, as in some cases one of the three constituents is a compound again, leading to entries such as *workplace education program, soybean research laboratory, classroom climate predictor, earthquake lethality potential, household insects research* or *newspaper headline*. Secondly, there is a category that has already been mentioned in Section 4.2.4 and affects sequences in which the first noun is not part of the compound but part of a preceding phrase, as in *city police department* and *lake community college*, which were almost certainly preceded by the name of a place. Besides, later scrolls through the data found instances that should have been dismissed following the principles described in the sections on improving precision such as, for example, sequences that include names (e.g. *king wood college, cannon air force, nassau community college, singer sewing machine, singer jennifer flowers, hill city council, nerve gas sarin*). Similarly, there are entries in which one of the supposed nouns is a verb, e.g. *fight breast cancer* or *heat vegetable oil*. As these possibilities had been ruled out by the script, this kind of noise can be traced back to incorrect tagging of the items in the corpus.

Other unwanted instances of juxtaposed nouns that do not form a compound are, for example, *sons birthday* or *zero breast cancer*. This kind of noise is probably the one that is most prevalent, as it could not be searched for systematically. All instances of noise mentioned here are still included in the 3N database. They were mostly detected in later stages of the work, in which frequency information had already been used for calculations, which is why no retrospective amendment was made. While in higher frequency levels of the 3N database unwanted items have been reduced to a minimum, a random sampling in the low-frequency area still yields a considerable amount of noise. However, the data cleansing was refined by random inspection and deletion until at this frequency level, too, the error rate was reduced to less than 10 percent. Accordingly, despite the continuing traces of noise, the 3N database can be claimed to be the best inventory of English three-noun compounds that is currently available.

Besides noise, the 3N database also contains instances that might not be regarded as compounds by all linguists. There are, for example, elements in which the first noun is pluralized and instances of what is commonly referred to as *descriptive genitives* (Huddleston and Pullum 2017: 1649), such as *boys football, news network, animal rights supporter, consumer affairs manager, grassroots organization* and *state workers compensation*. As these sequences denote one holistic concept, they still fit the concept of compounding as represented in this work. Furthermore, Lieber et al. (2015: 436) argue that descriptive genitives are more similar to compounds than to phrases, which is why there is no reason to exclude them from the concept of compounding.

Since many individual decisions had to be made about the inclusion of items, the 3N database is shaped by a touch of linguistic intuition and thus subject to criticism with regard to objectivity. This intervention, however, was unavoidable in order to do justice to the semantic differences between forms that look alike on the surface – something that computational methods cannot (yet) accomplish. Relying purely on automatized searching would have resulted in the inclusion of a massive number of unwanted items and their token frequencies, which would distort the data both quantitatively and qualitatively. Gaining exact token frequencies was considered indispensable, especially in view of the later operationalization of the concepts of entrenchment and productivity.

Despite the drawback in terms of time and effort, the database is seen as a major gain for research in the area of compounding, as it is not only of use for this research project but can be exploited by other researchers for further studies on complex compounding. Besides, the collection of three-noun compounds is not an end in itself but the database will provide the basis for all empirical investigations performed throughout this book and thus stands in the service of pursuing the larger goal of understanding the nature of complex compounding.

# 5 Annotation of internal structure

It has been explained in Section 3.1 that in a tripartite compound either the head or the modifier can be complex in that it contains another compound. This results in two different branching patterns: left-branching if the embedded compound is in the N1N2 position and thus constitutes the modifier, and right-branching if the embedded compound is in the N2N3 position and thus acts as a head. The overview in Figure 3 sketches the two branching patterns and exemplifies them with instances from the 3N database:

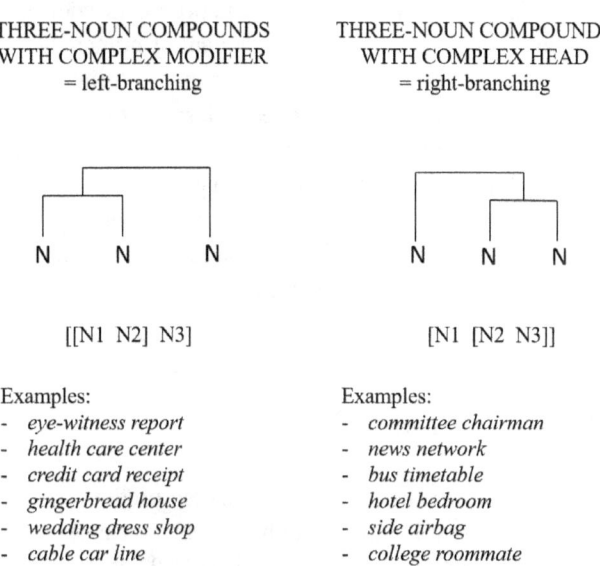

Figure 3: Branching patterns in tripartite nominal compounds.

It was suspected that these two structurally different types might also show their own formal and semantic characteristics. Therefore, information on the compounds' internal structure needed to be added to the database. Section 5.1 will present and discuss the criteria that are suggested in the literature to identify the morphological structure in complex compounds. Section 5.2 will explain the method that I have developed for the automated assignment of branching patterns.

## 5.1 Determining the branching pattern

In the morphological analysis of compounds consisting of three lexemes (N1N2N3) we are faced with the decision which noun pair is the complex base to which the third noun is added, as both the sequence of N1N2 and that of N2N3 can potentially be the embedded compound. The decision to be made is whether the second noun (N2) is part of the head or part of the modifier. For instance, in the three-noun compound *child safety seat*, is *safety* part of the head or of the modifier? Does this compound contain a complex head *safety seat* or a complex modifier *child safety*? To answer this question, criteria are needed that help determine the internal structure in polylexemic word-formation products. In this section, I will present (Section 5.1.1) and discuss (Sections 5.1.2 and 5.1.3) criteria for the assignment of branching patterns in complex compounds. I will show that the conventional criteria require more specification in order to be applicable to cases whose internal structure is not straightforward. I will present compounds where determining the internal structure proves problematic and will provide a categorization that is intended to help deal with the various kinds of intricacies encountered in the assignment of branching patterns (Section 5.1.4). In the last section, I will summarize the discussion and give an insight into the internal structure of compounds with more than three constituents.

### 5.1.1 Criteria suggested in other approaches

How do we know which of the items in complex word-formation products are immediate constituents? There are several linguists who have done research on this question, most of them focusing on the area of affixation. Plag (2003), for example, devotes a whole chapter to investigating the internal structure of multiply-affixed lexemes, but does not address this topic for compounds (or even mention that this phenomenon is to be encountered in compounds as well). Besides, it must be pointed out that scholars who touch on multiple affixation generally provide surprisingly little guidance for the identification of the morphological structure. This is probably because the default case in derivation is suffixation, where affixes are added consecutively and thus the branching pattern is straightforward. The morphological structure in derivation only becomes more intricate once prefixation also comes into play. Furthermore, many linguists who address complex affixation do not verbalize the need for criteria but simply use paraphrasing to demonstrate their choice of structure without explaining the principle that guides their decision, i.e. whether they are looking at the semantic plausibility of the resulting paraphrase or at the establishment of the lexemes used in the paraphrase. In those cases where criteria are explicitly introduced, three criteria are found repeatedly. I will present these criteria shortly, apply them to examples from the 3N database and demonstrate in this context in how far these criteria can benefit from further specification.

The first criterion used in complex affixation is formal, testing which of the potential root affixations exists as an independent lexeme (Schmid 2016: 201). I will refer to this criterion as "formal independence". A second proposal compares the plausibility of the meanings of the potential bases (Plag 2003: 39), which I refer to as the "semantic criterion". The third aspect that is commonly investigated is the distribution and productivity of the elements at question, e.g. which prefixes and suffixes tend to be added to which kinds of bases (Plag 2003: 39; Schmid 2016: 202); this aspect can be referred to as the "criterion of distribution". These three criteria per se are applicable to compounds as well; the criterion of distribution, however, is not helpful in the combination of nouns only.

There is only little literature that is explicitly dedicated to determining the structure in complex compounds. Haspelmath (2010) devotes a chapter to hierarchical structures in compounds, exemplifying the possible branching patterns for compounds consisting of three and four constituents. He justifies the different branching patterns through the semantic plausibility of the corresponding paraphrases (2010: 143). Carstairs-McCarthy (2018: 83–86) presents the branching patterns for a few complex compounds but does not reveal the criteria on which his decisions are based and exclusively uses clear, undisputable cases. Schmid (2016: 206–207) is one of the few to actually name explicit criteria for determining the structure in polylexemic compounds, following his preceding analysis of polymorphemic affixations. He settles on two criteria for revealing the internal structure of complex compounds, the first of which is modelled in analogy to the criterion of formal independence used in affixation. It examines which of the two potential noun pairs (i.e. N1N2 and N2N3) occur independently as lexemes. The second criterion is the semantic criterion used in affixation, which Schmid applies by using a paraphrase to support his choice of branching pattern. Based on these two criteria, Schmid determines the internal structure of the 75 tripartite compounds in his data set as either left- or right-branching. To exemplify his categorization, he uses sequences which are perfectly unproblematic, such as *Sunday newspaper* and *car boot sale*.

I will now apply these two criteria to the complex compounds *football coach* and *home health care*. In the case of *football coach*, the criterion of formal independence would argue that *ball coach* does not occur independently, while *football* does. Semantically, the description 'coach who trains football' is the only acceptable solution (as opposed to 'ball coach for foot'). Thus, both criteria converge in that *coach* by itself is identified as the head, while the combination of *foot* and *ball* forms the complex modifier, which is why *football coach* can be assigned the structure [[foot ball] coach]. By contrast, in the sequence *home health care*, formally *health care* does occur independently, while *home health* is not generally used as a complex lexeme. Semantically, we are dealing with 'health care that takes place at home' (as opposed to health care at dedicated centres), rather than 'care for home health'. Accordingly, this analysis proposes the structure [home [health care]]. Thus, in these two examples the semantic criterion is in agreement with the formal one, resulting in clear decisions about the branching patterns, assigning a left-branching structure to *football coach* and a right-branching structure to *home health care*. The criteria set up by Schmid (2016) are thus a solid foundation for assessing the morphological structure in complex compounds. In the majority of cases, these two criteria will suffice to determine the morphological structure of a given polylexemic compound. Nevertheless, the following section will demonstrate that the criteria do not stand the application to a broader set of items that also contains instances whose internal structure is less obvious.

### 5.1.2 Critical evaluation of the criteria

In this section, I intend to suggest amendments to the criteria introduced in Section 5.1.1 to guarantee their correct application. Firstly, the criterion of formal independence, which Schmid formulates as the question of "which elements can actually stand alone as lexemes" (2016: 206), is not fully tenable as such. It suggests that only one of the two word pairs in a tri-constituent sequence constitutes an existing lexeme. There are, however, tripartite compounds in which both word pairs can stand as lexemes and are used as such. In the case of *bus stop sign*, for example, both the potential bases *bus stop* and *stop sign* do occur. The same is true for *football game*: both *football* and *ball game* can stand in isolation. It is true that at this point, the – generally more conclusive – semantic criterion comes into play. Nevertheless, these cases indicate that Schmid's criterion is not formulated precisely enough, as the question is not "Which elements can stand alone?" but should be re-formulated as "Can only one of the two pairs stand as lexeme?" If both word pairs can stand as lexemes, further criteria must be taken into account.

Before continuing with the semantic criterion, I will discuss the criterion of formal independence in those cases where both word pairs are potential bases. Is it reasonable to argue that the embedded compound is the more frequent word pair? In the case of *football game*, for example, this would lead to choosing *football* over *ball game* as the embedded compound. This kind of decision-making might be successful in the majority of cases, since it is based on the reasoning that the more common word pair is more likely to be extended into a more complex compound than the less common word pair. The inherent problem with this proposal is that it is not a conclusive criterion but rather an indication based on likelihood. It is still possible that the less frequent word pair in a complex compound is the embedded compound. Have a look at the example *user data analysis*, where the word pair *data analysis* is used significantly more often than *user data* (3,152 occurrences in COCA online for *data analysis* vs. 455 occurrences for *user data*). Still, *data analysis* is not the complex base, as the whole expression conventionally describes the 'analysis of user data' rather than a 'data analysis of users'. To estimate how likely such a mismatch between the embedded compound and the more frequent word pair is to occur, for 40 three-noun compounds in which both word pairs formally qualify as the base of the complex compound, the word pair frequencies were determined through the online edition of COCA. In the majority of cases (34 out of 40), the embedded compound did turn out to be the more frequent word pair. Consequently, in those complex sequences where formally both ways of branching lead to existing lexemes, the (intuitive) comparison of the frequencies of the two word pairs can at least be used as a guide in determining the internal structure.

Let us turn to the semantic criterion. There are some aspects in the presentation and application of this criterion in the works cited above that cannot escape criticism. A major shortcoming is the absence of specificity. Schmid (2016: 206) stresses the importance of the semantic aspect, assigning it a crucial role, but does not further specify what exactly it involves. He gives no account of how he conceives the semantic criterion but simply paraphrases his items of *Sunday newspaper* as 'newspaper which is published on Sundays' and *car boot sale* as 'sale where people sell things from their car boots' (2016: 206). However, in order to be able to perform analyses for more delicate instances of complex compounds, we need a more thorough understanding of the aspects that the semantic criterion is supposed to encompass.

Specifying the semantic criterion in analogy to the formal criterion to the question "Which of the two word pairs makes sense?" is obviously not sensible, as in those cases where both word pairs exist both of them will be meaningful. In the examples of *football game* and *bus stop sign*, both the word pairs *football* and *ball game*, as well as *bus stop* and *stop sign* make sense. Rather, the semantic criterion needs to take into account the relationship between the word pairs and the meaning of the whole compound. Accordingly, it could be formulated as "Which of the competing interpretations comes closer to the meaning of the whole sequence?" On these grounds, we could argue that the structure underlying *bus stop sign* is more likely to be [[bus stop] sign], as this three-noun compound usually refers to a sign where the bus stops rather than a stop sign for the bus. In this way of structuring the sequence, *stop* is part of the complex modifier, while the head consists of *sign* only. It can be assumed that this reasoning reflects Schmid's understanding of the semantic criterion, as his way of operationalizing it through paraphrases incorporates the relation between the meaning of the whole sequence and the meanings of the word pairs.

At the risk of splitting hairs, it must be pointed out that even this account of the semantic criterion is not fully accurate, as it ignores the fact that two competing interpretations can exist for a particular complex compound. The branching patterns that Schmid (2016) and Carstairs-McCarthy (2018) present are absolute; there is no mention of whether other options are conceivable or a reasoning why only this solution is applicable. However, it is not true that the structure [[bus stop] sign] is the only correct option for *bus stop sign*. The alternative structure [bus [stop sign]] applies if the complex compound refers to a sign that tells buses where to stop (as they are sometimes allowed to drive further into roads than normal cars). Similarly, for Schmid's example of *car boot sale*, semantically the option [[car boot] sale], i.e. 'sale from car boots', is very salient. However, at least theoretically the option [car [boot sale]] needs to be considered as it is semantically plausible, describing a 'boot sale in a car'. This I would deem just as true for *Sunday newspaper*, where the structure [Sunday [news paper]], describing a newspaper distributed on Sundays, is straightforward. However, in a neutral spelling (i.e. *Sunday news paper*), the structure [[Sunday news] paper] is also conceivable, resulting in the interpretation 'paper with Sunday's news' (i.e. a sheet with the news for Sunday written down for a broadcaster to be read out on TV). It is true that in these cases one of the two analyses is more likely than the other one; still, it needs to be acknowledged that there are alternative structures, which is why it might be infelicitous to portray one solution as the only option. Accordingly, I would like to specify the semantic criterion as to "Which of the interpretations comes closer to the meaning of the whole sequence in this particular context?" For the compound *user data analysis*, the more likely interpretation is 'analysis of user data', as it usually represents the procedure commonly applied when information about users is collected on platforms and made use of. Still, the interpretation 'data analysis for users' could be valid in a context where a marketing agency performs the data analysis for their users (i.e. customers).

The points of criticism raised in this section might seem trivial but are still worth pointing out in order to provide an adequate toolkit for the analysis of polylexemic compounds. Before I can proceed and make a claim for additional criteria in Section 5.1.4, the next section will discuss the value of paraphrasing as a means to operationalize the semantic criterion.

### 5.1.3 Discussion of the value of paraphrasing

A critical point in the semantic criterion is the application of paraphrasing per se as a tool for determining the morphological structure. What does paraphrasing ultimately do? It seems to be an operationalization of both the formal and the semantic criterion, as it demonstrates which of the word pairs can be used independently and at the same time allows to test which of the alternative solutions is semantically more equivalent to the complex sequence. However, I have gained the impression that paraphrasing can be a pitfall, as we – not just the "naïve" native speaker, but even the linguist – might be led by what is conventionalized, not necessarily by what is more suitable from a semantic perspective. To check this impression, I performed two small-scale experiments in which I confronted native speakers with three complex compounds in two different tasks.

The first task was designed for the test item *children's bookstore*. This compound can theoretically be subject to two different branching patterns, as displayed in Figure 4:

**Figure 4:** Morphological structures for *children's bookstore*.

These two ways of structuring result in different interpretations. In the first version on the left side, where the sequence is assigned a left-branching structure, the N2 constituent *book* is part of the complex modifier. The complex compound describes a store where books for children can be bought. The second version with the right-branching structure suggests the interpretation of a bookstore for children, which is a store that is designed in a way to fit the needs of children, i.e. with small stools and a reading corner decorated with pets, etc. The more commonly found concept is obviously the first one, in which the N1N2 word pair *children's book* forms the embedded compound. Still, the N2N3 word pair *bookstore* is highly conventionalized, which is why despite the left-branching structure, the complex compound is generally spelt as N NN, a format that would rather suggest a right-branching structure. Based on this mismatch, *children's bookstore* was deemed a good candidate to test in how far paraphrasing is an efficient tool for performing a morphological analysis.

In the small-scale study, ten native speakers, three of whom are linguists, were presented with this complex compound in the written sentence: *As I needed a present for my niece, I went to a <u>children's book store</u> to get her a book about farm animals.* The target word was presented in the format N N N to avoid the candidates being influenced by the spelling. The sentence was not read out loud in order to avoid them being influenced by stressing. The participants were asked to replace the underlined sequence by a paraphrase. In their answer, all participants unanimously used the paraphrase "bookstore for children". When asked whether a *children's bookstore* is a bookstore that is designed for children, i.e. with small stools, etc., or whether it is a (normal) bookstore in which there are books for children, all the participants went for the second option. This suggests that although the speakers chose the structure [[children's book] store] from a semantic perspective, in their paraphrasing they opted for the opposite version.

The second task in the study consisted of two three-noun compounds with a parallel internal structure but different word pair frequencies, namely *food research center* and *cancer research center*. *Food research* is not a very common compound, occurring 59 times in COCA, while *research center* is quite established with 5,200 tokens. *Cancer research* has a token frequency of 1,494 and is thus fairly established. It is debatable whether these two three-noun compounds are instances of left-branching or right-branching, as according to the formal and semantic criteria both solutions seem plausible. However, obviously they are either both instances of left-branching or both instances of right-branching. For these items, ten native speakers, half of whom were linguists, were divided into two groups. The first group was given the test item *food research center*, the second group was confronted with the item *cancer research center*. Both test items were presented in written format in the format N N N. The participants were asked to paraphrase the items quickly and spontaneously. All participants in the first group paraphrased *food research center* as "research center for food". In the second group, four participants paraphrased *cancer research center* as "center for cancer research", while one opted for "research center for cancer". Accordingly, although both test items have the same morphological structure, the participants used different paraphrases.

These results support my intuition that when formulating paraphrases, speakers might not exclusively draw on semantic aspects. The behaviour of the participants in the two experiments suggests that speakers are not always guided by the underlying semantic structure but also by what sounds more natural, which is rather a reflection of the conventionalization of the word pairs involved. It is, of course, conceivable that the test item *children's bookstore* was not an ideal choice, as the internal genitive could have had an influence on its perception. Obviously, this situation requires further research; nevertheless, these observations indicate that the use of paraphrases in its function to operationalize the semantic criterion is not unproblematic.

There is one more aspect that renders the effectiveness of paraphrasing questionable. I have pointed out in Section 2.2 that compounds are an efficient tool for naming since they permit expressing complex concepts while using only little material. As a consequence, their formal side is underdetermined. For this reason, in creating a paraphrase there is not always a straightforward expression that consists exclusively of the elements involved. To demonstrate this situation, let us examine the example *suicide bomb attack*. Both paraphrases "suicide committed in the form of a bomb attack" and "attack by a suicide bomb[er]" are potential options. However, the first paraphrase is rather lengthy, while the second one requires an additional element, which renders both options somewhat clumsy. Semantically, I would argue that this complex compound has the structure [suicide [bomb attack]], as it is a bomb attack in the first place that is specified in that is has been performed by a person committing suicide. In the choice between the two paraphrases, however, the second option might be chosen simply because it sounds less clumsy than the alternative option. Another instance of this kind is provided by the sequence *child safety seat*. In paraphrasing it, the option "seat for child safety" might be preferred, simply because the alternative "safety seat for a child/children" requires either an article or the transformation of *child* into *children*.

For these reasons, if paraphrasing is used as a tool for deciding about the internal structure of complex sequences, it should be used with the awareness that firstly, there are cases where an authentic paraphrase is not necessarily in line with the semantic structure of the compound, and, secondly, that paraphrasing is often merely a reflection of what sounds more natural. The criticism raised here is not intended to disparage the use of paraphrasing; instead, it is the aim of these comments to raise awareness of the fact that paraphrasing is not unproblematic and thus to promote more careful use. With these remarks, I want to conclude the discussion of the criteria used for determining the morphological structure.

### 5.1.4 Compounds with unclear internal structure

This section will report on three-noun compounds for which determining the internal structure is not as straightforward as in the examples used in the previous sections. There are cases in which the application of the proposed criteria – even in their refined version – fails to reach a conclusive decision. Consider the example of *witness protection program*. Is *protection* part of the head or of the modifier, i.e. do we have a left-branching item [[witness protection] program] or right-branching [witness [protection program]]? Both potential bases *witness protection* and *protection program* can stand as independent lexemes perfectly well, which is why the criterion of formal independence is not helpful here. Deciding which word pair occurs more frequently is not decisive either, as both word pairs *witness protection* and *protection program* occur equally frequently (695 vs. 674 tokens). Semantically, both variants are in agreement with the meaning of the whole sequence, as a witness protection program is just as much a 'program for witness protection/the protection of witnesses' as it is a 'protection program for witnesses'. Therefore, the application of the two standard criteria does not yield a satisfactory result. This not an isolated phenomenon: does the compound *infant mortality rate* describe the 'mortality rate of infants' or rather the 'rate of infant mortality'? What about the structures of *family research council*, *population growth rate* or *senate minority leader*? In all of these cases, the criteria provided so far cannot fruitfully be applied to identify the internal structure.

One could raise the question here whether this is a problem of the criteria or rather of the phenomenon itself. More precisely, do we need a more refined and extended set of criteria or are there simply items for which the branching pattern is not clear? If the latter is true, is there possibly a third type of complex compound with a neutral branching pattern or a ternary structure, qualifying as synthetic word-formation types (cf. Schmid 2016: 205)? Following the traditional view that – with few exceptions – word-formation products are the results of binary processes, the latter assumption is rejected. Consulting research on polymorphemic affixation is not helpful in this situation. Even for affixes, there is only little exploration of more delicate cases. Most linguists use examples that are perfectly clear and do not put themselves to the trouble of going more deeply into the topic.

Plag (2003: 40) points out that in some complex compounds even the semantic criterion does not suffice to determine the morphological structure. Still, he does not further comment on how to deal with these instances. He simply concludes that in cases with ambiguity the differences in the competing interpretations are very subtle anyway (2003: 40). Haspelmath (2010: 143) states that "[s]ometimes a compound with more than two nouns may allow two hierarchical structures simultaneously. For example, a compound like *nuclear power station* can be grouped as [[nuclear power] [station]] or as [[nuclear] [power station]] with equal justification, because both make sense semantically and both the compounds *nuclear power* and *power station* exist in English." Lieber (2010: 44–45) admits that there are compounds whose structure is ambiguous and which can therefore be represented in more than one way, but only works with cases in which the two options result in different interpretations (e.g. [arctic [cat observer]] vs. [[arctic cat] observer]). I intend to explain why these proposals are simplified and hardly distinctive. Firstly, these authors refer to different kinds of unclarity as will be demonstrated later, and secondly, at least in some cases there are additional criteria that can be used to determine the internal structure. Therefore, I will attempt to derive a categorization for compounds with an unclear internal structure and show to what extent further criteria can be applied.

The first category of three-noun compounds that shows a peculiarity with regard to branching pattern is a group that I propose to call "homonymous complex compounds". In these cases, two different concepts are concealed within the same form. Accordingly, we are dealing with two complex compounds that are formally identical but differ semantically because they are related to different branching patterns, each of which results in a different output with a different meaning. This phenomenon has already been addressed in Section 5.1.2 with the example of *bus stop sign*, which can have two readings, both of which are plausible. Lieber's (2010) above cited example of the *arctic cat observer* clearly also belongs in this category. A further notorious but popular example for demonstrating this phenomenon is the German compound *Mädchenhandelsschule*, which probably goes back to Augst (1975). It could denote a 'Handelsschule für Mädchen' ('commercial college for girls') if categorized as right-branching; if read as a left-branching compound it denotes a 'Schule für Mädchenhandel' ('school for trafficking girls'). Obviously, this example is generally used rather humorously, as the two interpretations only exist theoretically while pragmatically the branching pattern is relatively clear.[7] Still, in theory we are dealing with two different, homonymous three-noun compounds: *Mädchenhandelsschule*$_1$ [[N N] N] and *Mädchenhandelsschule*$_2$ [N [N N]]. In these cases, the criterion that is required for the identification of the relevant structure is context information.

Another example of this category is the earlier mentioned sequence of *children's book store*. If the word pair N2N3 is chosen as the complex base, i.e. the structure [N [N N]] is assigned, it denotes a bookstore for children; if N1N2 is regarded as the embedded compound, the sequence has the structure [N N [N]], which results in the interpretation of a store with children's books. A further example of this kind is *air traffic control*. In the structure [N [N N]], this compound denotes 'the control of (street) traffic from the air', e.g. with the help of a drone. In the structure [[N N] N], however, it denotes 'the control of air traffic', i.e. of airplanes. An example found outside the 3N database is *winter sports equipment*. In the structure [[winter sports] equipment], this complex compound refers to 'equipment for winter sports', e.g. for skiing, while the structure [winter [sports equipment]] denotes 'sport equipment for the winter', which could also be warm running gear. A further example is the advertisement by a famous German furniture store for a *Kindergartenstuhl* ('kinder garden chair'), which could both be a 'chair for a kindergarten' or a 'garden chair for children'. Only the picture next to the advertisement made it clear that the correct interpretation in this case was the second option.

It has been pointed out above that in these cases, which are semantically ambiguous in isolation, context is the criterion that helps decide which interpretation is intended in the particular instance. Furthermore, in spoken language these compounds can presumably be disambiguated by means of stress, as it can be assumed that in the structure [N [N N]] the N2 will receive a main stress. Moreover, often one of the two possibilities is more conventionalized, which makes one of the interpretations more likely. Accordingly, homonymous three-noun compounds do not actually have an unclear internal structure.

---

7 Besides, if the latter interpretation was intended, it would probably be called a *Mädchenhandelschule*, i.e. lacking the linking element.

The next group of complex compounds that defies a straightforward determining of branching pattern falls into a category that I would categorize as instances of laymen insecurity. In these cases, there is only one "correct" (as in *intended*) interpretation. Still, it is not necessarily clear to the average language user which one it is but only to speakers who have some degree of expertise in the field in which the compound is used or has been created. I will provide a few examples to illustrate this kind of unclarity. Any person involved with medicine will probably be aware that the *blood sugar level* is 'the level of the blood sugar'. A layman, however, might just as well consider the interpretation 'sugar level of the blood'. Similarly, for the compound *business management system*, I claim that the average speaker does not know whether it denotes 'a system for business management' or rather 'a management system for businesses'. Furthermore, is a *reader service card* a 'card for/with reader services' or a 'service card for readers'? Is a *mortgage tax relief* a 'tax relief on the mortgage' or a 'relief of the mortgage tax'? In these cases, semantically, there is a slight difference between the two available interpretations, which are barely noticeable for the layman. A person more familiar with the area that the respective complex compound was coined in could probably argue in favour of one interpretation or the other. Still, in some cases, only the person that created the expression will know for sure, as is the case, for example, in *support evaluation list* ('evaluation list for support' vs. 'list for support evaluation'). In some of these instances, one of the two paraphrases sounds slightly more natural, which is, however, not necessarily the one that shows the underlying structure correctly but might be the word pair that is more conventionalized (cf. Section 5.1.3). In these types of unclear three-noun compounds, background knowledge and expertise are potential criteria that could help resolve the internal structure. However, in practice speakers do not have any problems understanding these compounds even without knowing the underlying structure, as in most cases the two interpretations are only marginally different and speakers are seldom faced with situations in which they require such explicit knowledge of these concepts that the tiny nuances that distinguish the two potential interpretations would become obvious. It is probably this category that Plag (2003: 40) has in mind when he talks of alternative morphological structures that result in marginal differences in meaning.

For the next category of complex compounds that are unclear with regard to their branching pattern, it is debatable whether they form a category of their own or must be seen as an extreme subtype of the category just presented. Either way, a gradient can be assumed between the category just mentioned and this one, which I suggest calling "unbiased compounds" (which might sound clumsy but is a means to avoid the term "neutral", the reason for which will be explained below). In the previous category, technically there is a difference between the two available interpretations, which is why the underlying structure can be identified with the help of background knowledge or expertise. In unbiased compounds, by contrast, there seems to be no tangible difference between the two competing interpretations. If we look at the complex compound *traffic control system*, for example, is it a 'control system for traffic' or a 'system for traffic control'? Both variants sound natural from a formal perspective and are semantically plausible. As far as the meaning is concerned, there seems to be no difference with regard to which word pair is regarded as the embedded compound as both interpretations seem to describe the same concept. This is similarly true for the compound *population growth rate*: does it denote 'the growth rate of the population' or 'the rate of population growth'? Again, there seems to be no difference between the two interpretations that come with the different branching patterns. This phenomenon is quite prevalent, as there are plenty of further examples in the 3N database that I would put into this category:

- *aggression prevention program*
- *cancer research center*
- *currency exchange rate*
- *data management system*
- *depression danger zone*
- *infant mortality rate*
- *missile defense system*
- *office lunch bill*
- *party membership card*
- *program planning process*
- *project evaluation process*
- *prosecution team member*
- *safety monitoring board*
- *soil conservation program*
- *transportation safety board*
- *system development process*
- *teacher education program*
- *behavior assessment system*
- *college entrance exams*
- *drug rehabilitation program*
- *highway traffic safety*
- *sea surface temperature*
- *teacher preparation program*
- *turtle observation rate*
- *university entrance requirements*
- *vehicle registration number*
- *violence prevention program*
- *voter registration number*
- *water filtration system*

In all of these cases, both word pairs are plausible embedded compounds as they are similarly acceptable from a semantic and formal perspective and the two competing interpretations seem to be identical in meaning. For these compounds, there are no criteria that can help decide for one of the two branching patterns. This category is probably what Haspelmath (2010: 143) is referring to when he states that for some complex compounds there can be more than one branching pattern. What does this mean for the categorization system? Do we need a further category of neutral branching, besides left- and right-branching? I venture to suggest that this would not be adequate, as these items do have a particular morphological structure, i.e. are instances of either left- or right-branching, but we simply fail to identify it. Accordingly, I do not agree with Haspelmath (2010: 143) when he states that some complex compounds may permit two hierarchical structures simultaneously, but would rather argue that in some complex compounds the underlying branching pattern remains unclear as we lack criteria that are sensitive enough to yield a conclusive solution.

### 5.1.5 Summary and conclusion

The previous sections have demonstrated that the criteria that have been applied so far for the identification of the internal structure in complex word-formation products are a sound base but can benefit from further refinement. It has been argued that the formal criterion as formulated by Schmid is not fully accurate, as it ignores the fact that both word pairs in a complex compound can be existing lexemes. Accordingly, it was argued that this criterion needs to be specified to "Does only one of the word pairs occur?" It has furthermore been proposed that in those cases where both word pairs are used as lexemes, a comparison of the word pair frequencies can help identify the embedded compound. With regard to the semantic criterion, an attempt has been made to specify what is actually being examined in applying this criterion. The discussion has led to the conclusion that the semantic criterion must investigate the competing interpretations in relation to the meaning of the whole compound in a particular context. This explanation is not claimed to be an unprecedented insight; but to my knowledge it has never been defined in this specificity. Finally, it has been argued that the way in which the semantic criterion is commonly operationalized, namely by means of paraphrasing, entails the risk of not actually representing the morphological structure of a complex compound but being misled by other formal aspects.

Furthermore, it has been shown that there are instances of complex compounds which require further criteria for the identification of their morphological structure, such as background knowledge, expertise or context. Nevertheless, even with this extended set of criteria the question of branching pattern cannot be resolved without doubt in all cases. It was shown that there is a considerable number of three-noun compounds for which the available criteria cannot successfully be applied to determine their morphological structure, which is why for these items the categorization into right-branching or left-branching remains blurry. Those compounds that seem to refuse a categorization are not only intriguing from a structural perspective but might also be interesting when it comes to their cognitive status, an aspect that could be investigated in studies concerned with the processing of left-branching and right-branching compounds.

I have also mentioned that difficulties in determining the branching pattern barely affect the speaker, as in those cases where both structures are conceivable, the differences between the competing interpretations are mostly negligibly small or not existent at all. Therefore, these instances are rather a problem for the linguist but not so much for the language user. Native speakers do not consciously make a decision for branching patterns, as they generally do not concern themselves with the morphological structure of complex words. They do, however, sometimes contemplate the internal structure of complex sequences – even if not consciously – when it comes to spelling. The relation between orthography and the internal structure of complex compounds will be the subject of Section 6.3.

The discussion in the previous sections must not lead to the belief that the internal structure of complex compounds is predominantly a delicate issue. In the majority of tripartite compounds, determining the morphological structure is quite straightforward and the two criteria presented at the beginning suffice to make a decision for left-branching or right-branching. In this light, the discussion and the venture to refine the criteria might seem petty and hair-splitting. However, it was an aim of this section to raise awareness of the fact that there are gaps in the methods suggested for determining the internal structure of complex lexemes. The weaknesses that have been addressed indicate that previous accounts of morphological structure leave room for improvement. It would be desirable for them to explicitly explain the criteria they employ and to refrain from presenting uncontroversial examples only.

While for tri-constituent compounds the situation might still be manageable, the call for better developed criteria becomes more crucial the more complex the sequences under investigation become. For complex compounds consisting of four lexemes, for example, there are already up to five different potential morphological structures, as illustrated in Figure 5:

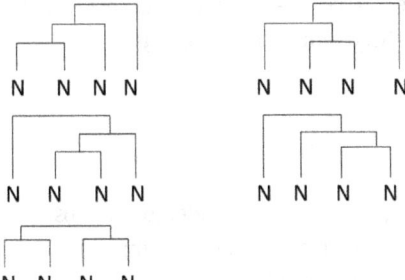

**Figure 5:** Potential morphological structures for four-constituent compounds.

Whether all of these morphological structures are actually used needs to be explored in a different project. However, it is obvious that here the decision-making process will become even harder. If we look at the complex compound *data safety*

*monitoring board*, for example, there are several legitimate options regarding the internal structure and thus the possible interpretations, e.g.
- [[data safety] [monitoring board]] i.e. 'monitoring board for data safety'
- [[[data safety] monitoring] board] i.e. 'board for the monitoring of data safety'
- [data [[safety monitoring] board]] i.e. 'board for safety monitoring of the data'

Evaluating which of the proposed structures and thus interpretations is correct is indisputably considerably more difficult than with tri-constituent compounds. It is conceivable that in such constructs the line between the different interpretations becomes even more blurry, since the semantic nuances become even finer, which supports my call for more precision when it comes to the criteria that can be used to determine the branching pattern.

Considering that even a manual assignment of branching patterns has proved to be delicate in some instances, it will be intriguing to see to what extent the internal structure in three-noun compounds can be identified in an automated way, which is the challenge that the next section will be dedicated to.

## 5.2 Automated assignment of branching pattern

As it was desirable to have information on the branching pattern for all items in the 3N database, the full set of almost 58,000 compounds needed to be annotated. Such venture obviously requires an automated tagging system. The following sections will present the technique developed for this purpose. Section 5.2.1 will explain which of the criteria that have been discussed in Section 5.1 can be operationalized in a way that allows an automated application. Section 5.2.2 will introduce the methodology that was developed for this purpose, the results of which will be presented in Section 5.2.3, including an evaluation and discussion of the proposal.

### 5.2.1 Choice of criteria

From a theoretical point of view, the semantic criterion is considered the most substantial criterion to determine the internal structure of a complex compound. From a methodological perspective, however, there is no feasible method to operationalize this criterion in such a way that it could be used for an automated categorization. The same is true for the criteria of context and background knowledge. Accordingly, the operationalization over a large data set requires a trade-off with regard to the criterion deemed appropriate, which is why the semantic criterion needs to be sacrificed to the more operationalizable formal criterion.

The formal criterion has been refined to the question of whether only one of the two word pairs occurs as a lexeme. As has been pointed out, however, it is possible that both word pairs are existing lexemes. Section 5.1.2 reported on the observation that in the majority of instances the embedded compound is the word pair that is more frequent. Accordingly, the determination of the morphological structure will be based on the comparison between the frequencies of the word pairs N1N2 and N2N3 in a three-noun compound, based on the reasoning that the more frequent pair is more likely to be the embedded compound. This approach to the assignment of branching patterns is of course only an indirect way of identifying the morphological structure, which is why a certain error rate must be allowed for. Wrong tagging is expected to occur firstly in complex compounds in which both word pairs are used frequently. In these cases, the more frequent pair will be selected, even if there is only a small discrepancy. Furthermore, it must be expected that there are cases in which the more frequent word pair is simply not the embedded compound, as has been pointed out in Section 5.1.2.

To test the suitability of this proposal, the procedure described in Section 5.1.2 was repeated for a sample of 100 tripartite compounds from the 3N database. For each of them, the usage frequencies of the noun pairs were manually extracted from the online edition of COCA and compared. The noun pair which reached a higher usage frequency was marked as the potential embedded compound. At the same time, the internal structure of these test items was identified manually by means of the application of the criteria presented in Section 5.1. A comparison of the results of the frequency-based decision making and the criteria-based assignment of morphological structure yielded an agreement of 89 percent. Accordingly, this method was evaluated as a good approximation to determining the internal structure of the complex compounds in the 3N database.

### 5.2.2 Operationalization

The procedure described in the previous section was automated through a self-written Python-script. It splits each three-noun compound (e.g. *law enforcement official*) into the combination of the first and second noun N1N2 (e.g. *law enforcement*) as well as the combination of the second and third noun N2N3 (e.g. *enforcement official*). These word pairs serve as an input for a frequency search in the offline version of COCA. The script includes a step of lemmatization, which tracks back different spellings and singular and plural forms of the word pairs to a lemmatized form, in order to yield correct word pair frequencies.

In order to minimize the error rate, it is important to not simply count the overall occurrences of each word pair, as this gives rise to what I propose to call "fake word pairs". These occur mainly in left-branching compounds, in which the N2 and N3 occur with a high number of different N1. The paradigmatic variation of the N1 in this set of tripartite compounds falsifies the branching pattern because it makes the N2N3 combination look like the more prominent word pair based on its co-occurrence. To exemplify this phenomenon, the following listing is an extract of three-noun compounds whose N2 is *rights* and whose N3 is *movement*, including the token frequencies of whole sequence:

- *animal rights movement*     60
- *abortion rights movement*     19
- *gay rights movement*     14
- *property rights movement*     12
- *disability rights movement*     11
- *migrant rights movement*     4
- *human rights movement*     3

These tripartite compounds are clearly instances of left-branching, with the complex modifier consisting of a variable N1 and the N2 *rights*. However, as the combination of *rights* and *movement* accompanies a high number of different N1s, it yields a higher number of occurrences than the pairs of N1 + *rights* and thus appears as the more frequent word pair. In this small sample of 7 items alone, there are 125 occurrences for *rights* + *movement* but only 60 for *animal* + *rights* and less for all other N1 + *rights* combinations. Consequently, in these instances the word pair *rights movement* would be falsely categorized as the embedded compound. Similar three-noun compounds that are prone to the phenomenon of fake word pairs are, for example, the following:
- N1 (e.g. *foot/cancer/animal*) *research center*
- N1 (e.g. *teacher/pupil/student/adult*) *training program*
- N1 (e.g. *health/day/child*) *care center*

To avoid false tagging for these kinds of items, the code for Python was specified to not simply count the overall token frequencies of the word pairs but to instead search for the word pairs not preceded or followed by another noun.

The result of this frequency search is a table that lists both word pairs of a tripartite compound with their frequencies, e.g. *law enforcement*: 1,394, *enforcement official*: 10. Based on the comparison of the frequencies, the script classifies the more frequent word pair as the embedded compound. Depending on whether the embedded compound is located in the N1N2 or the N2N3 position, it tags the three-noun compound as left-branching or right-branching. Accordingly, in comparing the word pair frequencies of *law enforcement official, law enforcement* is recognized as the more frequent word pair and marked as the embedded compound, which is why *law enforcement official* is tagged as left-branching.

With the help of this methodology, each item in the database was assigned a branching pattern. This information was added to the 3N database in the form of an additional column for each compound, which has the manifestations of "left" and "right", thus reporting the location of the embedded compound within the complex sequence. The next section presents the quantitative results as well as the flaws of this method.

### 5.2.3 Results and discussion

Among the 57,741 three-noun compounds in the 3N database almost two thirds (62.82%, i.e. 36,271 items) were tagged as left-branching compounds and about one third (36.95%, i.e. 21,335 items) was assigned a right-branching structure. A small proportion of compounds (0.23%, i.e. 135 items) could not be assigned a branching pattern by the code because both word pairs showed the exact same word pair frequency.

These results confirm that the complex constituent in a three-noun compound is more likely to be the modifier than the head. This finding is generally in line with the results gained by Schmid (2016: 208), who determines the branching pattern for a sample of tripartite compounds and finds that left-branching is the more dominant pattern. Schmid, however, observes an even stronger proportion of left-branching items, as he gives figures of 83% for left-branching and 17% for right-branching. This deviation is probably due to the fact that his analysis is based on a sample of 75 items only, which might not be fully representative. Nevertheless, as his categorization was done manually, precision in this set is probably maximally high, while it can be expected to be lower in the automated tagging applied in this project. At the same time, an examination of the automatically assigned branching pattern of 100 randomly picked items from the 3N database produced an error rate lower than 7 percent, which is why the accuracy of this method can be regarded as high. Consequently, the procedure applied here can be assessed as well qualified for the determination of the internal structure of complex compounds.

As expected, the method resulted in wrong tagging in instances where the noun pair that occurs more frequently is not the embedded compound. This, for example, applies to the items *prescription drug use* and *prescription drug problem*, which are clearly instances of left-branching. They were categorized as right-branching by the code due to the fact that *drug use* and *drug problem* occur frequently enough to overrule the frequency of *prescription drug*. The same is true for several complex compounds containing *law enforcement* as N2N3. As *law enforcement* is a quite frequent compound, *drug law enforcement* and *immigration law enforcement* have been erroneously tagged as right-branching. Further mistagged items are, for example, *winter survival skills, summer day time, drug market research* and *circle reader service*, all of which were erroneously marked as instances of right-branching because *daytime, market research* and *reader service* are each more frequent than *summer day, drug market* and *circle reader*, respectively. This kind of error had been foreseen and accepted as a trade-off for the practicability of the method.

Quite surprisingly, even though this possibility was estimated to be extremely low in the preparation of the Python-script, there were about 700 cases in which no branching pattern could be determined because both noun pairs received identical frequency counts. Examples for this category of unclear items are provided in Table 1. Note that in those cases where 0 occurrences are given, this does not mean that the respective word pairs do not exist, but that they do not occur by themselves without being preceded or followed by another noun (due to the design of the code aiming to prevent fake word pairs, see page 61). *Routine patrol*, for example, seems to be always preceded or followed by a further noun.

**Table 1:** Compounds with identical word pair frequencies.

| 3N | Frequency N1N2 | Frequency N2N3 |
|---|---|---|
| soil conservation program | 50 | 50 |
| college entrance requirements | 37 | 37 |
| pizza delivery guy | 34 | 34 |
| forest product companies* | 5 | 5 |
| safety monitoring board | 3 | 3 |
| city commuter lot* | 2 | 2 |
| health exercise advisor* | 1 | 1 |
| nut crunch cereal* | 1 | 1 |
| theft claim frequencies* | 1 | 1 |
| parent success indicator* | 1 | 1 |
| population standard deviation* | 0 | 0 |
| behaviour coding system | 0 | 0 |
| earth diver myth* | 0 | 0 |
| moving picture experts* | 0 | 0 |
| routine patrol stop | 0 | 0 |
| support evaluation list | 0 | 0 |

Those items marked with an asterisk were subsequently manually assigned to the categories of left-branching or right-branching based on the criteria presented in Section 5.1. The instances *earth diver myth, moving picture experts, forest product companies, health exercise advisor, theft claim frequencies* and *parent success indicator*, for example, were declared to be instances of left-branching, whereas *population standard deviation* and *city commuter lot* were categorized as right-branching. This revision left the category of unclear compounds with 135 items in the 3N database which are tagged for none of the two branching patterns but have received the attribute "unclear".

How did this technique perform for those instances which had been discussed as unclear cases in Section 5.1.4? Table 2 shows the word pair frequencies and the assigned branching pattern (BP) for some of these three-noun compounds:

**Table 2:** Branching patterns assigned to 3N categorized as "unbiased".

| 3N | Frequency N1N2 | Frequency N2N3 | BP |
|---|---|---|---|
| infant mortality rate | 562 | 449 | left |
| turtle observation rates | 0 | 6 | right |
| depression danger zone | 0 | 185 | right |
| health placement decisions | 14 | 45 | right |
| hurricane recovery efforts | 8 | 140 | right |
| flight crew member | 172 | 346 | right |
| income tax rate | 1,772 | 904 | left |
| sea surface temperature | 65 | 174 | right |

It can be seen that in most cases, based on the competing word pair frequencies a fairly clear decision was taken for one of the two branching patterns. As a manual decision-making would have not been able to opt for either of the two branching patterns, in all of these cases the automatically assigned branching pattern was maintained, which is why instances that had been classified as "unbiased" are not necessarily listed as unclear cases in the 3N database.

It can be concluded that although frequency of occurrence was not considered a reliable criterion in determining the morphological structure of complex compounds from a theoretical perspective, this criterion has yielded a high degree of agreement with a manual assignment of branching patterns. Considering that even a manual assignment is not always straightforward as has been set out in Section 5.1, the degree of accuracy yielded by this method is deemed acceptable. The analysis of the wrongly tagged items shows that erroneous tagging takes mainly place in those cases where both word pairs are existing lexemes – a risk that had been foreseen and accepted. To improve the error rate of this method, it might be useful to mark instances in which both word pairs receive a very similar token count, which then need to be subjected to a manual assignment. This, however, is of course only practicable for smaller data sets.

As most instances of erroneous tagging were only noticed in later stages of the project, the tagging remained unchanged in order not to create mismatches in the numbers already used for calculation. Mistagging predominantly affects three-noun compounds which were categorized as right-branching but are instances of left-branching instead. Consequently, the numbers reported for the branching patterns can be assumed to be slightly distorted in that left-branching is even more frequent than suggested by the results of the tagging script, while the number of right-branching items is lower than calculated. In this regard, it must furthermore be noted that the rate of noise (in the sense of items that cannot be accepted as compounds) is considerably higher among items that were tagged as right-branching than among those tagged as left-branching. Therefore, those sequences in the 3N database that are most likely to be instances of noise are not just items in the very low frequency area, as was concluded in Section 4.3, but within the low-frequency category it is predominantly items that are supposed to be right-branching which do not fall under the scope of compounds as defined in this project. Eliminating instances of low-frequency right-branching noise would definitely further increase the dominance of left-branching items over right-branching ones, which might be an additional aspect that explains the discrepancy in the relation between the two branching patterns as calculated in this project and as found by Schmid.

With these remarks, I want to conclude the documentation of the data retrieval and annotation process. The procedures described in Chapters 4 and 5 have resulted in a sound inventory of three-noun compounds of the English language, embedded in a database that provides information on their frequency and internal structure. In the following chapters, I will proceed to a detailed examination of the compounds in the database in the context of different research questions.

# Part III: Formal and functional description of three-noun compounds

# 6 Formal analysis of three-noun compounds

This chapter will examine tripartite compounds from a formal perspective. Several aspects that are commonly the subject of investigation in simple compounding will be addressed in order to provide a clearer picture of the formal characteristics of three-noun compounds in English. What do they typically look like? Are they composed of polysyllabic nouns, or are they preferably composed of fairly short words? Do they overwhelmingly consist of three bare nouns or are the constituents morphologically complex themselves? How homogeneously do three-noun compounds behave when it comes to their stress pattern? Which orthographic formats do three-noun compounds tend to be used in? In the investigation of these aspects, I also aim to reveal potential differences between left-branching and right-branching compounds: Are there any categorical differences when it comes to the formal characteristics of these two types of three-noun compounds? Do right-branching compounds, for example, tend to occur in different orthographic formats and show a different stress pattern than left-branching ones? In order to answer these questions, Section 6.1 will look into the length and morphological complexity of tri-constituent compounds. Section 6.2 will examine whether left-branching compounds and right-branching ones show a different behaviour regarding these aspects. In Section 6.3, the orthographic realization of the compounds will be in the focus of interest, exploring the use of the available spelling formats. Section 6.4 will approach the aspect of stress with the aim of evaluating whether stress in complex compounding is inherently different than in simple compounding. It will furthermore discuss to what extent left- and right-branching compounds[8] differ regarding their stress pattern.

All the analyses performed will be based on items from the 3N database. For quantitative investigations the whole data set will be used, while when qualitative aspects or features that cannot be analysed in an automated way are being examined, smaller sub-samples will be selected. Throughout the sections, I will work with different samples in order to provide a broad and comprehensive picture of three-noun compounds in English.

---

**8** In using the phrase "left- and right-branching compounds" henceforth, I will be referring to left-branching compounds and right-branching compounds, and not compounds that could be left- and right-branching, i.e. which have an unclear internal structure.

## 6.1 How complex are three-noun compounds formally?

When I presented my field of research at linguistic conferences, before starting the presentation I asked the linguists present whether they could think of examples of three-noun compounds in English. They created lengthy and clumsy sequences such as *law enforcement authority, gender identity disorder* or *trade union association* and acted with surprise when I pointed out that more typical examples of three-noun compounding are instances like *football game, birthday party, bus timetable* or *bedroom door*. This anecdote illustrates that the image of tri-constituent compounds seems to be one of clumsy, unnatural sequences. The term *complex compound* itself indicates that these items are indeed complex. However, the notion of *complex* in this sense merely denotes that they have a hierarchical internal structure, it does not necessarily mean that they contain morphologically complex constituents. In the following sections, I will explore the formal complexity of three-noun compounds as manifest through their length and number of morphological constituents, in order to evaluate how long and complex these word-formation products typically are. In this context, the compounds will not just be investigated as a whole but their constituents will also be examined with the aim of gaining insights into the composition of these items.

The operationalization of the variables length and morphological complexity was not automatized but performed manually, which is why the examination was not applied to the whole data set but merely to a sample of 600 compounds from the 3N database. In order to investigate a potential contrast between more and less frequently occurring items, the sample was composed of the 300 most frequent and the 300 least common compounds in the database.

### 6.1.1 Length of compounds and constituents

As English contains many silent letters, counting the number of letters was not deemed appropriate for operationalizing the length of a compound. Instead, the number of syllables, i.e. a compound's phonological complexity, was chosen to be a better reflection of how long an item is (or felt to be). The syllables of the items in the sample were counted and compared. Table 3 displays the average number of syllables for the three-noun compounds in the two different frequency levels.

On average, the 600 items under investigation show a syllable count of 5.44. The table shows, however, that the length of the compounds differs between the frequency levels. While the 300 most frequently occurring compounds have a length of just under five syllables, the rarer instances tend to have up to six

**Table 3:** Average number of syllables for 3N in different frequency levels.

| Frequency level | Average number of syllables |
| --- | --- |
| all 600 items | 5.44 |
| 300 most frequent 3N | 4.94 |
| 300 least frequent 3N | 5.93 |

syllables. These numbers indicate that there is a tendency for more conventionalized three-noun compounds to be slightly shorter than less conventionalized ones. These results become even more distinct when looking at the median for these two frequency categories: the median for the 300 most common items is 4, whereas the median for the 300 least common compounds is 6.

The discovery that more frequent compounds tend to be shorter than less frequent ones is not surprising as this phenomenon holds true in general for linguistic elements of differing complexity (cf. Krott et al. 1999). The intention of this comparison is rather to show that among those three-noun compounds that are used to a higher extent, lengthy sequences are quite atypical. This impression is further strengthened when we focus on sub-categories in the higher frequency level: the 50 most frequent items have an average length of 4.69 syllables; the ten most common items tend to be even shorter with a length of 4.1 syllables, comprising items such as *peanut butter, birthday party, college football* or *health care reform*. Among the most frequent items there are even minimally short items that consist of three syllables only, such as *football team, baseball game, health care costs* and *air force base*.

Nevertheless, it cannot be denied that there are three-noun compounds which are remarkably long. The following words are examples from both frequency levels that are much longer than the average, comprising between 9 and 11 syllables:[9]

| 300 MOST FREQUENT 3N | 300 LEAST FREQUENT 3N |
| --- | --- |
| – *government accountability office* | – *university student association* |
| – *security council resolution* | – *music library association* |
| – *emergency management agency* | – *acquisition quality assurance* |
| – *deputy assistant secretary* | – *university law professor* |
| – *health maintenance organization* | – *eating disorder association* |

---

[9] It is important to remember that – as explained in Section 4.3 – differences in citation form (some examples being reported in the singular, others in the plural) are based on the form in which the respective three-noun compound occurs more frequently.

(continued)

| 300 MOST FREQUENT 3N | 300 LEAST FREQUENT 3N |
|---|---|
| – student government representative | – catastrophe theory metaphor |
| – community college president | – drug enforcement administration |
| – attention deficit disorder | – traffic safety administration |
| – temperature measurement applications | – victims compensation coordinators |
| – personnel development coordinators | – exchange commission investigators |

These examples show that lengthy three-noun sequences do not only occur in the low frequency area but are also to be found among the more conventionalized ones (e.g. *government accountability office* or *emergency management agency*). They are, however, clearly untypical members of the category of three-noun compounds since they have about double the length of an average three-noun compound. Some of these, especially those in the category of the more frequently used items, are ones that might at some point be replaced by an abbreviation (e.g. *drug enforcement administration*). It is noticeable that the majority of these lengthy terms are titles (e.g. *president, coordinator, investigator*) or names of institutions (e.g. *office, agency, faculty, administration, committee, association* or *organization*) and thus terms which are probably used in more formal and bureaucratic contexts. (These instances will in Section 8.8 be described as "drawing-board compounds".)

Based on these results, it can be stated that frequently occurring three-noun compounds are relatively short, comprising four syllables only, which means that on average they consist of two monosyllabic lexemes and one bisyllabic lexeme. Less frequently used three-noun compounds tend to comprise up to six syllables. This cannot be considered short; however, these instances are still significantly shorter than the items of *law enforcement authority* and *trade union association* cited at the beginning of this chapter, which encompass eight syllables each and are thus not typical representatives of three-noun compounds as regards their length.

How is the length of the compounds distributed over their constituents? According to the figures in Table 3, each constituent tends to have a length of 1.81 syllables. Do all the three nouns tend to have the same length? If not, do the longer constituents occur overwhelmingly in a particular position? In the two examples of *law enforcement authority* and *trade union association*, the first noun is considerably shorter than the others – is this symptomatic? To answer these questions, the length of the compounds will now be viewed in more detail for the individual constituents. Table 4 again displays the average word length as approximated through syllable counts for the most and least frequent compounds but differentiated for each of the constituents N1, N2 and N3.

**Table 4:** Average number of syllables distributed among constituents.

| Frequency level | Syllables total | Syllables N1 | Syllables N2 | Syllables N3 |
|---|---|---|---|---|
| 300 most frequent 3N | 4.94 | 1.56 | 1.45 | 1.93 |
| 300 least frequent 3N | 5.93 | 1.98 | 1.77 | 2.18 |

There are two pieces of information that can be derived from Table 4. It can firstly be seen that with a decrease in frequency not just the overall number of syllables increases but each individual noun component tends to be longer in less frequently used compounds than in frequent ones (as opposed to only the N3 increasing in length, for example). This indicates that more frequently used compounds are generally composed of shorter constituents than less frequent ones. Secondly, a comparison of the average length shows that the syllables are not distributed evenly on the constituents but there are clear tendencies for each position. The figures suggest that in any three-noun compound, irrespective of the frequency level, the longest constituent tends to be the furthest right noun N3. This element has on average close to two syllables, while the other constituents tend to have one or two syllables. These observations suggest that there is some systematicity in the combination of the elements used to form tri-constituent compounds.

To summarize, it has been demonstrated that three-noun compounds are generally not as long as might be assumed, having a length of between five and six syllables on average. Highly frequent instances are considerably shorter, typically consisting of three or four syllables. Less frequent compounds tend to be longer that frequent ones but still typically stay within a length of six syllables. Furthermore, the individual constituents of three-noun compounds do not have the same length but the third noun tends to be the longest.

### 6.1.2 Morphological complexity

What is further of interest with regard to the "load" of a complex compound is its morphological complexity. To investigate this aspect, the items in the sample were analysed with the help of the *Munich UCL Morphology Corpus* (MUMC). The MUMC was compiled and used by Schmid (2016) and is based on the British component of the *International Corpus of English* (ICE-GB). It is not publicly available owing to copyright restrictions. The MUMC is an inventory of 20 texts containing approximately 7,400 lexemes of the English language that are tagged morphologically.

Tagging in the MUMC does not always seem coherent[10] and the inventory does not contain all the nouns in the sample; however, it was used owing to the lack of alternative tools that are openly accessible. When words were not listed in the MUMC, the number of morphemes was counted manually in accordance with a consultation of the OED. The MUMC does not acknowledge zero-morphemes, i.e. instances of conversion are not marked as morphologically complex (e.g. *work* is marked as monomorphemic both as a noun and as a verb). Table 5 displays the results of the morpheme counts for the items in the two frequency subsets of the sample.

**Table 5:** Average number of morphemes for 3N in different frequency levels.

| Frequency level | Average number of morphemes |
| --- | --- |
| all 600 items | 3.84 |
| 300 most frequent 3N | 3.76 |
| 300 least frequent 3N | 3.92 |

It can be seen that on average, three-noun compounds consist of just less than 4 morphemes, i.e. typically one morpheme per noun, with one of the constituents potentially being morphologically complex. The maximum number of morphemes is six, as found in *law enforcement official* or *government accountability office*. However, of the 600 items under investigation less than 15 show this degree of complexity. It had been expected that a decrease in frequency would be coupled with an increase in complexity, i.e. the more complex a tripartite compound is, the less frequent it is morphologically. This cannot be confirmed, as the figures show that there is only a vanishingly small discrepancy between the highly frequent items and the less frequent ones with regard to their morphological complexity. Instead, three-noun compounds seem to be generally limited to sequences with only one complex, i.e. affixed, constituent. Typical instances from the 3N database are thus, for example, *health care system, football player, classroom teacher* or *computer network*.

---

**10** The items *service* and *border*, for example, are tagged as consisting of one morpheme only, while *university*, *welfare* and *environment* are categorized as complex with *environ* being marked as a lexical free form. Also, there are inconsistencies within the same items: in *unconventional*, *convention* is tagged as consisting of two morphemes, while *convention* itself is listed as monomorphemic. The same is true for *research*, which is tagged as monomorphemic, but in combination with other words (e.g. in *AI research*) it is marked as complex.

Is there any systematicity in the allocation of the affixed constituent? The examples just cited convey the impression that the complex element occurs predominantly in the N1 or N3 position. From a theoretical perspective, the affixed constituent is most likely to be located in the head constituent, i.e. the N3, for example in the form of an -er agent (e.g. *football player, trade union leader*). This expectation is also supported by the findings of the previous section, where it was shown that the N3 constituent tends to be the longest element. To verify this assumption, Table 6 focuses on the morpheme distribution for the individual constituents of the items in the sample.

**Table 6:** Average number of morphemes distributed among constituents.

| Frequency level | Morphemes total | Morphemes N1 | Morphemes N2 | Morphemes N3 |
|---|---|---|---|---|
| 300 most frequent 3N | 3.76 | 1.28 | 1.19 | 1.29 |
| 300 least frequent 3N | 3.92 | 1.27 | 1.30 | 1.35 |

The table shows that each of the constituents of a three-noun compound tends to be morphologically simple, i.e. monomorphemic nouns. In analogy to the diagnosis given above for the whole forms, the individual constituents in more frequently used compounds are barely more complex than those in less common instances. With regard to the location of the affixed constituent, it can be seen that the average number of morphological constituents is highly similar for all constituents, with only a small tendency for the complex constituent to be the furthest right element, i.e. the N3 constituent (which sounds obvious at first, as these have also been shown to be the longest elements; however, these two features are not necessarily directly connected as there are monosyllabic but complex words, such as *health*, for example). This difference, however, is too small to permit a generalization being derived about the distribution of the affixed constituent. Rather, these numbers seem to suggest that the three elements in a three-noun compound are similarly likely to be the affixed constituent.

To give an impression of what the affixed constituents can look like, I will exemplify these numbers with instances from the 3N database. In both frequency levels, both in the N1 and the N3 position, the affixed elements are overwhelmingly deverbal nouns. In the N3 position, these complex items are often agent nouns (e.g. *player, teacher, carrier, worker, officer, student*). Other affixed N3 constituents are nouns denoting products and institutions, such as *edition, organization, management, committee, association* or *training*. There are also a few instances of prefixation in the N3 position, such as *reform, income* or *inmate*. In the N1 constituent, the affixed elements are mainly nouns derived from verbs or (more rarely) from adjectives, such as *health, emergency, education, treatment, security* or *death*. A common deverbal suffix in the

N1 position is *-ing*, as for example in *dining room table* or *eating disorder association*. Examples of derived nouns in the N2 position in both frequent and infrequent three-noun compounds are, for instance, *enforcement, department* and *management*.

A qualitative comparison of the affixes within the frequency subsets shows that those that are used in more frequent three-noun compounds tend to be of a different kind than those in less frequent ones. In the category of highly frequent items, the most commonly occurring affixed lexeme is *health*, a word that is probably not perceived as complex by the average speaker. The same is true of the affixed nouns *reform, service* and *computer*, which are derivations that are used more frequently than their bases, which is why it can be assumed that they are not necessarily perceived as complex by speakers (cf. Hay 2001). In infrequent compounds, by contrast, examples of commonly occurring complex words are *personality, association, treatment* or *surveillance*. This observation suggests that the complex nouns in more conventionalized tripartite compounds might be less overtly complex than those in less conventionalized compounds. This, however, is rather a tendency than an absolute categorization, as even among frequent three-noun compounds there are visibly complex components such as *–er* derivatives (e.g. in *player, leader, provider*) and complex lexemes such as *enforcement*, while some of the less obvious derivatives, such as *service*, also occur among the infrequent compounds. More data would be required to allow for conclusive statements about potential systematic differences in the quality of the affixed lexemes that are found in the two frequency levels.

The analysis suggests that the input for complex compounds is preferably morphologically simple words. On average, three-noun compounds contain only one morphologically complex constituent in the form of a suffixed noun. The affixed constituent is most likely to be the furthest right noun; however, this tendency is not very pronounced. The difference between frequent compounds and infrequent ones with regard to morphological complexity is vanishingly small, which means that in less frequent instances the morphological complexity of the formations (as opposed to their length) does not rise. Instead, it can be assumed that there is a general limit to the morphological complexity in polylexemic compounds. This is presumably due to the fact that additional morphemes would entail further conceptual input, which increases the effort for processing.

It can thus be stated that three-noun compounds do not tend to be overly complex from a morphological perspective, being generally limited to four morphemes that are represented through three lexemes, one of which is affixed. Accordingly, compounds such as *community development organization, trade union association* or *waste management authority* are rather untypical instances of polylexemic compounding, as even infrequent instances generally tend to contain maximally four morphemes only. More typical instances are provided by the forms of *stem cell research* or *health care bill*.

### 6.1.3 Conclusion

Based on the results obtained in Sections 6.1.1 and 6.1.2, it seems reasonable to claim that both from a morphological and from a phonological point of view, three-noun compounds cannot be said to be lengthy and clumsy sequences. It has been shown that the most frequent compounds are both fairly short and morphologically simple, while lengthy and morphologically highly complex sequences are an exception. If three-noun compounds are complex from a formal perspective, then this is due to a higher number of syllables but not necessarily due to an increased morphological complexity. The examples of *law enforcement authority, gender identity disorder* and *trade union association* that have been cited in the introduction to Chapter 6 can thus be discarded on an empirical basis as typical representatives of complex compounds. By contrast, more typical members of the category three-noun compound are four-syllable items with maximally one complex constituent, such as *football player, ice cream flavor, cable car line, car bomb attack* or *health care system*.

## 6.2 Do left- and right-branching compounds differ formally?

The analyses performed in the previous Section 6.1 aimed at conveying a first impression of three-noun compounds and have therefore treated them as a homogeneous group. However, Chapter 5 has detailed that we can distinguish two kinds of three-noun compounds based on their internal structure: left-branching compounds and right-branching ones. It is the aim of this section to examine whether these two types show differences in their formal characteristics. In order to give a first impression of the kinds of items found in these two categories, the following list provides examples taken from different frequency levels of the 3N database:

Do these two types of tripartite compounds show differences with regard to their formal characteristics? Are left-branching items, for example, shorter than right-branching ones? Are the affixed constituents located in different positions? In the following sections, left- and right-branching compounds will be contrasted

| Left-branching | Right-branching |
|---|---|
| – *bathroom door* | – *police headquarters* |
| – *keynote speech* | – *university law school* |
| – *death row inmate* | – *motor speedway* |
| – *newspaper story* | – *class warfare* |
| – *football coach* | – *mountain sunset* |
| – *newspaper article* | – *water theme park* |

(continued)

| Left-branching | Right-branching |
|---|---|
| – cowboy boot | – committee chairman |
| – sunflower seeds | – computer network |
| – death penalty case | – gas pipeline |
| – windshield wipers | – car salesman |
| – apple cider vinegar | – computer database |
| – breast cancer survivor | – terror network |
| – life insurance company | – school yearbook |
| – borderline personality | – summer weekend |
| – classroom climate | – picture postcard |
| – shoestring budget | – street flea market |
| – flight attendant call | – salmon fish farm |
| – nerve gas attack | – bus timetable |

with regard to their length and morphological complexity, applying the same methods as described in Section 6.1. I will also use the same data, i.e. the 300 most and the 300 least frequently used three-noun compounds but will now make a distinction between left- and right-branching compounds. Out of the 600 compounds in the sample, 430 are left-branching items and 170 right-branching ones.

### 6.2.1 Length of compounds and constituents

Section 6.1.1 has shown that the longest constituent in a three-noun compound tends to be the furthest right noun. Does this hold true if we make a distinction between the compounds with regard to their branching pattern? Table 7 again displays the word length through averaged syllable counts for each of the constituents N1, N2 and N3[11] for the 300 most and 300 least frequently used three-noun compounds but now enriched with information on the distribution on left- and right branching.

---

**11** Henceforth the use of the expressions "as N1/as N3" does not encompass all instances in which a word occurs in the first or third position respectively, but only those instances in which it occurs in first/third position AND acts as the outer noun, i.e. is not part of the embedded compound. To exemplify this, when talking of "*school* as N1", this will only refer to those instances of *school* in the N1 position that have the structure [school [N N]] and not those of [[school N] N]. Accordingly, the occurrence of *school* in *school band director*, for example, is not included even though *school* here is used in the N1 position, because it is part of the embedded compound.

## 6.2 Do left- and right-branching compounds differ formally? — 69

**Table 7:** Syllable counts distinguished for frequency levels and BPs.

| Frequency level | Syllables total | Syllables N1 | Syllables N2 | Syllables N3 |
| --- | --- | --- | --- | --- |
| 300 most frequent 3N total (LB + RB) | **4.94** | 1.56 | 1.45 | 1.93 |
| LB items among 300 most frequent 3N | **4.86** | 1.35 | 1.45 | 2.06 |
| RB items among 300 most frequent 3N | **5.23** | 2.23 | 1.49 | 1.51 |
| 300 least frequent 3N total (LB + RB) | **5.93** | 1.98 | 1.77 | 2.18 |
| LB items among 300 least frequent 3N | **5.80** | 1.71 | 1.77 | 2.32 |
| RB items among 300 least frequent 3N | **6.22** | 2.62 | 1.76 | 1.84 |

The first piece of information that can be gleaned from this table is the relation between the length of the two types of complex compounds. A comparison of the most common left-branching compounds with the most common right-branching ones (rows 2 and 3), as well as the same comparison within the infrequent compounds (rows 5 and 6) shows that in both frequency categories the average number of total syllables is generally lower for left-branching compounds than for right-branching ones. This suggest that left-branching compounds tend to be slightly shorter than right-branching ones. It has already been observed in Section 6.2.1 that infrequent three-noun compounds tend to be longer than those which are frequently used. These two observations together entail a hierarchy with regard to the length of tripartite compounds: the longest three-noun compounds are infrequent right-branching ones (6.22 syllables), while the shortest three-noun compounds appear to be frequent left-branching ones (4.86 syllables), with a discrepancy of 1.36 syllables.

This general tendency is also true for the individual constituents. It must be noted that in looking at the individual constituents what must be compared are not the N1 or N3 elements between each other but the elements that are in the same position with regard to the internal structure. Accordingly, the elements to be compared are the outer nouns (i.e. the elements that are not part of the embedded compound) on the one hand, which is the N1 constituent in right-branching items and the N3 constituent in left-branching ones, and the embedded compounds on the other hand, which is the N1N2 word pair in left-branching items and the N2N3 pair in right-branching ones. A comparison of the outer nouns shows that in both frequency levels the outer nouns of left-branching compounds are shorter than those of right-branching ones (2.06 vs. 2.23 syllables in the higher frequency area, and 2.32 vs. 2.62 in the low frequency area). The same is true for the constituents of the embedded compounds: the modifier and the head of the embedded compounds of left-branching items are shorter than the respective elements in right-branching ones. Accordingly, in each frequency level, each constituent of left-branching compounds tends to be shorter than the respective constituent in a right-branching compound.

Furthermore, it can clearly be seen that irrespective of the frequency level, the longest constituent is always the outer noun. Thus, in left-branching items the longest of the three nouns is the head, while in right-branching compounds the longest element is the modifier. On average, the outer nouns tend to have at least two syllables, while each of the constituents of the embedded compounds tend to have on average just less than two syllables. Independent of the frequency range or branching pattern, the first constituent of the embedded compound is generally minimally shorter than the second one. Accordingly, the result found in Section 6.1.1, where it was observed that the longest element in a tri-constituent compound is the third noun, does not hold true for both types of branching patterns and needs to be modified: only in left-branching compounds is the longest element the N3 constituent; in right-branching compounds the longest element is the noun in the N1 position.

To summarize, it can be stated that left-branching compounds are on average shorter than right-branching ones regarding both their overall length and the length of the individual constituents. Generally, frequent left-branching items are the shortest kind of three-noun compound, while infrequent right-branching ones tend to be the longest ones. The longest constituent in a three-noun compound tends to be the outer noun, i.e. the N1 constituent in right-branching compounds and the N3 constituent in left-branching ones.

### 6.2.2 Morphological complexity

Section 6.1.2 has shown that tri-constituent compounds generally tend to consist of morphologically simple nouns, with a tendency for one of the constituents to be bimorphemic. However, no significant difference could be determined for the allocation of the affixed constituent. We might get a clearer picture if we regard the data distinguished for the two branching patterns, as it is conceivable that left- and right-branching compounds differ with regard to the location of the complex noun. To evaluate this, Table 8 zooms in on the morpheme distribution for the individual constituents and branching patterns.

There are several observations that can be made from this table. Firstly, the numbers show more distinctively what has been observed in Section 6.1.2, namely that in both frequency levels and both types of branching patterns the constituents of three-noun compounds are predominantly morphologically simple elements. Thus, regardless of the branching pattern and the frequency level, three-noun compounds seem to typically consist of monomorphemic words.

**Table 8:** Morpheme counts distinguished for frequency levels and BPs.

| Frequency level | Morphemes total | Morphemes N1 | Morphemes N2 | Morphemes N3 |
|---|---|---|---|---|
| **300 most frequent 3N total (LB + RB)** | **3.76** | 1.28 | 1.19 | 1.29 |
| LB items among 300 most frequent 3N | 3.68 | 1.22 | 1.16 | 1.30 |
| RB items among 300 most frequent 3N | 3.61 | 1.32 | 1.17 | 1.12 |
| **300 least frequent 3N total (LB + RB)** | **3.92** | 1.27 | 1.30 | 1.35 |
| LB items among 300 least frequent 3N | 3.89 | 1.18 | 1.30 | 1.41 |
| RB items among 300 least frequent 3N | 3.95 | 1.48 | 1.28 | 1.19 |

The differences between left- and right-branching items in terms of complexity are vanishingly small. It might have been expected that left-branching compounds are less complex morphologically, as they are used more extensively. The figures show, however, that the constituents in left-branching compounds are not less complex than those in right-branching ones; quite the opposite: In the high-frequency category the constituents of the embedded compound (N1N2) in left-branching compounds even show slightly higher morpheme counts (on average 1.22 morphemes and 1.16 morphemes) than the constituents of the embedded compound in right-branching items (N2N3) (1.17 morphemes and 1.12 morphemes). These differences, however, are quantitatively very small. Both left- and right-branching compounds are only slightly more complex in the high-frequency area (on average 3.68 morphemes for frequent left-branching compounds and 3.61 for frequent right-branching ones) than in the low-frequency category (on average 3.89 morphemes for infrequent left-branching compounds and 3.95 for infrequent right-branching ones). Accordingly, it can be stated that there are no significant differences between left- and right-branching compounds when it comes to their morphological complexity.

There is a qualitative difference, however, between the instances of the two branching patterns with regard to the allocation of the morphologically complex constituent. As opposed to the observation made in Section 6.1.2, stating that the affixed constituent tends to be the element in the N3 position, it can be seen that this is not equally true for the two types of three-noun compounds. They clearly differ in this respect, as the constituent with the highest average complexity is the outer noun (on average 1.30 morphemes in frequent left-branching compounds, 1.32 in frequent right-branching ones, 1.41 morphemes in infrequent left-branching compounds and 1.48 in infrequent right-branching ones). Thus, in left-branching compounds the affixed constituent is most likely the noun in the N3 position, while in right-branching ones it is the noun in the N1 position. This is in line with the result gained in the previous section, which demonstrated that the longest constituent in a three-noun compound is the N1 constituent in right-branching compounds but the N3 constituent in left-branching ones. Accordingly, in a typical three-noun compound the embedded compound tends to consist of two simple nouns, while the outer noun tends to be an instance of derivation, which is instantiated through examples such as *classroom teacher*, *weekend edition* or *television network*.

To summarize, there are no significant differences between left- and right-branching compounds regarding their morphological complexity. They have a similar tendency to contain one morphologically complex noun and two simple nouns that form the embedded compound. There is a difference, however, when it comes to the position of the affixed element, as it is most likely to be the outer noun, which is the head in left-branching items and the modifier in right-branching ones.

### 6.2.3 Conclusion

It was the aim of Sections 6.2.1 and 6.2.2 to examine whether there are interesting insights to be gained from an examination of formal complexity distinguished for the two different types of three-noun compounds. Based on the quantitative analyses, it can be concluded that left-branching and right-branching compounds tend to have slightly different profiles when it comes to their formal appearance. The results gained in this section show that the observations made in Section 6.1 for the whole data set are not fully representative but that the numbers of syllables and morphemes for the individual constituents differ for left- and right-branching compounds. These findings demonstrate that an investigation of three-noun compounds needs to be fine-grained enough to distinguish between left- and right-branching items. It can be expected that these two types of three-noun compounds also behave differently in several other aspects, which is why this distinction will be taken into account as far as possible in the remainder of this work.

## 6.3 Orthographic aspects of complex compounds

This section will investigate the spelling of tripartite compounds. It has been explained in Section 2.2 that there is some degree of variability in English compound spelling. In tri-constituent compounds, spelling becomes theoretically more intricate as there are more constituents to be linked, which leads to more options with regard to their orthographic connection. Taking into account all the possible formats available, there are potentially nine orthographic realizations for the combination of three nouns:

| | | |
|---|---|---|
| – NNN | – N N N | – N-N-N |
| – NN N | – N N-N | – NN-N |
| – N NN | – N-N N | – N-NN |

Are all of these spelling formats actually employed? And if so, are they utilized to the same extent? A higher number of available formats potentially leaves even more room for inconsistencies and insecurities when it comes to the choices writers need to make. Does this mean that there is more variation between the different spelling formats than in simple compounds? Moreover, in contrast to simple compounding, in complex compounds spelling has a potential function: to mark the internal hierarchical structure of the constituents. Do speakers make use of this function? The following sections will address the orthography of tri-constituent compounds with the aim of creating a clearer image of their formal appearance. I will first outline the relationship between the orthography of complex compounds and their morphological structure on a theoretical basis (Section 6.3.1), before giving an insight into the utilization of this connection (Section 6.3.2). Based on this, I will investigate how much variation there is when it comes to the spelling formats found within individual types of three-noun compounds (Section 6.3.3).

### 6.3.1 How could spelling be related to morphological structure?

A highly interesting aspect in the spelling of complex compounds is its theoretical connection to morphological structure, as a compound's internal structure can potentially be replicated orthographically. This section will expound the potential of spelling when it comes to marking the hierarchical structure of tripartite compounds.

The formats that are available in the spelling of English three-noun compounds differ in their suitability for reflecting the internal structure. There are three spelling formats which are completely neutral, as the links between the three constituents are formally equally close or distant. This means that the first and the third noun are connected to the second, middle noun via the same means, which can be a hyphen, a space or no means of separation. This is the case in the following formats:

- NNN
- N-N-N
- N N N

As it is not obvious from the form which constituents belong together on the first level, these formats can potentially cause ambiguity in the interpretation of the respective compounds in those cases where both branching patterns are reasonable options and lead to competing interpretations (cf. Section 5.1.4).

In the remaining spelling formats, the orthography of a three-noun compound can potentially reflect its morphological structure. In these cases, solid spelling, hyphens and spaces meet, which means that the way in which the second noun is connected to the first noun differs from the connection to the third noun. As these orthographic cues express different degrees of connection, this results in two of the three constituents being more closely connected, thus reflecting a hierarchy in their combination. This situation is found in the remaining six formats:

- NN N
- N NN
- N-NN
- NN-N
- N-N N
- N N-N

It must be noted at this point that the nature of the hyphen in complex sequences is highly interesting. A comparison of the hyphen in the formats N-N N and N-NN shows that it takes two different functions here: while in the first tripartite compound the hyphen is a sign of the unification of the first and second noun, in the second compound the hyphen instead stands for separation, as it signals that the first and second noun are more remotely connected than the second and the third noun. Thus, the hyphen cannot per se be defined as an indicator of either unification or separation in tri-constituent compounds, but its status is defined relatively, depending on the second cue.

In the non-neutral formats presented above, a space is understood to indicate less closeness than a hyphen, while a hyphen is a less strong connector than solid spelling. Accordingly, in these non-neutral formats, the branching pattern of a three-noun compound could theoretically be derived from its spelling. More precisely, the mapping sketched in Figure 6 would be constructive:

| LEFT-BRANCHING | RIGHT-BRANCHING | |
|---|---|---|
| ⌐⎯⌐ | ⌐⎯⌐ | |
| N-N N | N N-N | |
| NN N | N NN | **Figure 6:** Mapping between orthography |
| NN-N | N-NN | and internal structure of 3N. |

The three spelling formats in which the N1N2 word pair is more closely related than that of N2N3 should be reserved for left-branching items, while the corresponding mirrored variants, in which the N2N3 word pair shows a stronger degree of orthographic unification, should be reserved for right-branching compounds. Especially in those cases where the morphological structure is not clear and two different interpretations are perfectly possible and reasonable, an orthographic format that reflects the morphological structure would be beneficial in order to disambiguate the meaning of the compound (see Section 5.1.4).

The orthography chosen by writers, however, does not always reflect a sensible pattern. Sometimes, spelling is a compromise that is not made on morphological or semantic principles but rather on practical considerations and conventionalization. In this respect, a very interesting case is provided by compounds whose conventionalized form is misleading, as it does not match the morphological structure. This is the case, for example, in the complex compound *animal bookshop* (cf. the analogue example of *children's book store* used in Section 5.1.3). *Bookshop* is a conventionalized compound that is overwhelmingly spelt as one unit. Although an *animal bookshop* is less a 'bookshop for animals' than a 'shop with books for animals', which would suggest the structure [[animal book] shop]], the sequence is overwhelmingly orthographically realized as *animal bookshop*, thus signalling the structure [[animal] [book shop]]. Clearly, the orthographic realization of this complex compound does not match its morphological structure. This phenomenon does not just occur in compounding but there are also instances of affixation in which the established spelling format of the relevant lexeme contradicts its morphological structure. The spelling of *open-mindedness*, for example, suggests the morphological structure [open [minded ness]], although both the semantic perspective ('the state of being open-minded') and the formal criterion (*open-minded* vs. *\*mindedness*) clearly demonstrate that *open-minded* is the base for the affixation. The hyphen used in this complex lexeme seems to be a compromise between the visual separation of an otherwise too long word and the awkward solution of splitting off a suffix with a hyphen. Instances of this kind, however, are not overly common.[12] Still, they indicate that spelling is not always a correct indicator of the internal structure of a complex word.

---

[12] German examples are *S-Bahntunnel* ('tunnel for the express train'), *E-Autobatterien* ('electric car batteries') or *Anti-Staubtuch* ('cloth against dust').

It can be concluded that the spelling of tripartite nominal compound bears the potential to reveal their morphological structure. However, a language user's awareness of this relationship cannot be presupposed. The next section will investigate whether native speakers make use of orthographic formats that reflect a compound's internal structure.

### 6.3.2 Which spelling formats are established in three-noun compounding?

Are all the nine spelling formats that have been presented in the previous section actually used in the spelling of three-noun compounds? Sanchez-Stockhammer (2018: 257) finds that compounds with three constituents disfavour solid spelling but rather occur in open or hyphenated format. She does, however, not specify, whether that means that there are spaces or hyphens between all three constituents or only between the embedded compound and the outer noun. Bauer (1998: 69) claims that "long words are written separately [. . .] while short words are more likely to be written together". It is, however, unclear, whether tri-constituent compounds qualify as long or short. Accordingly, this section will examine which of the available spelling formats are actually employed and can be considered established for the orthographic realization of three-noun compounds.

The 3N database cannot be utilized for this purpose, as it has stored the compounds in the neutral format N N N. Therefore, no quantitative analysis can be provided for the spelling of the whole set of three-noun compounds but only for a sample of 260 items which were drawn randomly from the 3N database. The sample contains items from all frequency levels, 197 of which are left-branching, 63 right-branching. With the help of a self-programmed Python-script, the offline version of COCA was searched for the occurrences of each three-noun compound in the sample in all 9 orthographic realizations. The script counts the tokens for each spelling format per three-noun compound, compares the token frequencies of the different spelling formats and lists each compound in its most frequent spelling. This most frequent spelling was understood to be the established spelling format of the respective compound. This way, each compound in the sample was attributed one established spelling format. Table 9 shows the quantitative distribution of the 260 test items among the nine available formats. It must be noted that a type count of zero does not mean that this spelling format does not exist for three-noun compounds but instead that this format is never found as the most frequently chosen orthographic realization for any three-noun compound in the sample.

**Table 9:** Use of available spelling formats.

| Spelling formats | Number of types of 3N |
|---|---|
| **FORMAT 1: N N N**<br>all components separated through spaces | 127 |
| **FORMAT 2: NNN**<br>all components orthographically united | 0 |
| **FORMAT 3: N-N-N**<br>all components united through hyphens | 0 |
| **FORMAT 4: NN N**<br>N1N2 orthographically united, N3 connected through space | 90 |
| **FORMAT 5: N NN**<br>N2N3 orthographically united, N1 connected through space | 36 |
| **FORMAT 6: NN-N**<br>N1N2 orthographically united, N3 connected through hyphen | 0 |
| **FORMAT 7: N-NN**<br>N2N3 orthographically united, N1 connected through hyphen | 0 |
| **FORMAT 8: N-N N**<br>N1N2 connected through hyphen, N3 connected through space | 7 |
| **FORMAT 9: N N-N**<br>N2N3 connected through hyphen, N1 connected through space | 0 |

The table shows that not all nine spelling formats can be considered established formats for the orthographic realization of tripartite compounds. Instead, only few of them appear as the most frequent format of a particular compound: format 1, in which all the items are separated by spaces (i.e. N N N), formats 4 and 5, in which the embedded compound is orthographically united and the outer noun is connected by a space (i.e. NN N and N NN), and format 8, in which the embedded compound is united by a hyphen and the head connected by a space (i.e. N-N N). Therefore, it can be stated that the nine spelling formats that are theoretically available for the realization of three-noun compounds only exist in theory; in practice only four formats can be considered established. To exemplify these formats, the following list provides instances for each of them from the 3N database:

- **FORMAT 1: N N N**
  e.g. *air defense system, baby boomer parents, child poverty rate, death penalty cases, health risk factor, home pregnancy test*

- **FORMAT 4: NN N**
  e.g. *airline pilots, bathroom mirror, crossword puzzle, airport hotel, birthday cake, weekend trip*
- **FORMAT 5: N NN**
  e.g. *tax loophole, surveillance videotape, paper placemat, pearl earring, employee handbook*
- **FORMAT 8: N-N N**
  e.g. *season-ticket holders, weight-loss program, problem-solving strategies*

A look at the quantitative distribution between these four spelling formats shows that about half the three-noun compounds in the sample are established in the spelling format N N N, while almost exactly the same number is realized in the formats N NN and NN N. The spelling format N-N N is established for considerably fewer three-noun compounds. Accordingly, it can be stated that the two most established spelling formats of three-noun compounds consist in an embedded compound whose constituents either form an orthographic unit or are separated through a space, and an outer noun that is connected by a space.

I will now contrast the spelling formats used for left- and right-branching compounds. The 63 right-branching compounds occur exclusively in the formats 1 (N N N) and 5 (N NN), with 27 items being realized as N N N and 36 items as N NN. Of the 197 left-branching compounds, by contrast, 100 occur in the format N N N, 90 in the format NN N, and 7 in the format N-N N. It is interesting to see that the right-branching format that corresponds to format 8 (N-N N), i.e. format 9 (N N-N), does not appear as an established spelling format for right-branching compounds. Thus, it can be stated that right-branching compounds occur commonly in both the format N N N and N NN, with the latter being slightly more dominant than the former. Left-branching compounds show a similar behaviour, also occurring most frequently in the formats N N N and NN N; however, here the preference is for the former rather than the latter. Besides, for left-branching compounds there is an additional spelling format that is used, namely N-N N, but to a much lesser degree than the other two formats.

What do the figures in Table 9 reveal about the relationship between orthography and morphological structure addressed in the previous section? Of the neutral formats N-N-N, N N N and NNN, only one presents an established format, namely N N N. The other two are not attested as established spellings for any item in the sample. Of the non-neutral formats, the variants used are NN N/N NN and N-NN. With 127 items established in a neutral format and 133 items in a non-neutral one, this leads to a fairly even distribution between these two categories. Obviously, language users make use of neutral formats and non-neutral ones to a similar degree. From a linguistic point of view, it is interesting to see that the neutral format is used so frequently, as this shows that language users do not make maximum use of the possibility of reflecting the morphological structure. Why does the mapping suggested in the previous section not happen? Obviously, language users do not feel the need to do so, which might be due to the fact that in the majority of complex compounds there is only one possible interpretation, and even if not, speakers seem to understand the concept behind the compound well enough. Accordingly, a match between orthography and internal structure might be only desirable from a formal point of view but does not seem necessary from a functional perspective.

To conclude, there are two dominant orthographic formats in the spelling of three-noun compounds: a neutral one, in which the three nouns are juxtaposed with a space between the constituents (N N N), and a non-neutral one, in which the embedded compound is realized as an orthographic unit, with the outer noun adjoined with a space (i.e. NN N and N NN). There are slight differences in the spelling of left- and right-branching compounds: while right-branching compounds are mostly realized in the format N NN, followed by N N N, left-branching ones are most often found in the format N N N, followed by NN N, and to a much lesser degree in the format N-N N. These results suggest that there is some regularity or degree of conventionalization in the spelling of English three-noun compounds.

### 6.3.3 Is there within-type variation?

The observations made in the previous section do not claim that three-noun compounds are never realized in any of the other available formats, but instead that these formats are never the most frequent and thus the most established realization of any three-noun compound. Whether these spellings are still used as an alternative to the established spellings is the main aspect that will be examined in this section. It will provide a more qualitative, item-based approach to the spelling of three-noun compounds and focus on the variation within individual compounds. I expect variation to occur between the spelling formats related to each of the branching patterns, i.e. on the one hand between the formats NN N, N-N N and NN-N for left-branching compounds, and on the other hand between N NN, N N-N and N-NN for right-branching items. I am furthermore interested in finding out whether compounds with an unclear internal structure show fluctuation between left- and right-branching spelling formats.

To verify these expectations, a sample of 60 compounds was drawn from the 3N database. In order to be able to observe variation, the items were primarily sampled from higher frequency areas, which means that low-frequency items are underrepresented. This is, however, not deemed problematic, as if it should turn out that among the more conventionalized items there is a high degree of fluctuation between different spelling formats, this can be assumed to be just as true for infrequent compounds. The sample items are displayed in Table 10; they have been numbered to facilitate referencing to them. Of the 60 three-noun compounds in the sample, 43 are left-branching (items 1–43) and 15 are right-branching (items 46–60). The remaining two compounds (items 44 and 45) are ones whose internal structure has been discussed as unclear in earlier sections. For all items in the sample, the online edition of COCA was searched for their occurrences in the nine available orthographic formats both in the singular and in the plural.[13] The table shows the distribution of the tokens on the different spelling formats for each item in the sample. Empty fields mean the respective compound has not been found in that spelling format. For each item, the spelling format that accounts for most tokens is marked as the primary spelling format (red colour). If additionally any of the other formats reach more than ten percent of the overall number of tokens of a particular compound, it is considered a significant variant and marked as a secondary spelling format (blue colour).

**Table 10:** Distribution of 3N tokens on spelling formats.

| | 3N | Total | NNN | N N N | N-N-N | NN N | N NN | NN-N | N-NN | N-N N | N N-N |
|---|---|---|---|---|---|---|---|---|---|---|---|
| 1 | football game | 4,963 | 1 | 1 | | 4,949 | | 10 | | 2 | |
| 2 | birthday party | 4,406 | | | | 4,382 | | 24 | | 0 | |
| 3 | trade union movement | 99 | | 84 | | | | | | 15 | |
| 4 | bedroom door | 1,626 | | 1 | | 1,625 | | | | | |
| 5 | roller coaster ride | 557 | | 267 | | 57 | | | | 233 | |
| 6 | gingerbread house | 380 | | 7 | | 363 | | 10 | | | |
| 7 | classroom teacher | 3,034 | | | | 3,033 | | 1 | | | |
| 8 | credit card company | 1,172 | | 1,012 | | 3 | | | | 157 | |
| 9 | credit card bill | 481 | | 425 | 1 | 1 | | | | 54 | |
| 10 | day care center | 1,718 | 1 | 761 | 4 | 341 | | | | 612 | |
| 11 | deathbed words | 5 | | | | | 5 | | | | |
| 12 | control group participants | 44 | | 39 | | | | | | 5 | |
| 13 | death row inmate | 550 | | 440 | | 2 | | | | 108 | |
| 14 | body mass index | 1,143 | | 1,046 | 3 | 2 | | 1 | | 91 | 1 |
| 15 | stem cell research | 1,521 | | 1,233 | | 4 | | | | 284 | |
| 16 | health care center | 188 | | 137 | | 38 | | | | 13 | |
| 17 | consumer protection agency | 124 | | 115 | | | | | | 9 | |

---

**13** Accordingly, the total frequencies given here do not concur with those given in other sections, as these are retrieved from the online edition of COCA instead of the 3N database.

6.3 Orthographic aspects of complex compounds — 81

**Table 10** (continued)

| | 3N | Total | NNN | N N N | N-N-N | NN N | N NN | NN-NN | N-NN | N-N N | N N-N |
|---|---|---|---|---|---|---|---|---|---|---|---|
| 18 | air traffic control | 733 | | 616 | 35 | 1 | | | | 80 | 1 |
| 19 | war crimes tribunal | 196 | | 171 | | | | | | 25 | |
| 20 | bathroom mirror | 517 | | | | 515 | | 2 | | | |
| 21 | law enforcement official | 2,446 | | 2,174 | | 1 | | | | 271 | |
| 22 | football league | 1,832 | | | | 1,832 | | | | | |
| 23 | baseball team | 1,955 | | | | 1,949 | | 6 | | | |
| 24 | aircraft carrier | 1,977 | | 11 | | 1,941 | | 24 | | 1 | |
| 25 | dining room table | 1,374 | | 1,090 | 1 | 15 | | | | 268 | |
| 26 | cowboy hat | 1,101 | | | | 1,096 | | 5 | | | |
| 27 | airline industry | 863 | | | | 858 | | 5 | | | |
| 28 | town hall meeting | 1,075 | | 913 | | 21 | | | | 141 | |
| 29 | birthday cake | 999 | | 1 | | 998 | | | | | |
| 30 | birth control pill | 1,101 | | 928 | 1 | 4 | | 1 | | 167 | |
| 31 | lifetime achievement | 620 | | 2 | | 597 | | 17 | | 4 | |
| 32 | newspaper story | 373 | | 1 | | 370 | | 2 | | | |
| 33 | sunflower seeds | 647 | | | | 634 | | 13 | | | |
| 34 | gunshot wound | 1,208 | | 23 | 1 | 1,176 | | 5 | | 3 | |
| 35 | carbon dioxide emissions | 816 | | 740 | 1 | | | | | 75 | |
| 36 | jigsaw puzzle | 727 | | 4 | | 699 | | 9 | | 15 | |
| 37 | attention deficit disorder | 555 | | 501 | | | | | | 56 | |
| 38 | life support machine | 31 | | 16 | | | | | | 15 | |
| 39 | video game addiction | 14 | | 9 | | 1 | | | | 4 | |
| 40 | toilet paper roll | 107 | | 97 | 1 | | | | | 9 | |
| 41 | food delivery service | 25 | | 18 | | | | | | 7 | |
| 42 | nail polish remover | 111 | | 95 | | 1 | | | | 15 | |
| 43 | internet service provider | 703 | | 694 | | | | | | 9 | |
| 44 | infant mortality rate | 503 | | 436 | | 1 | | | | 66 | |
| 45 | missile defense system | 657 | | 594 | | | | | | 66 | |
| 46 | senate finance committee | 693 | | 693 | | | | | | | |
| 47 | water theme park | 6 | | 6 | | | | | | | |
| 48 | camera video tape | 226 | | | | 226 | | | | | |
| 49 | documentary film maker | 381 | | 22 | | 350 | | | | 3 | 6 |
| 50 | home health care | 724 | | 579 | 9 | 134 | | 1 | | 1 | |
| 51 | hospital emergency room | 335 | | 335 | | | | | | | |
| 52 | beach volleyball | 369 | | | | 363 | | 5 | | | 1 |
| 53 | college roommate | 436 | | 3 | 2 | 431 | | | | | |
| 54 | history textbook | 269 | | 11 | | 257 | | | | | 1 |

**Table 10** (continued)

| 3N | | Total | NNN | N N N | N-N-N | NN N | N NN | NN-N | N-NN | N-N NN | N N-N |
|---|---|---|---|---|---|---|---|---|---|---|---|
| 55 | *university law school* | 591 | 588 | | | | | | | | 3 |
| 56 | *television network* | 1,363 | | | | | 1,36 | 3 | | | |
| 57 | *master bedroom* | 1,542 | | | | | 1,523 | | 19 | | |
| 58 | *sport utility vehicle* | 750 | | 444 | 1 | 1 | | | | 306 | |
| 59 | *committee chairman* | 204 | | | | | 204 | | | | |
| 60 | *school classroom* | 597 | | 3 | | | 594 | | | | |

There are several insights that can be gained from this table. Firstly, while all spelling formats are attested, they are used to very different degrees. The neutral format in which all constituents are orthographically united (NNN) is found only twice: There is one occurrence in this format for both the compounds [1] *football game* and [10] *day care center*. Looking into the relevant texts in the corpus, however, reveals that in both cases the whole text lacks spaces, which is why these occurrences cannot be counted as an actual realization of this format. It can thus be claimed that the format NNN is not used for the spelling of three-noun compounds in English (as opposed to German, for example). Similarly, the formats N-NN and N N-N are employed rather seldom and never constitute a serious variant. The same is true for the format N-N-N, which – apart from its occurrences in [18] *air traffic control* – is only rarely chosen. Accordingly, these four formats do not seem to be commonly used options for the spelling of three-noun compounds in English. The format NN-N is used sporadically as an alternative to other spelling formats; however, only to such a limited extent that it never presents a significant variant. The only formats that are relevant options in the spelling of three-noun compounds are those that have been shown to constitute established formats in the previous section: N N N, NN N, N NN and N-N N. Based on this observation, it can be stated that the utilization of spelling formats within types is comparable to that across types and, accordingly, these four formats are the only orthographic formats that are conventionally employed in the spelling of three-noun compounds.

Moving away from these quite general observations, I will shift the focus to the variation within the different types of three-noun compounds. Only in one single case is there noticeable variation between three formats, all of which seem established to some degree: the compound *day care center* [10] is commonly realized as *day care center, daycare center* and *day-care center*. This, however, seems to be an exception. For 36 out of 60 items in the sample, there is a quite clear preference for one particular spelling format. This is the case, for example, for [1] *football game,* [17] *consumer protection agency,* [43] *internet service provider* and

[52] *beach volleyball*, which are predominantly realized in one particular format, with other formats being infrequent occurrences that are not regarded as spelling variants as they account for less than ten percent of the tokens. For the remaining 24 three-noun compounds in the sample (those items which have an additional blue field), there is variation between two spelling formats. All of these items show a clear preference for one format but exhibit a considerable number of tokens in an alternative spelling, as in the cases of [5] *roller coaster ride*, [13] *death row inmate* or [50] *home health care*. Based on these observations, it can be stated that the majority of the items in the sample do not show remarkable variation between different spelling formats but are established in one particular format. Those items that do show variation only alternate between two spelling formats. Therefore, it can be concluded that the orthographic variation that occurs within individual three-noun compounds is rather low.

Are there any principles that guide the variation between two formats? In a search for systematicity in the alternation between spelling formats, the following observations can be made:
(i) those three-noun compounds that are established in the spelling formats NN N or N NN do not display any significant use of alternative spelling formats
(ii) variation occurs exclusively in those items whose most established spelling format is the format N N N
(iii) the alternative spelling chosen for items in (ii) is predominantly the format N-N N
(iv) there is no fluctuation between the most common formats N N N and NN N/N NN

It is interesting to see that for those compounds whose most established format is the neutral format N N N, language users show a tendency to use the non-neutral format N-N N as an alternative. This tendency might be an indication that in these cases language users *do* have an intuition that two of the constituents in the tripartite compound are more closely related and might have a reflex to mark this relation. This observation suggests that the connection between spelling and morphological structure is not just something linguists desire.

A comparison of left- and right-branching compounds with regard to variation suggests that there seems to be less variation in right-branching compounds, as 13 out of 15 items do not show wide variation, while in left-branching compounds there is remarkable alternation in 21 out of 43 instances. While in left-branching compounds the majority of items established in the format N N N show variation with another format (mostly N-N N), this variation does not occur for right-branching compounds established in the neutral format N N N. This observation indicates that the spelling of right-branching compounds might be more conventionalized than that of left-branching ones. However, the sample and the respective figures are too small to permit substantive generalizations, which is why further testing is needed to determine whether there are significant differences between these two types regarding the degree of variation they allow.

For those two items whose internal structure was considered unclear from a linguistic perspective, i.e. [44] *infant mortality rate* and [45] *missile defense system*, there is surprisingly little variance. Interestingly, for both items the same tendency can be observed: they are predominantly realized in the neutral format N N N. Still, language users employ the format N-N N as an alternative (i.e. *missile-defense system*, *infant-mortality rate*), a format that represents a left-branching structure. No right-branching formats were opted for. Contrary to expectations, there is no variation between the spelling formats related to the two different branching patterns. Being based on two items only, this observation does not permit generalizations. It is nevertheless highly interesting and calls for further research on items with a theoretically unclear structure. If the observation made here holds true, this could indicate that in linguistically unclear cases speakers simply choose a neutral pattern or, if they opt for a non-neutral one, they tend to choose the pattern they are more familiar with and are thus more likely to opt for a left-branching spelling format.

To conclude, this section has shown that the majority of three-noun compounds is predominantly realized in one particular spelling format. There is a considerable number of tripartite compounds that are used in more than one orthographic format; however, the usage of these compounds tends to alternate with only one other spelling format and not the full range of available formats. The type of three-noun compound that displays most variation are left-branching items that are conventionalized in the format N N N. In these instances, quite commonly the alternative spelling N-N N is chosen. Right-branching compounds that are conventionalized in the neutral format N N N generally do not show this kind of alternation. Accordingly, if there is alternation in the spelling of three-noun compounds, then it is predominantly between the formats N N N and N-N N. For items which are established in the formats NN N or N NN, language users do not tend to use alternative spellings. The observations made in this section need verification with larger data sets; nevertheless, they indicate that the variation in the spelling of three-noun compounds is systematic to some degree and that there is a certain degree of predictability of which kinds of items are affected by variation and which kind of variation they are likely to show.

## 6.4 Stress in complex compounds

As a last aspect of the formal analysis, this section will examine the stress pattern of three-noun compounds. In Section 2.2, I briefly sketched the general situation of stress in compounding, explaining that compounds tend to show fore-stress. Does this situation hold true for more complex compounds? Do three-noun compounds also predominantly show fore-stress? Or is stress in these instances more complicated as there are more constituents that can potentially carry stress? And do left- and right-branching compounds differ with regard to their stress patterns, i.e. are *college football* and *football game* stressed the same way? In an attempt to answer these questions, Section 6.4.1 will present the results of a small-scale experiment on stress in three-noun compounds, which aims at detecting whether they show the same stress pattern as simple compounds. This will be followed by theoretical considerations about the potential differences between the stress patterns of left- and right-branching compounds in Section 6.4.2.

### 6.4.1 Are complex compounds stressed like simple compounds?

As has been pointed out in Section 2.2, the stress pattern in compounds can be subject to fluctuation due to several factors (e.g. dependence on context, intra-speaker and inter-speaker differences, etc.). Still, there is general agreement that there is a dominant stress pattern to be found in compounds, which consists of a main stress on the first constituent, i.e. the modifier, and a weaker one on the second element, i.e. the head. As tripartite compounds contain a further constituent, it would be plausible if the stress pattern was modified quantitatively, as theoretically additional stress points could appear, which might also have an influence on the quality of the stress points. On the other hand, three-noun compounds just like simple compounds consist of two immediate constituents, with the only difference that one of these constituents is complex, which is why it is just as conceivable that the stress pattern of simple compounds holds true for tri-constituent compounds as well.

The coverage of this aspect in the literature is relatively scarce. Marchand (1960: 16) points out that "too long" compounds will always have two main stresses (e.g. 'concert per'formance). For tri-constituent compounds, Warren (1978: 32, 39) observes that left-branching compounds show fore-stress and that the weaker, secondary stress of the embedded compound moves to the last constituent (e.g. 'airplane but 'airplane ˌpassenger), while right-branching compounds seem to differ. She reasons that the differences in stress assignment between the branching patterns can be traced back to the concept of information structure (1978: 39). Giegerich (2009) explicitly addresses stress in tripartite compounds and demonstrates that the

Compound Stress Rule does not hold for all compounds. The question of stress in polylexemic compounding has also been raised by Carstairs-McCarthy (2018: 84). Based on his intuition, he considers the stress patterns of four selected compounds consisting of three or more lexemes (e.g. *dishwasher marketing brochure*). On these grounds, he concludes that left-branching compounds are stressed like simple compounds, with the main stress on the modifier. In right-branching compounds, however, he does not find fore-stress. Based on his example of *holiday car trip*, in which he assigns the main stress on *car*, he reasons that in right-branching compounds the main stress must be on the complex head so they tend to show the stress pattern of phrases (2018: 84–86). However, a sounder data basis would be desirable, as well as an evaluation of the items by a larger number of native speakers. Above all, Carstairs-McCarthy only looks into main stress points but does not mention secondary, weak stresses, which are informative as well, as they allow an insight into what happens to stress assignment if a word undergoes further word-formation processes.

While the following small-scale study is not fully representative either, it is based on a slightly larger set of test items and involves the judgement of other participants. Four participants, who are both native speakers of English and linguists, were asked to stress a list of test items on paper. They were instructed to imagine the test items embedded in a sentence. The test items consisted of 30 three-noun compounds from the 3N database, 15 of which were left-branching and 15 right-branching. The notation of the stress points was simply done by marking audible main stress points as well as weaker ones with upper and lower stress marks (' = strong, main stress, ͵ = weak(er), secondary stress). This was done in consultation and discussion with the study participants. Both the quality and the quantity of the stress points were examined without testing equipment but were merely evaluated by the examiner and the native speaker assessors, which is why the results are to be interpreted as observations which need to be subjected to proper empirical testing. Accordingly, this study does not claim to be representative or exhaustive but is to be seen as a starting point for further examination.

The following table shows the test items with the stress points as assigned by the participants, distinguished for left- and right-branching compounds. In those cases where speakers were unsure or different speakers opted for different results, the alternative stress points are marked with brackets or two alternative options are given, indicated by a slash.

In general, the stress points assigned by the participants were distinctive enough to assign a stress pattern to each three-noun compound in the sample. In all cases, the participants very noticeably assigned a main stress. This main stress was exclusively placed on the furthest left element, i.e. the modifier. This observation suggests that three-noun compounds show fore-stress and thus generally have the same stress pattern as simple compounds.

**Table 11:** Stress assigned to left- and right-branching 3N.

| Left-branching | Right-branching |
|---|---|
| ˈbaseball ˌplayer | ˈbus ˌtimetable |
| ˈbus driver (ˌ)seat | ˈcable ˌnetwork |
| ˈclassroom reˌform | ˈcommittee ˌ/ˈchairman |
| ˈcredit card ˌcompany | comˈputer ˌ/ˈnetwork |
| ˈfootball (ˌ)game | ˈhome ˈhealthˌcare |
| ˈfootball ˌplayer | hoˈtel ˈcarˌpark |
| ˈhealthcare reˌform | ˈmaster ˌ/ˈbedroom |
| ˈhealthcare ˌsystem | ˈnight ˈfootball |
| ˈmountain bike ˌrace | ˈschool ˈfootball |
| ˈnail polish reˌmover | ˈsport utˈility ˌvehicle |
| ˈnetwork ˌproblems | ˈstreet ˈfleamarket |
| ˈnewspaper deˌlivery | supˈport ˌnetwork |
| ˈpeanut (ˌ)butter | teleˈvision ˌ/ˈnetwork |
| ˈwater treatment ˌcompany | ˈtransporˌtation ˌ/ˈsafety ˌboard |
| ˈweekend eˌdition | uniˈversity ˌ/ˈlaw ˌschool |

However, the stress points aside from the main stress on the modifier present a much less clear picture. In some left-branching instances, the study participants did not agree whether there is a secondary, weaker stress or not (cf. *ˈbus driver (ˌ) seat*). If they did assign a secondary, weak stress, then it was audibly weaker than the main stress. In all of the right-branching compounds, by contrast, all the speakers did assign a second stress on the head. However, rather than disagreeing on whether was a second stress point at all as in the left-branching cases, here the study participants disagreed about the quality of the second stress point: some classified it as a secondary, weak stress, others realized it as a second main stress comparable to that of the modifier (cf. *comˈputer ˌ/ˈnetwork*). This second stress point may not be another main stress, but it was audibly clearly stronger than the non-modifier stress in left-branching compounds.

These results suggest that the Compound Stress Rule seems to generally hold true for three-noun compounds irrespective of the fact that one of the two constituents is complex, since fore-stress on the modifier was undisputed in all cases. Based on these results, I cannot agree with Carstairs-McCarthy's claim that right-branching compounds are stressed on the complex head, but rather suggest that at least some right-branching compounds show fore-stress as well, even though empirical testing in a larger-scale study is of course required to back up these initial results.

### 6.4.2 Does stress differ with regard to morphological structure?

The previous section suggested that the stress pattern in three-noun compounds generally does not seem to differ from that in simple compounds, identifying fore-stress on the modifier for both left- and right-branching compounds. However, the quality of the second, non-main stress remained unclear, as an evaluation of this aspect purely by ear is not reliable. Furthermore, a clearer idea of how left- and right-branching compounds differ with regard to stress is required. Therefore, this section will look more closely into the potential qualitative and quantitative differences in the stress patterns of left- and right-branching compounds from a theoretical perspective.

As has been stated before, in a typical two-noun compound the modifier receives the main stress and the head a secondary, weaker stress. What happens with these stress points once that compound combines with a further noun, either as a modifier or as a head? Are the original stress points replaced or added to the new stress points in the same place? To examine potential stress patterns in complex compounds, I will retrace the step of combining a compound with a further noun to form a three-noun compound. From a theoretical perspective, there are either two modifiers or two heads in three-noun compounds, depending on the branching pattern: a modifier and a head of primary rank, as part of the embedded compound, and additionally either another modifier or another head of secondary rank for the whole tri-constituent compound. Figure 7 illustrates the relationship between the heads and modifiers of primary and secondary rank for the two branching patterns as well as the corresponding stress patterns that theoretically result from the combination of these two ranks.

Let me clarify this illustration and start with left-branching items. When a compound, e.g. *football*, consisting of a modifier (N1) with main stress and a weakly stressed head (N2) (i.e. ˈfoot‚ball), is used to modify a further noun in a three-noun compound, the whole compound receives main stress: ˈ[foot‚ball]. The main stress in both the resulting three-noun compound (i.e. *football game*) and the original, now inner compound (i.e. *football*) thus falls on the same constituent, the N1. The second, weaker stress is assigned to the noun that is added on the second level, i.e. the N3 (i.e. *game*), which receives a weak stress (i.e. ‚game). What is unclear, however, is whether the original compound brings its head stress of primary rank (i.e. the weak stress on *ball*) into this relationship. If so, this would result in the stress pattern ˈN‚N‚N (i.e. ˈfoot‚ball ‚game). If not, the stress pattern would be ˈNNˌN (i.e. ˈfootball ‚game). Accordingly, the question is the following: Do speakers assign any stress to the N2 constituent in left-branching compounds? The observations in the previous section indicate that the head stress of primary rank is not realized in the complex compound, which would plead for the latter stress pattern ˈNN‚N. In the study, the

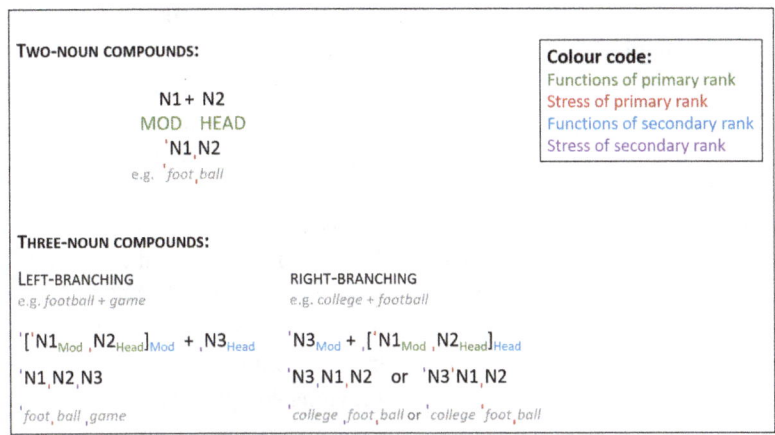

**Figure 7:** Distribution of stress points in left- and right-branching 3N.

participants did not even agree that there is a weak stress on the N3 constituent in all cases, i.e. that there is any kind of stress on *game* in the compound *football game*. In those cases where the N3 constituent does carry stress, is there a qualitative difference to the stress of the N2 constituent? To exemplify this, is the quality of the stress on the constituents of *ball* and *game* the same? Accordingly, what would be worth investigating empirically for left-branching three-noun compounds is the quality of the stress assigned to the N2 and the N3 constituent.

I will now regard right-branching compounds. If a compound with default main stress on the modifier and weak stress on the head (e.g. ˈfootˌball) is used as a head that is modified by another noun in a three-noun compound (e.g. *college football*), the modifier of second rank (i.e. *college*) receives the main stress (i.e. ˈcollege), while the inner compound (i.e. ˈfootˌball) receives a weak stress: ˈcollege ˌ[ˈfootˌball]. This combination theoretically results in an encounter of two different stress points in the N1 constituent *foot*. It is reasonable to assume that the stress of secondary rank, i.e. the weak stress, replaces the main stress of primary rank, which would result in the stress pattern ˈNˌNˌN. This would be in agreement with some of the observations made in the previous section, where study participants indicated a weak stress on the N1 constituent (e.g. ˈfood ˌnetwork). However, there were also right-branching items in which the stress assignment by the participants deviated, as in some instances the native speakers argued they would assign a further main stress to the N1 constituent (e.g. hoˈtel ˈcarpark, uniˈversity ˈlaw school, ˈnight ˈfootball). This would suggest that in some cases the modifier stress of primary rank is brought into the new combination, resulting in the stress pattern ˈNˈNˌN. Quite certainly, even if the N1 should receive another heavy stress, one would expect it not to be equal in strength to the main stress of the N3 constituent (i.e. the stress on *college*) but to be weaker. Accordingly, the stress of the N1 constituent in right-branching compounds is highly interesting: Is its strength more similar to the main stress of the N3 constituent or to the weak stress of the N2 constituent? It is conceivable that there is no absolute answer to this but that there are different types of right-branching compounds with regard to this aspect, i.e. a "type *night football*" ('N 'NN) and a "type *food network*" ('N ‚NN), which might be determined by semantic features of the modifiers. This assumption is supported by Giegerich (2015), who explains that compounds of the former type (which will be described as featuring ascriptive attribution in Section 7.5), favour end-stress (2015: 16).

The second question of interest in right-branching compounds is whether the N2 constituent keeps its weak stress of primary rank in the new combination, i.e.: Do speakers put any stress on the constituent *ball* in the sequence *college football*? A look at the results of the study suggests that this is true in some cases, cf. 'transportation '/‚safety ‚board or 'home ‚health ‚care, where the second element of the complex head (e.g. *board/care*) did receive a weak stress. In other cases, however, such as 'night 'football or 'master /'bedroom, this element was not assigned any kind of stress. It would thus be desirable to find out whether there are differences among right-branching compounds with regard to the stress assigned to the N2 constituent.

To summarize, what needs testing when it comes to the stress pattern in right-branching compounds are the following aspects:

(i) The quantity of stress points: Are there three or two stress points, i.e. does the N2 constituent carry a weak stress or no stress at all?
(ii) The quality of stress of the N1 constituent: Does it carry a heavy stress or a weak stress?
 a. If the N1 constituent carries a heavy stress, does it differ in quality to the main stress of the N3 constituent?
 b. If the N1 carries a weak stress, does it differ in quality to the weak stress of the N2 constituent?

What is to be tested in left-branching compounds is the stress of the N2 and the N3 constituent: Do they carry any stress? If so, do they have the same quality?

The largely theoretical considerations of this section must of course be subjected to an empirical study with appropriate acoustic phonetic equipment that is able to measure the quality and the quantity of the stress points precisely and thoroughly. Only then will it be possible to answer the question whether the stress patterns of left-branching and right-branching compounds differ systematically. On a theoretical basis, the questions posed at the beginning of this section can be answered to this extent: For left-branching three-noun compounds, stress does not seem to be more complex than for two-noun compounds, the only question is whether the embedded compound carries a further weak stress on the third constituent. For right-branching compounds, stress is potentially more complex, as there are several conceivable options for the stress points of both the second and third constituent. If it should turn out that there are qualitative and quantitative differences between left- and right-branching compounds when it comes to their stress pattern, then it would be highly intriguing to test which stress pattern native speakers assign to those complex compounds whose internal structure has been assessed as unclear in Section 5.1.4, such as *business management system*, for example.

## 6.5 Summary and conclusion

It was the aim of the different questions posed throughout Chapter 6 to determine the formal characteristics of three-noun compounds in general as well as the peculiarities of the instances of the two branching patterns. The analysis of samples from the 3N database has revealed several interesting features. It has shown that three-noun compounds cannot be said to be lengthy and formally complex sequences but tend to consist of two morphologically simple monosyllabic nouns that form the embedded compound, while the outer noun tends to be a bisyllabic suffixed noun. Less frequent compounds tend to be longer than more frequent ones but not more complex morphologically. Both among frequent and infrequent compounds there are compounds which are extremely long, such as *drug enforcement administration* or *deputy defense secretary*. Their length, however, is clearly above the average and thus, from a formal perspective, they are not typical representatives of three-noun compounds but rather exceptions, as opposed to instances like *football game* or *birthday party*.

A comparison of left- and right-branching compounds has shown that these two structurally different types can be distinguished formally in that left-branching items are generally shorter than right-branching ones. Still, they are not necessarily less complex. Instead, they tend to behave quite similarly when it comes to their morphological complexity, showing a tendency to consist of two monomorphemic words and one complex element each. There is a difference between these two types of complex compounds when it comes to the position of the affixed constituent, as it is in the position of the outer noun, i.e. the furthest left element in right-branching compounds and the furthest right element in left-branching ones.

Another formal feature that has been examined is orthography. It has been shown that although in theory spelling could be a good signpost for the internal structure of a tripartite compound, in practice orthography is not that closely tied to morphological structure. Language users make use of both neutral and non-neutral formats to the same degree. Furthermore, not all potentially available spelling formats are not made use of. Instead, the spelling of three-noun compounds is limited to the formats N N N, NN N/N NN and N-N N. Right-branching compounds are almost exclusively used in the formats N NN and N N N, with the first one being the more prevalent version, while the majority of left-branching compounds occur in the format N N N, a slightly lower number are realized as NN N and a comparatively small proportion are found in the format N-N N. Therefore, from an orthographic perspective, three-noun compounding is not significantly more complicated than simple compounding, as the theoretical abundance of spelling formats is not relevant, since only four formats can be considered established. Furthermore, variation in the spelling of three-noun compounds is clearly reserved to particular types. For those compounds that are most established in the neutral format N N N there is considerable variation, with writers employing the format NN-N as an alternative. Those compounds which are conventionalized in the formats NN N and N NN tend not to show variation.

The last aspect to be examined was the stress pattern of three-noun compounds. It has been argued that complex compounds can generally be assumed to show forestress just like simple compounds. A theoretical approach to the differences in stress for left- and right-branching compounds suggested that there are potentially qualitative differences in those elements that carry a non-main stress. Whether the instantiations of the two different morphological structures show quantifiable, measurable differences in terms of strength of stress needs to be tested in a larger scale study, for which the aspects discussed are to be seen as an inspiration and starting point.

To conclude, these sections have given a clearer idea of the formal characteristics of three-noun compounds in English. They have shown that tripartite nominal compounds do not form a homogeneous phenomenon but that there are remarkable differences between left- and right-branching compounds from a formal perspective. I hypothesize that a comparison of left- and right-branching items will be even more fruitful from a semantic point of view. This aspect will be examined in the next chapter, embedded in different research questions that provide a functional approximation to the phenomenon of tri-constituent compounds.

# 7 Functional analysis of three-noun compounds

This chapter will take a functional perspective on three-noun compounds by approaching the meaning and use of these word-formation products. In this context, there are many questions to be answered: Are there any three-noun compounds that are used frequently enough to be considered established in the English speech community? Which semantic fields do they come from? Are they used to describe everyday concepts or do they tend to denote abstract ideas in bureaucratic fields? Are three-noun compounds mostly shorter forms of syntactic phrases? Are they used in spoken language at all or are they generally reserved for formal registers? How transparent are these formations? And, importantly: Are there any differences between left- and right-branching compounds from a semantic and functional perspective? These are only some of the questions that will be addressed in the course of this chapter in order to complete the profile of three-noun compounds.

I will first provide a brief semantic categorization of three-noun compounds in Section 7.1. Section 7.2 will examine the frequency spectrum in which these complex compounds are used. Section 7.3 will be dedicated to exploring the quantitative differences in the use of left- and right-branching compounds. In Section 7.4, the focus of interest will be the embedded compounds of right-branching compounds in order to examine whether this branching structure allows only certain kinds of elements as a head. As a follow-up, Section 7.5 will take a closer look at the properties of the modifiers of right-branching compounds and point to potential semantic differences to the modifiers of left-branching compounds. After focusing on differences between the instances of the two branching patterns, the subsequent sections will be dedicated to the meaning and use of three-noun compounds as a holistic phenomenon. Section 7.6 will investigate whether these complex compounds are limited to certain areas of discourse. In Section 7.7, the semantic areas that three-noun compounds find their field of denotation in will be identified. Section 7.8 will be dedicated to the semantic compositionality of three-noun compounds, on the basis of which Section 7.9 will examine whether compounds are used as an alternative to syntactic phrases.

## 7.1 General semantic categorization

This section will provide a general semantic categorization of the compounds in the 3N database. For this, I will first briefly introduce the basic concepts for the semantic description of compounds and then present a semantic analysis for a sample of three-noun compounds.

As has been pointed out in Section 2.1, the notion of *head* is traditionally used in compounding to denote the constituent that determines the semantic category of the whole compound. Based on this concept, the most prominent way of categorizing compounds distinguishes between endocentric, exocentric and coordinative compounds (cf. Scalise and Vogel 2010; Scalise and Bisetto 2011). In endocentric compounds, the head element is semantically specified by the modifier (e.g. a *bus driver* denotes a kind of driver). Exocentric compounds are understood to be headless, i.e. their semantic head is not found within the compound (e.g. *egghead* or *red tape*). The respective compounds are often characterized by possessing the attribute described in the compound, in most cases in a metaphorical sense. Coordinative compounds can be generalized as having two heads. They are mostly used to describe parallel jobs or functions, such as *study-bedroom* or *editor-manager*. The most prototypical noun compounds in English are endocentric compounds which are determinative, i.e. hyponyms of the head, and thus have a modifier-head structure (Bloomfield 1933: 235; Quirk et al. 1985: 1567; Olsen 2000: 898) or *determinant-determinatum* structure in the terminology of Marchand (1969: 54).

Based on these explanations, I will attempt a portrayal of the semantic characteristics of three-noun compounds. It is expected that similarly to two-noun compounds, most items will be endocentric determinative compounds. Bauer and Huddleston (2017: 1648) also provide an example of a tri-constituent coordinative compound, namely *secretary-treasurer-editor*. It is, however, expected that these kinds of items are rather rare as in most cases coordinative compounds describe parallel jobs or functions performed by one person and the need to connect three concepts in this way is rather unlikely.

For the semantic analysis, all the items in the samples used so far were examined, i.e. the 300 most and least frequent three-noun compounds used in Chapter 6, as well as the 260 items used in the sections examining orthography, resulting in a sample of 560 items. They were manually classified as either endocentric, exocentric or coordinative. Not all of the items could be categorized conclusively. The compound *consumer product safety*, for example, could be an instance of a determinative compound with an embedded coordinative compound if it describes 'the safety of the product as well as the safety of the consumer'. Alternatively, it could be a determinative compound which describes either 'the product safety for the consumer', or 'the safety of the consumer product', depending on the branching pattern assigned. Such items, in which without context no decision could be made, were excluded from the categorization, which left 523 items in the sample.

The overwhelming majority of 511 three-noun compounds were categorized as endocentric, determinative compounds, such as, for example, *trade union leader*, which denotes a type of leader, or *birthday party*, denoting a type of party. No instances of exocentric compounds were found. However, the embedded compounds within determinative compounds can be exocentric to some degree, as is the case in *football coach*, for example. Here, *ball* does not refer to a kind of ball, but the embedded compound *football* is used in a metonymic sense, referring to the sport in which this kind of ball is used. The sample did not contain any fully coordinative compounds in which the three nouns are coordinated on the same level. There are, however, 8 instances of coordinative compounds that feature the coordination of *two* constituents on the same level, more precisely of the embedded compound and the outer noun, as, for example, in *singer-songwriter*. Furthermore, there are a very small number of hybrid forms, in which the embedded compound features coordination but the relation between the three-noun compound and the embedded compound is determinative (e.g. *parent-teacher conference*).

This evaluation suggests that three-noun compounds almost exclusively consist of determinative compounds. They thus behave similarly to two-noun compounds but seem to display an even stronger use of the determinative pattern and a very scarce exploitation of the alternative types. The category of hybrid forms (i.e. determinative tripartite compounds whose embedded compound is coordinative) might further be interesting in terms of formal features, as their stress pattern can be expected to deviate from that of determinative three-noun compounds that are based on a determinative embedded compound, e.g. *parent-teacher conference* might show two main stresses on the embedded compound (i.e. ˈparent ˈteacher ˌconference). A more thorough evaluation of the embedded compounds within determinative compounds might be insightful to see to what extent three-noun compounds tend to be based on non-determinative embedded compounds. Having described the general semantic setup of three-noun compounds, the following sections will look into more precise research questions.

## 7.2 To what extent are three-noun compounds used?

Does complex compounding give rise to items that can be considered conventionalized? Or does the word-formation process in which three nouns are combined predominantly produce terms that are only temporarily salient? To answer these questions, this section will explore the frequency spectrum of the compounds in the 3N database and in this context also give a qualitative insight into the most and least frequent three-noun compounds of the English language.

For this, I will first provide insight into the type-token distribution. The 3N database contains 57,741 different types of three-noun compounds, attested by a total of 678,737 tokens. Accordingly, each type of three-noun compound occurs on average about ten times. To examine this distribution more closely, the compounds in the database were categorized in 5 groups based on their token frequencies: extremely frequent items which occur more than 1,000 times, highly frequent ones occurring between 500 and 1,000 times, frequent compounds with token frequencies between 100 and 500, fairly frequent ones occurring between 50 and 100 times, barely frequent items occurring between 50 and 10 times, and rather infrequent compounds, which are used less than 10 times. Table 12 presents the type counts for these token frequency ranges as well as the respective proportions.

**Table 12:** Count of 3N types in different token frequency ranges.

| Token frequency | < 10 | 10–49 | 50–99 | 100–499 | 500–1,000 | > 1,000 |
|---|---|---|---|---|---|---|
| NUMBER OF TYPES | 45,094 | 10,892 | 1,017 | 660 | 48 | 30 |
| % | 78.10 | 18.86 | 1.76 | 1.14 | 0.08 | 0.05 |

The chart shows that the majority of three-noun compounds have very low token frequencies: almost eighty percent occur ten times or less (to be precise between 3 and 10 times, as 3 was the frequency threshold in the n-gram sets, cf. Section 4.1). In comparison, the number of types in the higher frequency areas is relatively low: only about three percent of three-noun compounds show token frequencies of 50 or higher. There are only about 700 types of three-noun compounds which occur more than 100 times. Of these, a tiny proportion of 30 types is used more than a thousand times. These results are not unexpected: Kim and Baldwin (2006) report a similar distribution for two-noun compounds, finding that half the types encountered in the BNC are single occurrences. This exploitation of the frequency spectrum, featuring a small amount of types with high token frequencies and an extremely long tail of low-frequency types, is not surprising but follows a Zipfian distribution that is commonly found in various kinds of linguistic phenomena (cf. Zipf 1935).

These figures indicate that there are only a small number of three-noun compounds which are used extensively, while most three-noun compounds are used fairly infrequently. In saying this, it must not be forgotten that the low-frequency area contains a considerable amount of noise, which is why the actual number of infrequent three-noun compounds can be expected to be lower. Nevertheless, the high number of low-frequency types indicates that three-noun compounds are dominated by such items which are only established to a limited degree. Obviously, speakers make extensive use of the word-formation process N+N+N to coin instances that might only be of temporary use (One might be inclined to say that these figures qualify the word-formation process in which three nouns are combined as a *productive* one, which might generally be true; however, the concept of productivity will be approached in more depth in Chapter 8). This ad-hoc character is typical of products of compounding, especially of noun compounds, which are commonly used to name "disposable concepts" (Schmid 2016: 143).

In order to give a qualitative insight into the items in the low-frequency area, the following list provides a selection of three-noun compounds from the 3N database with token frequencies below 10:

- doorway greeting
- farming systems information
- mountain sunset
- crash test ratings
- heart transplant candidates
- night-time concerts
- water torture approach
- nerve gas story
- eating disorder clinic
- life support machine
- wedding dress designer

- coefficient growth curve
- manslaughter sentence
- sunflower galaxy
- support telephone number
- airport café
- date rape victim
- weekend fighting
- flea market monkey
- flea market table
- video game addiction
- student network

Some of these items are clear instances of the above-mentioned disposable character, such as *manslaughter sentence* or *flea market monkey*. They have a deictic function which does not exceed a temporary need, as they are references made in a certain context to then current events or people. Other sequences have a naming function but refer to concepts that are not conventionalized in the speech community as they are either only established among a limited number of speakers (e.g. *sunflower galaxy, nerve gas story*) or are not in the focus of discourse so explicitly often enough to be commonly referred to in this way (e.g. *flea market table, eating disorder clinic, weekend fighting*). The list also contains items which are presumably syntactic in nature, such as *night-time concerts, mountain sunset, crash test ratings, support telephone number* or *wedding dress designer*. These compounds might be alternative forms of referring to a concept that is more commonly expressed through a syntactic phrase (e.g. *sunset in the mountains, telephone number for support, designer of wedding dresses*). Considering that among the low-frequency items there are both such with a naming function as well as such that have a syntactic function but denote concepts that are not just of temporary importance, this qualitative insight does not fully support the characterization of infrequent compounds as tools to denote disposable, temporary concepts.

Before giving an insight into higher-frequency items, I want to address the fact that some compounds in the list of low-frequency items feel more familiar than their token frequency suggests, such as *student network, life support machine* or *airport café*, for example. This – presumed or real – discrepancy can be traced back to three different roots. The first of these concerns formations whose motivation is syntactic in nature. In these cases, there can be a discrepancy between the degree to which a concept is established and the establishment of the form used to refer to it. While the concepts might be encountered quite frequently, they are not exclusively expressed via a compound but might in most cases be denoted by a different form, e.g. a syntactic phrase. Accordingly, speakers encounter the concept more often than the compound form, which is why the presumed familiarity with the form might be confused with familiarity with the concept. This could, for example, be the case for the compound *airport café*, which might in most cases be simply referred to as *café* without the modifier *airport*, since if this concept is referred to in a situation at the airport, the specification through the modifier is not required. Another explanation for the discrepancy between the intuitive degree of establishment of some concepts and the token frequencies of the relevant compounds can be due to a cognitive feature of compounding. Through the mechanism of hypostatization, speakers are able to create a meaningful concept from the combination of given concepts. Accordingly, some of the compounds listed above might actually not describe very common concepts but the relevant concept is so plausible that the respective compounds feel more familiar than they actually are, which could be the case in *doorway greeting*. A last aspect that can explain why for some items the token frequencies intuitively are too low is not compound-specific but related to corpus data in general. It is possible that the token frequencies found in the corpus are lower than the degree to which the items and the respective concepts are established in the speech community. Token frequencies do not always adequately reflect the degree to which speakers are confronted with words and the concepts they describe, as will be discussed in more detail in Section 8.6.2. These three aspects may explain why some of the low-frequency items feel more established than their token frequencies suggest.

Having provided a qualitative insight into low-frequency three-noun compounds, I will now turn to the other end of the frequency spectrum. The small number of types in the higher frequency levels gains more prominence when looking at the proportion of their token frequencies. Table 13 shows the number of tokens in the different frequency ranges (for reasons of clarity, the three highest frequency ranges have been subsumed into one category).

**Table 13:** Distribution of types and tokens among frequency ranges.

| Frequency range | Types | Types % | Tokens | Tokens % |
|---|---|---|---|---|
| > 100 | 738 | 1.27 | 206,008 | 30.35 |
| 50–99 | 1,017 | 1.76 | 69,466 | 10.23 |
| 10–49 | 10,892 | 18.86 | 204,178 | 30.08 |
| < 10 | 45,094 | 78.10 | 199,085 | 29.33 |

The table shows that the huge number of 45,094 types of three-noun compounds which occur less than 10 times accounts for a relatively small number of tokens (199,085 tokens). Almost the same number of tokens is covered by the comparatively few 738 types which occur more than 100 times (206,008 tokens). Although only about one fifth of all types occur more than ten times in the corpus, these types form more than 70 percent of all tokens. Accordingly, the use of and exposure to three-noun compounds is not dominated by low-frequency items; instead, when speakers use or encounter a three-noun compound it is more likely to be an item that is established to some degree.

What do these frequently occurring three-noun compounds look like? And are they used frequently enough to be regarded as established in the English speech community? To give a qualitative insight into the items in the high-frequency area, Figure 8 displays the 30 most common three-noun compounds in the 3N database, i.e. all items with token frequencies higher than 1,000. The compound types are located on the x-axis, with the respective token frequencies displayed on the y-axis. The tokens encompass all spelling formats found for the relevant item. Each item is listed in its most frequently found format.

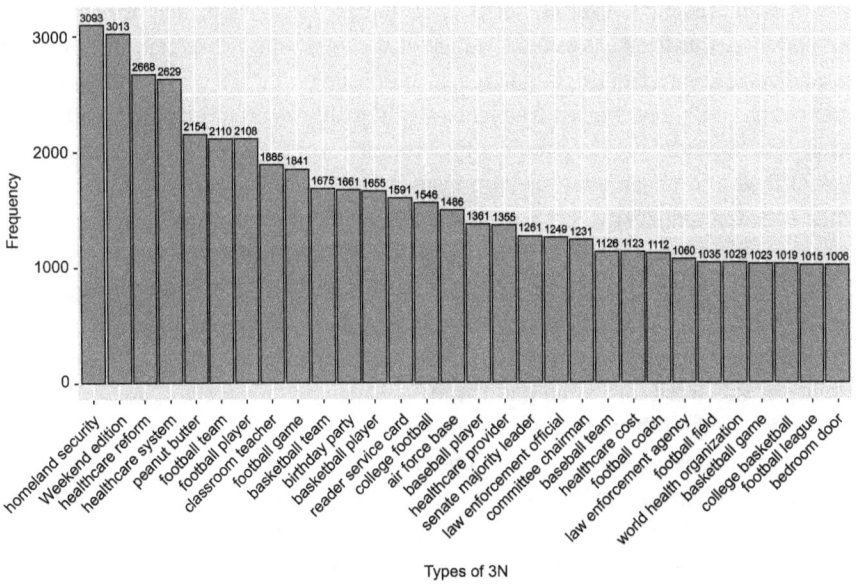

**Figure 8:** Most frequent three-noun compounds.

These 30 most frequent types, which constitute only 0.05 percent of all types of three-noun compounds, account for 48,120 tokens, which is 7 percent of all the tokens in the 3N database. Accordingly, they can be said to be strongly prevalent among three-noun compounds, as on average almost every tenth token of three-noun compound a speaker encounters will be one of the items displayed in the figure. Among these high frequency types, the two most frequent ones, *homeland security* and *weekend edition*, occur more than 3,000 times each. There are a handful of types with token frequencies higher than 2,000, such as *peanut butter, health care system* and *football team*, and another 23 types that occur between one and two thousand times in the corpus, such as *college football, air force base* and *bedroom door*. Can these complex compounds be considered conventionalized? Schmid (2016: 139) determines the status of conventionalization of the (simple) compounds in his sample by checking whether the items under investigation have entries in the *Oxford Advanced Learner's Dictionary* (OALD). However, not all English compounds are consistently listed in dictionaries. A random check in the OED confirms that this is even more true for three-noun compounds, which is why this proposal is not deemed fruitful here. Even without any way of empirically measuring the degree of establishedness of these items, the majority of the three-noun compounds displayed in the table can be reasonably claimed to be established expressions of the English language. Compounds like *basketball game, bedroom door* or *football league* are clearly not marked or clumsy word sequences but constitute perfectly customary expressions that are commonly employed in this form. As establishedness is a continuum, there is no threshold beyond which a word can be categorized as established, which is why even three-noun compounds with lower token frequencies will qualify as established to a certain degree. It is, however, not the aim here to determine which three-noun compounds are established and which ones are not; instead, the intention is to show that despite their seeming complexity, there are tri-constituent noun compounds that can be considered conventionalized expressions of the English language.

To summarize, this section has given an insight into the frequency spectrum covered by three-noun compounds, indicating that, on the one hand, there are a large number of types with only few instances, which is an indication of the suitability of this word-formation pattern for the naming of more and less temporary concepts. On the other hand, there are three-noun compounds that have become an established part of the lexicon of the English speech community. In this account of the use of three-noun compounds no distinction has been made between left- and right-branching compounds, which is why the following section will examine whether these two types differ when it comes to the extent to which they are used.

## 7.3 Are left-branching compounds more frequent than right-branching ones?

Section 5.2.3 has shown that there are more types of left-branching compounds than right-branching ones. A look at the most conventionalized items on page 99 shows that these are almost exclusively left-branching items. Are right-branching compounds rather to be found among the low-frequency items? Theoretical considerations would suggest quite the contrary, namely that right-branching items can be found mainly among the conventionalized compounds, while newly formed instances may be exclusively left-branching items, as this pattern is more prevalent and might consequently be more accessible for speakers. To assess this situation, this section will approximate the quantitative relation between the two kinds of three-noun compounds with regard to both types and tokens.

The categorization into branching patterns in Chapter 5 showed that almost two thirds of the compound types in the 3N database feature a left-branching structure (63%), leaving about one third of items for right-branching (37%). This relation is averaged across all instances of three-noun compounds. In order to investigate whether it is stable across the frequency spectrum, the proportion of left-branching and right-branching items was determined for subsets with different token frequencies. Figure 9 displays the quantitative relation between left- and right-branching compounds distinguished for different token frequency ranges.

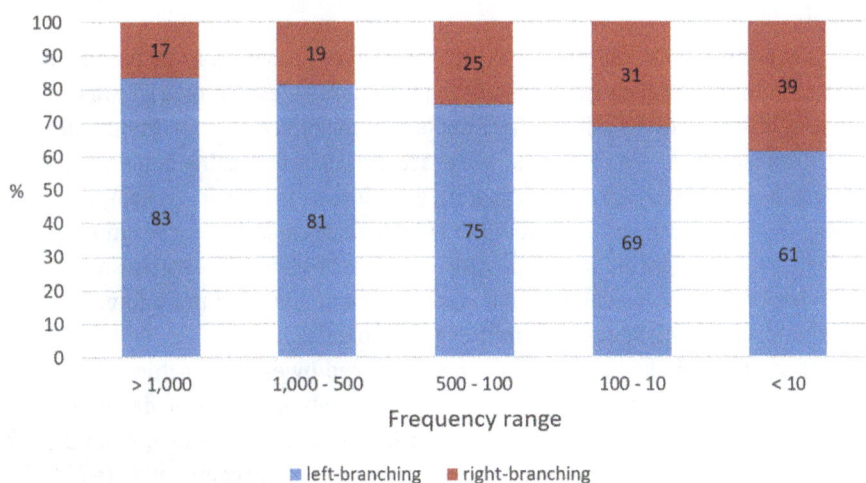

**Figure 9:** Relationship between branching patterns across frequency ranges.

The diagram shows that in all frequency ranges there are more instances of left-branching than right-branching, with at least 60 percent of the types featuring this morphological structure in each frequency category. Not only are there fewer infrequent formations with a right-branching structure but also among the more conventionalized three-noun compounds are left-branching items the dominant type. What can also be seen, however, is that the quantitative dominance of left-branching items over right-branching ones depends to a considerable degree on the frequency range, as the relationship between the two types of three-noun compounds does not remain stable: the higher the frequency range, the lower the share of right-branching items becomes. While the number of right-branching items among the most frequent three-noun compounds is comparatively small, accounting for less than 20 percent, the share of right-branching items increases with a decrease in token frequency. Among the rather infrequent three-noun compounds, right-branching types make up almost 40 percent, a proportion almost double that in the high-frequency area. At this point, it must be remembered that this category (low-frequency items tagged as right-branching) is the one that contains a large amount of noise (cf. Section 4.3). Therefore, it would not be fully accurate to claim that four out of ten low-frequency formations are right-branching items. The actual number of right-branching items can be assumed to be lower, which suggests that the dominance of left-branching items in the low-frequency area is stronger than suggested by the figures. According to these results, left-branching items are prevalent among three-noun compounds in all frequency ranges.

Nevertheless, the diagram also shows that there are right-branching items to be found in the low-frequency range, which demonstrates that the right-branching pattern is sufficiently available for speakers to make use of it for the creation of new compounds. At the same time, there are also right-branching items among the conventionalized three-noun compounds, even if their proportion is comparatively small. Instances such as *college football* or *committee chairman*, for example, occur more than 1,000 times in the corpus and can thus be considered established. Thus, both left-branching compounds and right-branching ones are to be found among the established and among the infrequent compounds.

Having merely looked into the types produced by each branching pattern so far, I will now focus on the tokens. Based on the observations made so far, it is suspected that there are not only fewer types of right-branching compounds, but that furthermore the token frequencies of right-branching compounds tend to be lower than those of left-branching ones. To test this assumption, the average number of tokens per type was calculated for the two branching patterns:

The table shows that on average, each type of three-noun compound is used around twelve times. A comparison of the two branching patterns reveals a

## 7.3 Are left-branching compounds more frequent than right-branching ones?

**Table 14:** Type-token relationship distinguished for branching patterns.

| Category | Types | Tokens | Tokens per type |
|---|---|---|---|
| 3N TOTAL | 57,607 | 678,463 | 11.78 |
| LEFT-BRANCHING 3N | 36,271 | 479,987 | 13.23 |
| RIGHT-BRANCHING 3N | 21,335 | 196,927 | 9.23 |

discrepancy between their type-token relationships: While compounds with a left-branching structure have a token frequency of 13 on average, right-branching compounds tend to comprise 9 tokens only. Therefore, the token frequencies of right-branching compounds can be said to be generally lower than those of left-branching ones, which suggests that left-branching compounds tend to be used more often than right-branching ones.

This impression is further supported by a direct comparison of the token frequencies for the most frequent instances of each branching pattern. Figure 10 depicts the frequencies for the 300 most frequent left-branching compounds (green line), as well as for the 300 most frequent right-branching ones (blue line).

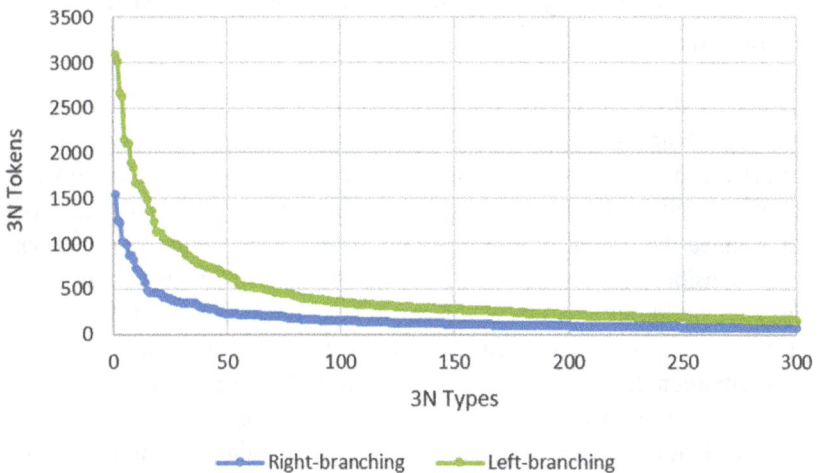

**Figure 10:** Token frequencies of most frequent left- and right-branching 3N.

The figure clearly illustrates that the most frequent left-branching compounds have higher token frequencies than the most frequent right-branching ones. While left-branching compounds include 25 instances in the 4-digit area, there are only 5 types of right-branching compounds with token frequencies higher than 1,000. The most frequent left-branching compound, *homeland security*, occurs 3,093 times, while the most frequent right-branching one, *college football*, has a token frequency of 1,546 only. While the 20 most frequent left-branching items cover a frequency range from 3,093 to 1,112, the range for the 20 most frequent right-branching items is from 1,546 to 443. These numbers confirm that right-branching compounds in general feature lower token-frequencies than left-branching ones, or, to phrase it differently, left-branching items tend to be used more frequently than right-branching ones.

To summarize, left-branching compounds are the dominant type of three-noun compound as regards both types and tokens. There are not merely more different compounds of this branching pattern, but each of these compounds also tend to be used more frequently. At the same time, it has been observed that the quantitative relationship between the branching patterns depends on the frequency range. This finding might provide a further explanation for the deviating ratio between left-branching and right-branching reported by Schmid (cf. page 62), as in his data the token frequencies of the items under investigation are not provided.

## 7.4 Do right-branching compounds require special kinds of heads?

The previous section has shown that left-branching compounds are more prevalent than right-branching ones in terms of both types and tokens. The reason for this difference in use can presumably be traced back to the cognitive effort required for the processing of these two kinds of complex compounds. It can be reasonably claimed that the head in a compound is the more important constituent as it is responsible for general reference. It might be less favourable to have a complex element in this position, as this might be to the detriment of the processing effort. This reasoning would put right-branching compounds at a disadvantage. This situation, however, clearly needs empirical investigation, for example in the form of an eye-tracking experiment in which the processing effort required for left- and right-branching compounds is contrasted, which can unfortunately not be provided within this book. Nevertheless, it can be reasonably assumed that complex heads in a compound are a less favourable constellation for processing than simple heads.

This explanation, however, raises the question why there are still right-branching compounds if this format is not ideal. The reason for this might lie in the quality of the complex heads. This impression is gained by Schmid (2016: 208), who observes for the right-branching three-noun compounds in his sample that the embedded compounds are overwhelmingly established instances, such as *girlfriend, playmate, newsagent, warfare, deadline, bedroom, headmaster, newspaper* or *timetable*. This leads him to reason that "[t]he potential for the formation and syntactic use of poly-morphemic compounds whose head is a compound in itself, is obviously more limited [than that of compounds whose modifier is a compound in itself]. Since the head is the decisive constituent from a grammatical, semantic and conceptual point of view, it seems to be preferred if it is an already established lexeme [. . .]" (2016: 208). Schmid draws his observation from a small sample of 75 compounds only. Does his assumption hold true for larger data sets? Do right-branching compounds tend to be based on established compounds? It is the aim of this section to find out whether only particular kinds of embedded compounds are suitable as heads in right-branching compounds.

To do so, the heads of 150 right-branching compounds that were drawn randomly from the 3N database was analysed in a fairly simple setup. The heads, i.e. the embedded compounds, were rated as either established or less so based on their token frequencies in the online edition of COCA. The embedded compounds were searched for in isolation, i.e. not being part of a complex compound. Token frequencies of 50 or lower led to a categorization as "rather less established", compounds with higher token frequencies were categorized as "established". Based on this classification, 116 out of 150 tripartite compounds were categorized as being based on an established compound, such as, for example, *campus newspaper, music classroom, company newsletter, college football, master bedroom, pearl necklace, student network, computer database, side airbag* or *history textbook*. Among the remaining 34 complex compounds that were classified as containing a less established embedded compound are, for example, *senate majority leader, senate judiciary committee, senate finance committee, sport utility vehicle, missile defense system, security trust fund, library media specialist, rape crisis center* and *sea surface temperature*.

This analysis suggests that the complex heads in right-branching items are predominantly established compounds, such as *football* or *network*. This does, however, not mean that right-branching compounds cannot feature less established compounds as heads, as there are a fair number of right-branching compounds whose embedded compounds cannot be considered established (e.g. *sport utility vehicle*). Accordingly, it cannot be confirmed that right-branching compounds require established compounds as heads, as they also permit embedded compounds which are established to a lesser degree. Nevertheless, embedded compounds that are established to some degree are clearly the preferred format for heads in right-branching compounds.

In order to examine whether this situation is reserved to the embedded compounds in right-branching compounds and thus attributable to the function of the head, or whether it holds true for the embedded compounds in left-branching instances as well, the same analysis was performed for the complex modifiers of a sample of 150 left-branching compounds. Surprisingly, it yielded nearly the same result: Out of the 150 sample items, only 41 three-noun compounds were categorized as containing a rather less strongly established compound, as for example *hormone replacement therapy, health maintenance organization, substance abuse treatment, emergency management agency, venture capital firm, information literacy skill* or *senate confirmation hearing*. The remaining 109 items were classified as being based on an embedded compound that was evaluated as relatively established, e.g. *weekend edition, peanut butter, health care reform, classroom teacher, bedroom door, football league, baseball player, stem cell research, newspaper article, cowboy hat, airline industry, breast cancer survivor* or *birthday cake*.

Accordingly, out of 300 tripartite compounds, 41 left-branching compounds and 34 right-branching ones were assessed as being based on a rather unestablished embedded compound. This comparison indicates that right-branching compounds are not more strongly based on established compounds than left-branching ones. Instead, these results suggest that established compounds are not only advantageous as heads but also as modifiers. It must of course be acknowledged that the methodology applied here is highly simplistic, based on a plain either-or decision regarding the establishedness of the compounds in question. Obviously, finer distinctions would be sensible for a more thorough analysis of the degree of establishedness of the embedded compounds. Nevertheless, it can be assumed that the general observation made, namely that complex compounds preferably contain embedded compounds that are established to some degree, does hold true. For both left-branching and right-branching compounds it seems to be favourable if the embedded compound is an established lexeme. These observations support Warren's assumption cited in Section 3.1, namely that complex compounds seem to be easier to process – and thus more likely to be formed – if they contain "ready-made" components (Warren 1978: 15). The cognitive background that can account for this connection will be detailed in Chapter 8.

## 7.5 Do simple and complex modifiers differ in quality?

While the previous section compared the embedded compounds in left- and right-branching compounds and thus focused on a formal constituent, this section will contrast those elements that share the same function in the two types of three-noun compounds, namely their modifiers. Obviously, the modifiers differ formally as those in left-branching compounds are compounds, while those in right-branching compounds are simple words. In this section, I will suggest that these two kinds of modifiers also differ in quality.

In order to allow a comparison of the modifiers, Table 15 presents the 50 most common left-branching three-noun compounds and the 50 most common right-branching ones, extracted from the 3N database. The subsequent claims are based on the observation of a much larger data set; this extract is intended to give an insight into the inventory of modifiers, as it is fairly representative of the phenomena to be described. Those modifiers in the column of right-branching compounds which are marked with one or two asterisks show semantic commonalities and have thus been assigned to two distinct categories that will be explained below.

**Table 15:** Most frequent left-branching and right-branching compounds.

| Left-branching | Right-branching |
| --- | --- |
| homeland security | college football** |
| weekend edition | senate majority leader** |
| health care reform | committee chairman |
| health care system | world health organization** |
| peanut butter | college basketball** |
| football team | master bedroom |
| football player | television network |
| classroom teacher | world trade organization** |
| football game | senate judiciary committee** |
| basketball team | cable network |
| birthday party | news network |
| basketball player | computer network |
| reader service card | school football** |
| airforce base | boys basketball* |
| baseball player | senate finance committee** |
| health care provider | girls basketball* |
| law enforcement official | transportation safety board |
| baseball team | vanilla ice cream* |
| health care cost | home health care |
| football coach | sport utility vehicle |
| law enforcement agency | support network |
| football field | university law school** |
| basketball game | night football* |
| football league | missile defense system |
| bedroom door | police headquarters |
| campaign finance reform | music classroom |
| basketball coach | gas pipeline |
| baseball game | education classroom |
| health care plan | school basketball* |
| aircraft carrier | food network |
| household income | senate minority leader** |
| security council resolution | motor speedway |

**Table 15** (continued)

| Left-branching | Right-branching |
| --- | --- |
| dining room table | commission chairman |
| cocktail party | school classroom** |
| day care center | deputy district attorney** |
| health care worker | deputy assistant secretary** |
| health care professional | class warfare |
| basketball court | student newspaper* |
| railroad track | university law professor** |
| law enforcement officer | hospital emergency room |
| bedroom window | city councilman** |
| baseball bat | beach volleyball |
| stem cell research | security trust fund |
| teacher education program | radio network |
| health care bill | news headline |
| newspaper article | computer keyboard |
| bathroom door | senate banking committee** |
| cowboy hat | school newspaper** |
| airline industry | car salesman |
| cowboy boot | side airbag* |

The first of these categories concerns the items marked with one asterisk. Their modifiers are deemed special with regard to their morphological properties, as these lexemes can act as both nouns and adjectives. In their function of modifying a compound, their role resembles that of an adjective, compare, for example, *vanilla ice cream, night football, side airbag, boys basketball* and *girls basketball*. Especially in the first three examples, the morphological status of the modifiers in this constellation is debatable, as a classification as both noun and adjective would be conceivable based on their attributive characteristics. A similar observation has been made by Tarasova (2013: 62), who contrasts the behaviour of nouns in their use as a modifier with that as a head. She observes that many of the nouns that are used as modifiers are ambiguous regarding their word class, often qualifying for an attributive function (cf. also Bauer et al. 2019).

Theoretically, the modifiers in left-branching compounds could have an adjectival quality as well, as they also modify a noun and the role of noun-modification is typically taken by adjectives. However, in left-branching compounds the modifier takes the form of a two-noun compound, which is conceptually rather unlikely to have adjectival features, as a combination of two nouns is more prone to describe thing-like entities (cf. Langacker 1987b). Therefore, the phenomenon of modifiers that resemble adjectives seems to be exclusive to right-branching compounds. It is exactly this aspect that has contributed to intricacies in the data collection process for the 3N database, as it was these kinds of items (*silver earring, plastic water bottle*, etc.) which were challenging in the decision-making process about which sequences to include (cf. Section 4.2.3). The following overview is an attempt to classify these adjectival modifiers, grouping them by the kinds of concepts they denote:

- HUMANS: *boys, girls, child, adult, student, volunteer, youth*
  e.g. *boys soccer team, girls volleyball, child behavior problems, adult stem cell, student research project, volunteer food preparers, youth risk behavior, youth behavior problems*
- TIMES: *night, summer, winter*
  e.g. *night skyline, summer sunlight, summer air temperature*
- MATERIAL: *metal, leather, silver, pearl, plastic, vanilla*
  e.g. *metal bedframe, leather briefcase, silver earring, pearl necklace, vanilla ice cream*
- TITLES: *executive, deputy*
  e.g. *executive conference center, executive fashion editor, deputy police chief, deputy art director*
- OTHERS: *side*
  e.g. *side airbag*

Clearly, these modifiers are not adjectives, as they do not display the behaviour of adjectives. They cannot, for example, be modified by adverbs, e.g. *\*a very summer air temperature, \*an extremely leather briefcase*. Still, they have a "less nouny" and more adjective-like character than other modifiers, which raises the question whether the respective three-noun compounds denote one holistic concept or instead rather describe the modification of a concept. This situation has some nontrivial implications, as it challenges the status of these instances as three-noun compounds. Are we still dealing with a morphological phenomenon or rather a syntactic one? Giegerich (2015) uses similar instances to discuss the divide between the lexicon and syntax. He explains that in such instances the relevant nouns function as ascriptive attributes – a behaviour that is not typical for nouns as they usually perform associative attribution (Giegerich 2015: 10–12). The resulting three-noun sequences tend to resemble syntactic formations in which a noun phrase is premodified by an adjective and are thus formally and semantically less characteristic of compounding than other three-noun sequences. In those instances that use *boys* and *girls* as modifiers, this impression is furthermore strengthened through the genitive-like nature of these modifiers.

The second category of modifiers concerns those items in the table that are marked with two asterisks. In these cases, the combination of the modifier and the compound formally has the flavour of an elliptic co-joint that would be expressed more naturally in the form of HEAD PREPOSITION (ARTICLE) MODIFIER. This is

to be observed primarily in right-branching compounds with a syntactic function, in which the modifier denotes a place or an institution:
- INSTITUTIONS: *college, school, university, senate, committee*
  e.g. *college transfer rate, school football, university law school, senate committee members, senate ethics rules, committee press secretary*
- PLACES: *home, world*
  e.g. *home health care, home network, world health organization, world oil demand*

Interestingly, it seems to be exactly these kinds of compounds which showed peculiarities in their pronunciation, featuring a stress pattern that deviates from the other items, with a second heavy stress on the embedded compound (cf. Section 6.4.1). This behaviour is associated more with syntactic constructions than with compounds. Based on these observations, the items in this category can be claimed to be less typical instances of the formal and semantic units which compounding is generally known to produce.

To conclude, this section has pointed out that there are modifiers in right-branching compounds that are somewhat peculiar as they contribute to the impression that the character of the respective three-noun compounds is distinct from the formally and semantically holistic nature associated with compounds. Instead, these complex compounds resemble syntactic phenomena in which the modifier and the modified concept are less strongly connected than they generally are in compounds. This is not an absolute characterization but more of a tendency and only affects a certain proportion of modifiers. It might, however, contribute to the impression that some instances of right-branching compounds are less typical examples of compounding than left-branching ones, for which this phenomenon has not been found.

## 7.6 Which areas of discourse are three-noun compounds used in?

Is the usage of complex compounds limited to certain areas of discourse? Schmid (2016: 141–142) has investigated this situation for two-noun compounds, examining their distribution in the fields of CONVERSATION, LETTERS, FICTION, REPORTAGE and ACADEMIC WRITING and finds that they are more strongly used in formal and abstract registers than in conversations and personal letters. Considering that three-noun compounds are formally more complex than two-noun compounds, this raises the question of whether they predominantly occur in formal and written genres. To explore this situation, this section will investigate the usage spectrum of tripartite nominal compounds with regard to the genres in which they are employed.

To do so, a sample of 100 items was drawn randomly from the 3N database. To explore the fields of discourse they are used in, the chart function of the online edition of COCA was consulted. This function displays the distribution of the tokens over the five genres SPOKEN, FICTION, MAGAZINES, NEWSPAPERS and ACADEMIC TEXTS,[14] which contain approximately the same number of words. For each complex compound in the sample, the distribution of the token frequencies among these genres was determined. The average distribution of the tokens across the genres is displayed in Figure 11.

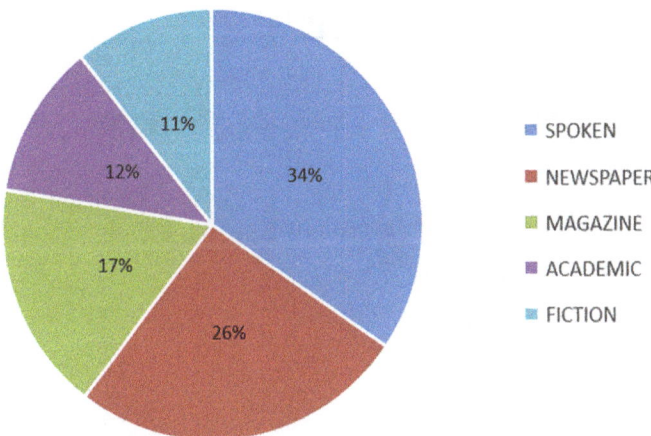

**Figure 11:** Distribution of 3N tokens among registers.

The diagram shows that the usage of three-noun compounds is spread across all five genres covered by the corpus. There is no register in which tripartite nominal compounds are not used at all, although the number of tokens in the fields of fictional literature and academic journals is comparatively low, covering just about one tenth of tokens each. Considering the fact that the sample items occur in all genres to some degree, the idea that complex compounds are reserved for certain areas of discourse can be rejected. On the contrary, three-noun compounds can be claimed to be relatively unmarked concerning their usage in different registers. Besides, it is noticeable that one third of all tokens are found in the field of spoken

---

[14] Date: January 2020. In the meantime, the corpus has been extended to include three further sections, namely BLOG, WEB and TV/MOVIES.

language. It can thus be explicitly refuted that three-noun compounds are formally too complex to be used in informal and spoken discourse.

Nevertheless, this quantified report of the occurrences in the different genres should not stand alone, as quite certainly the individual items display idiosyncratic behaviour in this respect. In order to give a qualitative insight into the usage of three-noun compounds, for exemplary sample items the distribution of the tokens on the genres spoken (SPOK), fiction (FICT), popular magazines (MAG), newspaper (NEWS) and academic texts (ACAD) is displayed in Table 16.

**Table 16:** Distribution of 3N tokens among registers.

| 3N | TOKENS | SPOK | FICT | MAG | NEWS | ACAD |
|---|---|---|---|---|---|---|
| air traffic control | 532 | 225 | 29 | 117 | 141 | 20 |
| airport security | 539 | 209 | 41 | 118 | 149 | 22 |
| bedroom window | 949 | 44 | 687 | 102 | 104 | 12 |
| birth control pill | 437 | 158 | 32 | 127 | 89 | 31 |
| birthday present | 364 | 55 | 182 | 59 | 55 | 13 |
| body mass index | 739 | 32 | 3 | 154 | 46 | 504 |
| bone marrow transplant | 409 | 166 | 18 | 64 | 133 | 28 |
| breast cancer survivor | 263 | 52 | 3 | 97 | 77 | 34 |
| classroom guidance | 119 | 0 | 0 | 0 | 0 | 119 |
| consumer protection agency | 76 | 30 | 0 | 18 | 21 | 7 |
| control group participant | 37 | 0 | 0 | 0 | 0 | 37 |
| cowboy hat | 869 | 91 | 347 | 160 | 248 | 23 |
| credit card company | 633 | 151 | 21 | 182 | 256 | 23 |
| death row inmates | 352 | 115 | 10 | 49 | 156 | 22 |
| dining room table | 855 | 76 | 472 | 141 | 142 | 24 |
| drug use abstinence | 8 | 0 | 0 | 0 | 0 | 8 |
| eyewitness account | 377 | 132 | 31 | 67 | 80 | 67 |
| ginger bread house | 199 | 33 | 49 | 53 | 61 | 3 |
| health care reform | 3,243 | 1,742 | 6 | 498 | 701 | 296 |
| health insurance coverage | 292 | 47 | 0 | 59 | 78 | 108 |
| information system development | 7 | 0 | 0 | 0 | 0 | 7 |
| internet service provider | 486 | 62 | 6 | 172 | 202 | 44 |
| newspaper article | 840 | 136 | 123 | 127 | 179 | 275 |
| population growth rate | 188 | 5 | 0 | 33 | 28 | 122 |
| roller coaster ride | 343 | 93 | 31 | 84 | 117 | 18 |
| skin surgery center | 9 | 0 | 0 | 9 | 0 | 0 |
| snack food personality | 3 | 0 | 0 | 0 | 3 | 0 |
| stem cell research | 234 | 45 | 1 | 72 | 99 | 17 |
| trade union leader | 43 | 6 | 3 | 6 | 12 | 16 |
| war crimes trial | 164 | 74 | 1 | 22 | 48 | 19 |
| weekend edition | 3,031 | 2,991 | 2 | 10 | 24 | 4 |
| workplace safety | 119 | 18 | 1 | 31 | 34 | 35 |

A comparison of the distribution for the individual items shows that only in a few instances does the spread of the genres coincide with that determined on average, i.e. occurring most frequently in spoken language, followed by usage in newspapers, magazines, academic writing and fiction. This is true, for example, for the instances of *bone marrow transplant, death row inmates, eyewitness account* and *weekend edition*. In all other cases, the items under investigation behave quite distinctly. *Birth control pill*, for example, is mainly found in the spoken register and in magazines, several times in newspapers but comparatively seldom in academic writing or fiction. *Birthday present*, by contrast, has a completely different distribution, barely occurring in academic texts but overwhelmingly in fictional writing and is to be found to a similar degree in newspapers, magazines and spoken language. *Internet service provider* is mainly reserved for academic texts and newspapers; *body mass index* is predominantly used in academic contexts and in magazines. *Bedroom window* and *dining room table*, by contrast, are mainly reserved for fictional writing. *Stem cell research*, surprisingly, occurs more often in magazines and newspapers than in academic writing and is used comparatively frequently in spoken language but almost never in fictional texts.

These comparisons illustrate that the individual three-noun compounds display different behaviour when it comes to their distribution among the various registers. Clearly, each complex compound has a very own, individual profile regarding their usage, which is not surprising but simply related to the concepts they denote. The figures in Table 16 show that although most three-noun compounds show a preference for one or more registers, the majority of items occurs in all genres to some degree, except for items with low token frequencies, which of course have little room for variation. It is true that there are three-noun compounds which are limited in their use, as some of them – not surprisingly – do not occur in fictional texts (e.g. *health insurance coverage, trade union leader* or *population growth rate*). Only a minority of words occurs solely in one genre, such as *skin surgery center* or *snack food personality*. However, for these items (as for most other items which are absent in more than one genre), the token frequencies are too low to evaluate their distribution properly and to draw generalizations. Academic writing is the only area that comprises several complex compounds which seem exclusively reserved to this genre, such as *classroom guidance, information system development, control group participant* and *drug use abstinence*. This is, however, clearly related to the concepts denoted by these compounds instead of being attributable to the phenomenon of complex compounding.

The table furthermore shows that there are also a considerable number of compounds that occur mainly in the spoken genre, such as *eyewitness account, air traffic control, airport security, birth control pill, health care reform* and *weekend edition*. This observation is clearly a reason to explicitly reject the potential assumption that three-noun compounds are a phenomenon that is reserved for written discourse and might be too formally complex to be used in the spoken discourse. Instead, it can be claimed that three-noun compounds are commonly found in spoken language.

This depiction of the token distribution among the registers of COCA demonstrates that the use of three-noun compounds is determined pragmatically similarly to that of less complex words. Abstracting away from individual types, it can be stated that three-noun compounds are neither reserved for a certain part of discourse nor limited in their use in different genres but are employed in a variety of genres, including the spoken register. In this context, Schmid points out that the distribution of compounds among the different registers depends on their kind, stating that phrasal compounds are to be found more often in press texts, while technical compounds are predominant in academic writing, and compounds with a lexical function again are rather to be found in more informal registers (2016: 141–142). Clearly, the sample used here is too small to verify this situation for three-noun compounds; however, it would be intriguing to conduct further research on this topic that investigates whether the use of three-noun compounds in certain genres corresponds to different functional types.

## 7.7 What semantic areas do three-noun compounds come from?

What semantic areas do the concepts that are expressed by three-noun compounds stem from? Do these word-formation products typically denote concepts in everyday life, as is the case in *football game* or *school classroom*, or are typical instances rather ones which refer to concepts in administrative areas, like *drug control administration* or *law enforcement official*? Schmid (2016: 114) claims that compounding generally produces instances in all subject areas. Is this also true for three-noun compounds? To answer these questions, this section will scrutinise the semantic fields in which the complex compounds in the 3N database find their field of denotation.

This semantic field is understood to be hosted by a compound's modifier, as this is the component that sets the semantic frame, while the head denotes the kind of referent that is selected within that frame (e.g. a *football game* denotes an event in the semantic area of sports; a *wedding cake factory* denotes a building in the semantic area of food, etc.). For the analysis of the semantic fields that are covered by three-noun compounds, the 100 most frequently occurring modifiers in the 3N database were identified. These modifiers occur in 10,179 types of three-noun compounds, i.e. one sixth of all types, and can thus be seen as a representative sample of the whole set of modifiers used in three-noun compounds. The modifiers were determined irrespective of the branching pattern of the three-noun compounds, which is why the sample comprises both simple modifiers and complex modifiers (i.e. compounds), more precisely 64 complex modifiers and 36 simple ones. This sample of modifiers was analysed with the help of the *UCREL Semantic Analysis System* (USAS), which is an open access online tool that provides a framework for the semantic categorization of lexemes.[15] With the help of USAS, the meaning of a lexeme can be assigned to one of 21 major semantic fields, which are displayed in Figure 12. Most of these semantic categories are again divided up into further, more fine-grained subcategories.[16]

| A<br>general and abstract terms | B<br>the body and the individual | C<br>arts and crafts | E<br>emotions |
|---|---|---|---|
| F<br>food and farming | G<br>government and public | H<br>architectur, housing and the home | I<br>money and commerce in industry |
| K<br>entertainment, sports and games | L<br>life and living things | M<br>movement, location, travel and transport | N<br>numbers and measurement |
| O<br>substances, material, objects and equipment | P<br>education | Q<br>language and communication | S<br>social actions, states and processes |
| T<br>time | W<br>world and environment | X<br>psychological actions, states and processes | Y<br>science and technology |
| Z<br>names and grammar | | | |

**Figure 12:** Semantic fields established by the USAS.

UCREL also provides a tagger that is intended to automatically assign lexemes to one of the proposed categories. However, there are several intricacies related to the tool on the one hand and the specific data on the other, which render it ineffective for this project. Firstly, the categorization performed by the tagger is often subject to debate, which is why the results of the automatic tagging require manual

---

15 http://ucrel.lancs.ac.uk/usas/.
16 The detailed categorization can be found on http://ucrel.lancs.ac.uk/usas/USASSemanticTagset.

inspection and correction. *Classroom*, for example, is labelled as H2 (PARTS OF BUILDINGS) but could just as well be P1 (EDUCATION). Secondly, the tool frequently suggests more than one category. An automatic tagging of *cowboy*, for example, suggests the categories S2 (PEOPLE) and F4 (FARMING). Therefore, the work with the tool requires post-processing of the results by means of a manual selection of one main category, which is why it does not necessarily save time. Besides these general issues, the tagger is able to deal with compounds only to a limited extent, as it can only process sequences that have the form of an orthographic unit. It does not recognize compounds spelt with a blank in the input (e.g. *health care*) but analyses and treats them as two separate words. Compounds containing a hyphen are not accepted as words at all; the response to such sequences is "unmatched". For these reasons, the automated tagging system was not employed. Instead, assigning the 100 test items of the modifier sample to the semantic fields provided by UCREL was done manually.

Figure 13 displays the distribution of the modifiers into the semantic categories displayed above. The names of the categories have been slightly adapted in that they were specified according to the data assembled in these categories.

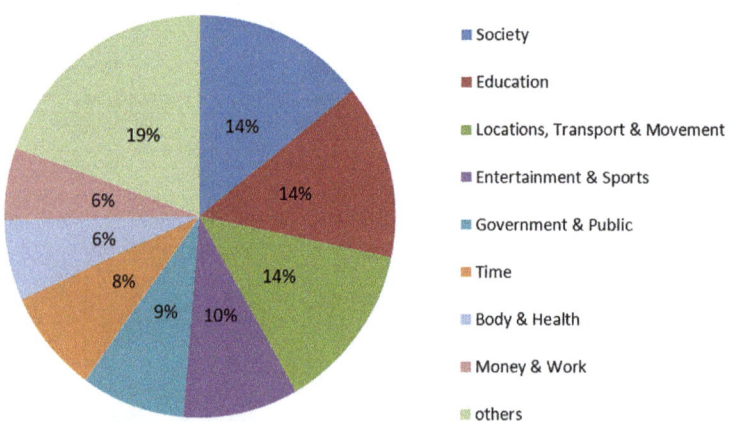

**Figure 13:** Categorization of semantic areas denoted by 3N modifiers.

The chart shows that the most prominent subject areas that three-noun compounds are used in are SOCIETY, EDUCATION and LOCATIONS, TRANSPORT & MOVEMENT. To be more precise, what is mostly referred to in the area of SOCIETY are the following subcategories:
- GROUPS AND AFFILIATION: compounds containing the modifier *community* (e.g. *community newspaper, community health center*)

- KIN: compounds containing modifiers such as *household* (e.g. *household income, household product*) or *family* (e.g. *family network, family newspaper*)
- PEOPLE: compounds with modifiers such as *adult* (e.g. *adult bookstore, adult literacy rate*) or *youth* (e.g. *youth football, youth violence prevention*)
- POWER RELATIONSHIP: compounds with modifiers like *deputy* (e.g. *deputy chairman, deputy police chief*) or *executive* (e.g. *executive committee member*)

The field of EDUCATION is not further subdivided in the UCREL system but the sub-categories that can be identified among the modifiers are the following:
- INSTITUTIONS: compounds with modifiers such as *school, university, college* or *community college* (e.g. *school newspaper, classroom environment, university faculty member, college roommate, community college instructor*)
- PERSONS AT SCHOOL: compounds with modifiers such as *students* and *teachers* (e.g. *student newspaper, teacher workshop*)
- OBJECTS USED AT SCHOOL: compounds with modifiers such as *textbook* (e.g. *textbook use*)

With regard to the category LOCATIONS, TRANSPORT & MOVEMENT, the modifiers are spread over the sub-categories LOCATION/PLACES (e.g. *city, bay area, park*) and OBJECTS relevant for movement and transportation on land or air (e.g. *railroad, airport, street, aircraft, roadside, motorcycle, aerospace*).

To give a brief summary of the categories that are encountered to a lesser degree, in the area of ENTERTAINMENT & SPORTS, the modifiers refer mainly to specific sports (e.g. *basketball, baseball, football*). The modifiers related to issues of GOVERNMENT & PUBLIC stem mainly from the area of warfare (e.g. *air force, army, navy*), concern general issues connected with government (e.g. *government, senate, state department*) or the field of law and order (e.g. *law enforcement, security, court room, police*). Modifiers in the category of TIME are, for example, *lifetime, wartime* or *summer*. In the category of BODY & HEALTH, the most common modifiers are *health care, health, breast cancer, health insurance* and *hospital*. In the area of MONEY AND WORK, the dominant modifiers are *workplace, credit card, business, consumer, stock market* and *company*. The category of OTHERS contains modifiers from a variety of areas, such as SCIENCE & TECHNOLOGY (e.g. *computer, database, internet*), HOUSES & THE HOME (e.g. *home, bathroom, bedroom*) or WORLD & ENVIRONMENT (e.g. *rainbow, mountain, water*).

The intention of this analysis is to show that the modifiers in three-noun compounds stem from a variety of subject areas. This means that the semantic areas in which the items under investigation are used and find their field of denotation are quite diverse. This is in line with Schmid's claim for compounding in general, demonstrating that three-noun compounds are not limited to specific subject areas but are used to refer to instances in all common spheres of everyday life, such as sports, social relationships or work-related issues. Accordingly, from a semantic perspective, examples such as *school classroom, community newspaper* and *football game* can be classified as just as typical products of three-noun compounding as *drug control administration, executive committee member* and *law enforcement official*.

## 7.8 How compositional are three-noun compounds?

A further relevant topic connected to the meaning of compounds, which has already been introduced in Section 2.2, is their compositionality. This aspect is highly popular in research into compounding, as it is closely related to the aspect of compound processing and has therefore been the subject of several studies that aim to develop models of morphological processing (e.g. Libben and Jarema 2006; Juhasz 2007; Ji et al. 2011). Compositionality is concerned with the question to what extent the meaning of a complex sequence can be accounted for through its parts. Typically, the meaning of a compound is richer than the combination of the meanings of its constituents: a *bedroom* is not simply a room with a bed, just as a *wheelchair* is not simply a chair with wheels.

The lack of compositionality in compounds, i.e. a certain degree of lexicalization, is often assumed to be the result of a diachronic change. This can happen if the referent undergoes changes but the form used to refer to it stays the same, as is the case in *blackboard* (cf. Schmid 2016: 79–80). It can also be due to metaphorical or metonymical shifts of the whole compound or one of its constituent, as is the case in *football* if used to denote the sport instead of the ball (cf. Bell and Schäfer 2013). However, it can also be present from the outset in the moment of coinage (cf. Ungerer and Schmid 2013: 78). This is due to the fact that compounds are a means to express diverse concepts and ideas with relatively little material, which is why in their form necessarily some aspects are foregrounded while others are omitted. Accordingly, even newly formed compounds can be non-compositional, which I will illustrate with an example. Imagine a company where employees who are leaving the company are bid farewell at the yearly staff meeting. After praising the work of the employee and emphasizing how valuable this employee was to the company, the boss proudly hands over the standard gift, a mug that has the company's logo printed on it. While the employee receives the gift and tries to get out of the spotlight, the other employees try to ignore the awkwardness of being given a mug after ten years of work. At the start of one of these meetings, the boss asks for the audience's attention and holds a mug in their hands. One of the employees whispers to another one, "Oh no, it's going to be one of those mug moments again."

The newly formed compound *mug moment* will be fully comprehensible for any member of the staff who has witnessed one of these scenes before. Still, it is not compositional, as the actual context and negative association related to it cannot be derived from the constituents of the compound.[17]

Traditionally, only non-compositional word sequences were accepted as compounds (cf. Ball 1938: 169, 1951: 3; Foley 1943: 444). Ball explicitly required a compound to express an "idea that is entirely different" from that of its components (1951: 3). This corresponds to a very narrow and not tenable understanding of compounding. Nowadays, most scholars also count instances as compounds that can be interpreted in a highly literal manner, such as *passenger seat* (Sanchez-Stockhammer 2018: 34), which is in line with the broader understanding of compounding employed in this project. However, the example of *mug moment* has illustrated what also Ungerer and Schmid (1998) have demonstrated, namely that even for apparently compositional compounds there is often an additional conceptual content associated with the word-formation product that is not necessarily part of the constituents (cf. also Taylor 2002: 100; Schmid 2008: 4–5). This aspect will be taken into account here by not speaking of full compositionality but rather of a high degree of compositionality. Against this backdrop, compositionality must be conceived as a scalar concept that reaches from strongly lexicalized compounds to highly compositional ones whose meaning is strongly predictable (cf. Schäfer 2018: 1). "In between, there are combinations with varying degrees of relatedness between the constituents' meaning and the meaning of the whole, and with varying degrees of predictability based on typical ways of combining these constituents" (Schäfer 2018: 1).

With regard to terminology, the notion of *compositionality* encompasses the question to what extent the meaning of a compound can be accounted for (i.e. predicted) by the meanings of its constituents. The notion of *transparency* refers to the question whether the meanings of the constituents are synchronically related to the meaning of the compound (Zwitserlood 1994: 344; Schäfer 2018: 1). Accordingly, while a compound like *weekend* might be transparent, it is still not compositional, as the compound includes additional semantic aspects that cannot be derived from the constituents, such as the aspects related to the idea of leisure time. Compounds that are not transparent (e.g. *cocktail*) are generally referred to as *opaque*. Schmid (2016: 78) mentions an even more extreme case, namely *obscured compounds*, such as *lord* or *gospel*. These items are neither compositional nor transparent, as they are formally not identifiable as compounds anymore.

---

[17] This compound could become lexicalized over time if at some point the mug was replaced by another gift, for example a pen, but the situation was still referred to as a *mug moment*.

In the context of compositionality, there are several questions to be raised when it comes to multi-word compounds: Does the English language have any three-noun compounds that are lexicalized to such degree that they can be considered opaque? Or do tripartite compounds tend to be compositional, including a high proportion of compounds with a syntactic function? Besides answering these questions, this section intends to illustrate to what extent the aspect of compositionality in complex compounding differs qualitatively (and potentially also quantitatively) from that in simple compounding.

In order to provide the basis for a model of compositionality in three-noun compounds, I will first try and sketch such a model for two-noun compounds. The illustration in Figure 14 is an attempt to arrange two-noun compounds along a scale of semantic compositionality. The examples were collected from the set of embedded compounds in the 3N database. The illustration ranges from fully opaque compounds at the bottom of the image to highly compositional ones at the top, with the transition between the compounds being on a sliding scale. Although compositionality is understood to be a gradual phenomenon, there are four qualitative stages that can be distinguished, illustrated along the scale on the left-hand side in the form of letters. The letters A and B are used to denote the two nouns in a two-noun compound. The cloud-like arrangement of the exemplary compounds on the right side in the illustration is used in order not to suggest a strictly sequential order in the arrangement of the compounds.

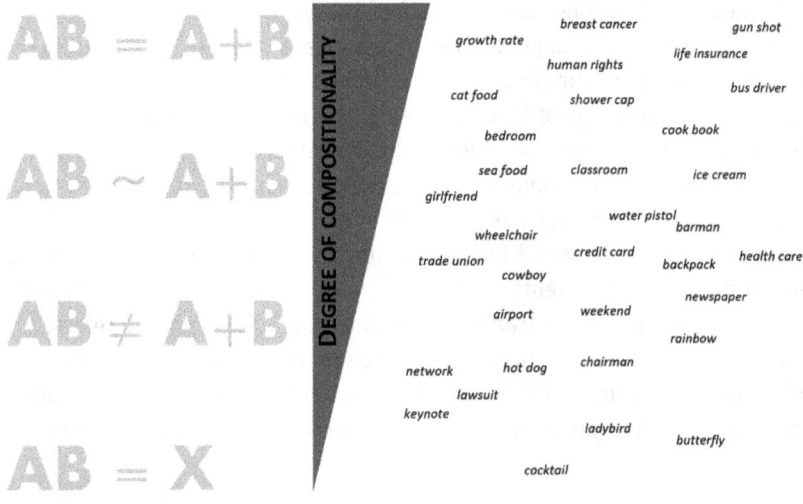

**Figure 14:** Degrees of compositionality in 2N.

The top of the illustration displays a category described as AB = A+B, which is supposed to express that the combination of the meanings of the constituents equals the meaning of the compound. This category displays the highest degree of compositionality. It contains compounds which are both highly compositional and transparent. Their meaning is mostly predictable from the summation of the meanings of the components. In compounds like *growth rate*, for example, it can be argued that there is no discrepancy between the compound meaning and that of the summed parts, as the meaning of *growth rate* can substantially be described through 'the rate of growth'.

The next category further down along the scale of compositionality is described as AB ~ A+B. This is intended to express that the compounds in this category are transparent, as the meanings of the constituents are contained in that of the compound. Still, these compounds are not compositional as the compounds display a certain degree of lexicalization and thus the content of the compound is richer than the summed meanings of its parts. Nevertheless, the combination of the meanings of the constituents at least comes close to the concept expressed through the compound, i.e. the compound's meaning is to a stronger or lesser degree predictable. This category is the most heterogeneous class as the degree to which the meaning of a compound can be richer than that of its constituents is vast. While *cook book*, for example, shows a fairly low degree of semantic specification, *barman* encompasses many semantic aspects that are absent in the combination of the constituent meanings.

Going further down along the scale of compositionality, the next category AB ≠ A+B consists of compounds which are barely compositional. These compounds are minimally transparent as the meaning of at least one of the constituents is at least remotely related to the meaning of the compound (as is the case, for example, in *cowboy*, *rainbow* or *newspaper*). These compounds are not compositional but highly lexicalized, leading to a gulf between the meanings of the constituents and the concept described by the whole form.

The compounds at the end of the scale of compositionality at the very bottom of the illustration in the category AB = X are opaque compounds. Their meaning cannot be derived at all from the meanings of the constituents, which is illustrated by the use of a different letter after the equal sign in the label for this category. The compounds in this category lack any compositionality and transparency, as is the case in the example of *cocktail*. Between this category and the category mentioned before of AB ≠ A+B, there are instances which are slightly more transparent, as at least one of the compound constituents shows a low degree of semantic relatedness to the meaning of the compound, as for example in *keynote* and *ladybird*.

To examine this situation for three-noun compounds, a sample of 250 items from various frequency levels was selected from the 3N database and matched to the categorization system sketched above for two-noun compounds. It must be pointed out at this point that the compositionality of non-established compounds can only be evaluated to a limited extent. Does the complex compound *wind row management*, for example, actually refer to something that has to do with wind rows? Since linguists are not present at the moment of coinage and thus lack context information, they can hardly assess the compositionality of unfamiliar items, as they cannot evaluate whether there are additional aspects contained in the concept of the compound that are not contained in its constituents or whether the compound requires a metaphorical interpretation. The items in the sample, however, seem to be established enough to assume that the description provided here is appropriate. The different degrees to which these three-noun compounds are semantically richer than the sum of their constituents are illustrated in Figure 15, which is analogous to the illustration used for two-noun compounds, with the exception that it includes an additional category. Again, the letters A, B, and C are used as representatives for the three noun constituents. For reasons of clarity, no separate illustration is given for left- and right-branching compounds, but the usage of AB + C has been chosen for reasons of simplicity and is intended to encompass the cases of both ab + c (*football game*) and a + bc (*school football*). The illustration does not contain all 250 compounds in the sample but only exemplary items in order to remain clear. The number of items displayed in each category is intended to approximate to the proportion of items found in the relevant categories. Again, the categories are to be understood as points of accumulation along a continuous scale of compositionality.

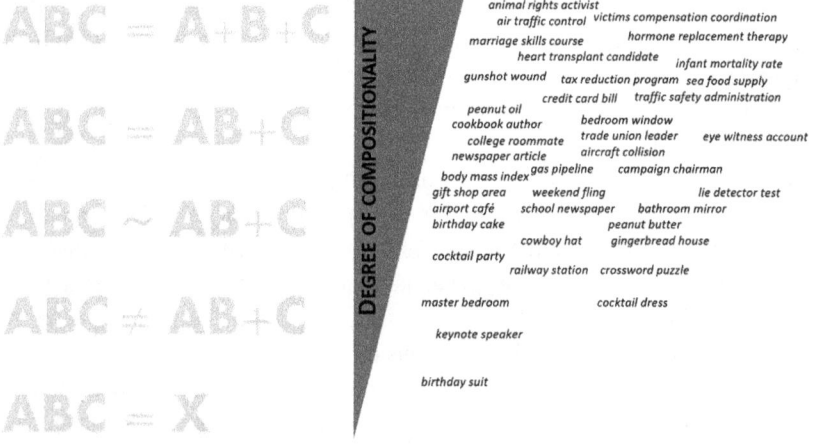

**Figure 15:** Degrees of compositionality in 3N.

The first stage of the scale at the top of the figure, which is described as ABC = A+B+C, is analogous to the same category for two-noun compounds. It comprises instances which are highly compositional and transparent. The meanings of the respective compounds can be almost fully accounted for by the summation of the meanings of the three nouns. The denotation of *animal rights activist*, for example, can be sufficiently predicted through its components, as it describes an 'activist who supports the rights of animals'. The same is felt to be true for the compound *hormone replacement therapy*, which denotes a 'therapy in which hormones are replaced', just as a *heart transplant candidate* is a 'candidate for the transplant of a heart'. There seems to be little or nothing that is semantically contained in the compounds that is absent in the summation of the meanings of their parts, but the meaning of the compounds can mostly be predicted from their constituents (provided, of course, that the appropriate sense of the words is chosen, e.g. *heart* in *heart transplant candidate* not being used in a figurative sense).

The next category of ABC = AB+C is one that does not exist in simple compounds, as here the compositionality of the embedded compound comes into play. This category contains tripartite compounds whose compositionality is limited in that the inner compound is lexicalized. Still, the complex compound ABC can be described by the combination of the meaning of the embedded compound and that of the outer noun, which is why these items can be labelled as partly compositional and relatively transparent. The simple compound *trade union*, for example, is lexicalized and non-compositional, which is why *trade union leader* cannot satisfactorily be described as 'the leader of a union to do with trade'. Given the meaning of *trade union*, however, the meaning of *trade union leader* can be adequately described as 'the leader of a trade union'. Similarly, while the simple compound *bedroom* is lexicalized and thus non-compositional, the complex compound *bedroom window* is evaluated to be partly compositional, as its meaning can be fully described by the lexicalized meaning of *bedroom* and that of *window*, as there seems to be nothing that specifically characterizes such a window. Therefore, for the items in this category, once the non-compositional meaning of the embedded compound is given, there seem to be no further relevant meaning components that are inherent in the complex compound that are not included in the sum of the embedded compound and the further noun.

The third group, which is described as ABC ~ AB+C, also encompasses tripartite compounds with a lexicalized embedded compound. These tripartite compounds are transparent given the lexicalized meaning of the embedded compound, as the meanings of the embedded compound and that of the third noun can be related to the meaning of the complex compound. However, these instances are not as compositional as those in the previous category. Instead, the complex compounds in this category express a concept that is semantically more specific than the combination of the meanings of the embedded compound and the outer noun. The semantic discrepancy that holds between the meaning of the complex compound and the summed meaning of the constituents ranges from fairly low to very high. There are complex compounds where the combination of the meaning of the embedded compound and that of the outer noun comes close to the three-noun compound but is not fully equivalent to it. A *cowboy hat*, for example, is not exactly the same as 'the hat of a cowboy', as the latter does not necessarily have the specifications of a typical cowboy hat (i.e. made out of leather and broad-brimmed) but can be simply any hat worn by a cowboy. In other instances in this category further down along the scale of compositionality, the three-noun compound is semantically far more specific than the sum of the embedded compound and the outer noun, as is the case in *cocktail party*, for example. A speaker who has never heard this lexeme before will manage to understand that it is some kind of party at which cocktails are served. This is true but lacks some components, as a cocktail party is not just any party at which cocktails are served, but a party that is a bit more chic, where people stand around at high tables (instead of dancing or dining at a table, for example). In addition, usually the drinks served are not exclusively cocktails. Accordingly, for the instances of this category the combination of the inner compound and the third constituent does not sufficiently describe the meaning of the corresponding compound. Instead, the whole three-noun compound displays a greater or lesser degree of lexicalization.

The fourth core area, which is described as ABC ≠ AB+C, is represented through sequences which feature only very low degrees of compositionality and transparency. For the items in this category, the meaning of at least one constituent is not directly found in the meaning of the whole compound. Many of them require a metonymic or metaphoric interpretation of the embedded compound, as is the case, for example, in *cocktail dress* or *keynote speaker*. In these instances, the meaning of the three-noun compound cannot be derived from the combination of the meanings of the embedded compound and the third noun, but the three-noun compounds as a whole are lexicalized.

The last category at the end of the scale of compositionality that is described as ABC = X is reserved for opaque compounds. This category lacks examples as almost no instances of three-noun compounds were found that were fully opaque and showed no compositionality nor transparency. The only compound that could be considered to fall in this category is *birthday suit*, as its meaning 'naked' is only metaphorically related to the meanings of the constituents. All other items in the sample showed at least some semantic connection to one of the components.

Based on this categorization, a qualitative and to some extent a quantitative comparison as well can be drawn between the compositionality in two- and three-noun compounds. The analysis has shown that three-noun compounds are not found along the full scale of semantic compositionality. As opposed to two-noun compounds, which include a considerable number of semantically opaque compounds, this category does not seem to be relevant for three-noun compounds. In three-noun compounding, opacity instead tends to be found *within* the three-noun compounds in the embedded compound. This gives rise to an additional category of partial compositionality, which applies if a part of the sequence, namely the embedded compound, is non-compositional and lexicalized to a stronger or lesser degree.

Besides these qualitative differences in the compositionality of simple and complex compounds, there seem to be quantitative differences regarding the disposition of the different categories. Although there are to my knowledge no figures available for the disposition of the differing degrees of compositionality of simple compounds, the categories with low degrees of compositionality (i.e. ABC ≠ AB+C and ABC = X) seem to be less strongly occupied by three-noun compounds than are the equivalent categories for simple compounds. By contrast, the categories of highly transparent and relatively compositional three-noun compounds seem to be quite strongly exploited compared to two-noun compounds, as the majority of three-noun compounds are located in the first, second and third category counted from the top, i.e. ABC = A+B+C, ABC = AB+C and ABC ~ AB+C.

Although this impression needs empirical quantification, the analysis has conveyed the impression that complex compounds can generally be claimed to be more compositional than simple compounds. It is conceivable that this situation is related to the fact that polylexemic compounds may hold a higher proportion of compounds whose formation is syntactically motivated. To verify this situation, a large-scale analysis would have to be performed that analyses whether complex compounding encompasses more instances which have a syntactic or deictic function instead of a lexical one.

## 7.9 Do compositional three-noun compounds compete with syntactic phrases?

Having found that the meaning of a large proportion of three-noun compounds is at least partly compositional, this section is interested in examining whether this situation is reflected in usage. Is there an onomasiological competition between three-noun compounds which are fully or partly compositional and equivalent syntactic phrases containing the individual constituents? Do speakers alternate, for instance, between the expressions *trade union leader* and *leader of the trade union*? If only some three-noun compounds show this kind of alternation, can this behaviour be attributed to specific kinds of compounds? It is conceivable, for example, that only compounds with a syntactic function or only non-established compounds allow variation. In those cases where there are syntactic phrases that are used to refer to the same referents as the respective compounds, are there any factors that determine the usage of these variants? It is the aim of this section to answer these questions in order to gain a clearer picture about the usage of complex compounds.

The items that will be subject to investigation are 50 three-noun compounds from the 3N database that can be classified as highly or partly compositional in the sense defined in the previous section, i.e. instances in which the tripartite compound is semantically equivalent to the combination of the meanings of the three nouns or to the combination of the meanings of the embedded compound and the outer noun. Section 7.9.1 will provide the details of the collection of the relevant syntactic phrases in the corpus. Section 7.9.2 will assess whether the morphological and the syntactic variants are used to the same degree. Section 7.9.3 will consider factors that might explain in which situations speakers use phrases and in which ones they prefer compounds. On this basis, Section 7.9.4 will investigate what characterizes those compounds that permit variation with syntactic phrases.

### 7.9.1 Which syntactic phrases exist as alternatives to three-noun compounds?

To collect syntactic equivalents for the 50 three-noun compounds in the sample, the online edition of COCA was searched for alternative expressions. For the complex compound *consumer protection office*, for example, the following syntactic phrases are conceivable: *office for consumer protection*, *office for the protection of consumers*, *office for protection of consumers* and *office for the protection of the consumer*. In order to find every potential variant, including both singular and plural forms and different spelling formats, as well as instances with and without the division of the embedded compound, the search queries were designed as tolerantly as possible. The following instances are an account of the general patterns that were searched for, the first of which is the query without the division of the embedded compound, the second one is an explicit search for the phrase where the constituents of the embedded compound are divided (PREP = preposition; DET = determiner):

- N3(s) PREP (DET) N1(-)N2(s)
   e.g. *office(s)* PREP (DET) *consumer(-)protection(s)*
- N3(s) PREP (DET) N2(s) PREP (DET) N1(s)
   e.g. *office(s)* PREP (DET) *protection(s)* PREP (DET) *consumer(s)*

The item of determiner includes not just searches for definite and indefinite articles but also for possessive pronouns, in order to find instances such as *present for his birthday* in the query for *birthday present*, for example. All hits yielded with these queries were checked to see if they could be accepted as semantic equivalents to the relevant complex compound. Matches in which the syntactic solution was followed by another noun were excluded, e.g. in the search for alternative phrases for *trade union leader*, the results *leader of the trade union group* and *leader of the trade union confederation* were not included. Besides, the individual hits were examined in context in order to accept only instances where the compound constituents constitute nouns in the corresponding phrases, e.g. in the search for syntactic variants of the compound *rollercoaster ride*, only those instances among the matches of *ride on a rollercoaster* were included in which *ride* represents a noun. In accordance with the open-faced fashion of the recall, the decision about which results could be accepted from a semantic perspective was fairly tolerant. If the semantic similarity was considered high enough in that the syntactic solution did not lack any semantic aspects inherent in the compound, the phrases were categorized as equivalents.

Table 17 displays the types of syntactic phrases found for the 50 three-noun compounds under investigation. Similar variants among the syntactic phrases for the same tripartite compound (e.g. singular and plural forms) are summarized under one entry. An empty field means that no alternative phrase was found.

The table shows that for 11 out of 50 three-noun compounds, i.e. about a fifth of all items, no syntactic solutions were found. In some cases this was not surprising. For words like *snack food personality* or *butter cookie dough*, for example, syntactic solutions are conceivable from a semantic perspective; formally, however, they would sound rather clumsy. In a large number of cases, however, finding no syntactic alternatives was quite counter-intuitive as they were deemed to sound perfectly natural, as for example in the case of *consumer affairs manager* (*\*manager for consumer affairs*), *witness protection program* (*\*program for witness protection/program for the protection of witnesses*) or *water treatment plant* (*\*plant for water treatment/plant for the treatment of water*). Similarly, for *credit card bills*, for example, forms such as *bill(s) for your/his/her/the credit card* had been expected, likewise a paraphrase *area(s) protected by the police* for the compound *police protection area*.[18] A subsequent explicit search for these instances, however, did not yield any matches, neither did a more tolerant query for different formats. This suggests that

---

[18] For *police protection area* due to the unclear status of the branching pattern, both left- and right-branching options were searched for, e.g. *area(s) protected by the police*, *area(s) with police protection*, *area(s) with protection by the police*, *protection area(s) of the police*.

**Table 17:** 3N and corresponding syntactic phrases.

| 3N | Alternative syntactic phrases |
| --- | --- |
| air traffic control | |
| airport transfer | transfers from the airport |
| bedroom window | window(s) of the bedroom <br> window(s) of my/his/her/your/their bedroom(s) |
| birthday present | present for my/your/his/her birthday <br> presents for the birthday |
| bone marrow transplant | transplants of bone marrow |
| breast cancer survivor | survivor(s) of breast cancer |
| butter cookie dough | |
| campaign chairman | chairman of campaign <br> chairman(/men) of the campaign <br> chairman of his campaign <br> chairman of your campaign <br> chairman of their campaign <br> chairman of my campaign <br> chairman of her campaign <br> chairman on the campaign |
| car salesman | salesman of cars |
| carbon dioxide emissions | emission(s) of carbon dioxide |
| classroom guidance | guidance in the classroom |
| college roommate | roommate in college <br> roommate from college |
| community swimming pool | swimming pool for the community |
| consumer affairs manager | manager of consumer affairs |
| consumer protection agency | |
| consumer protection office | office(s) of consumer protection |
| control group participants | participant(s) in the control group <br> participants for the control group |
| credit card bills | bills for a credit card <br> bill for a credit card |
| death bed words | words on her deathbed <br> words from his deathbed |

**Table 17** (continued)

| 3N | Alternative syntactic phrases |
|---|---|
| death row inmates | inmates on death row<br>inmates from death row<br>inmates of death row |
| drinking water source | source(s) of drinking water<br>source(s) for drinking water |
| drug use abstinence | abstinence from drug use |
| eyewitness account | accounts of eyewitnesses |
| football player | player(s) in football<br>players at football |
| health care bill | bill for health care |
| health care reform | |
| health insurance coverage | coverage through the health insurance<br>coverage in their health insurance<br>coverage on the health insurance |
| heart disease risk | risk of heart disease<br>risk for heart disease |
| hormone replacement therapy | |
| information system development | development of an information system |
| internet service provider | providers of internet service |
| marriage skill course | |
| missile defense system | systems for missile defense<br>system of missile defense |
| newspaper article | article in the newspaper |
| newspaper editor(s) | editor of the/a newspaper |
| newspaper reporter | reporter for the/a newspaper<br>reporter from the newspaper<br>reporters from this newspaper |
| population growth rate | growth rate of the population<br>growth rate of a population |
| pumpkin seed pesto | |
| roller coaster ride | ride on a roller coaster |

**Table 17** (continued)

| 3N | Alternative syntactic phrases |
|---|---|
| security council staff | |
| stem cell research | research on stem cells |
| sunflower seeds | seeds of sunflowers |
| support network | network(s) of support |
| television anchorwoman | anchorwoman on television |
| trade union leader | leaders of the trade union |
| trade union movement | |
| war crimes trial | trial(s) for war crimes<br>trial on war crimes<br>trial of war crimes |
| water treatment plant | |
| witness protection program | |
| workplace safety | safety in the workplace<br>safety at the workplace |

the lack of alternative syntactic solutions for these instances is not due to an inaccuracy of the queries performed but that such phrases simply do not exist in the corpus. This finding stresses the importance of working with corpus data instead of relying on (sometimes misguided) linguistic introspection.

It can be seen in the table that for almost half the 39 items for which alternative paraphrases were registered, more than one type was found. The different syntactic versions are semantically almost identical and formally mostly differ from each other only in the preposition, e.g. *trials for war crimes, trials on war crimes* and *trials of war crimes*, or *safety at the workplace* and *safety in the workplace*.

With regard to the formats found, most paraphrases follow the general pattern 'N3 PREP *the* EMBEDDED COMPOUND'. In no case was the embedded compound split up in the syntactic solution. This is rather surprising for those cases that were understood to belong to the category ABC = A+B+C, such as *drug use abstinence* or *witness protection program*. These complex compounds are highly compositional, including a non-lexicalized embedded compound. From a formal perspective, a syntactic phrase that separates the constituents of the embedded compound does not sound marked in any way (e.g. *\*abstinence from the use of drugs, \*program for the* *protection of witnesses*), which is why in these tripartite compounds it had been expected that there would be competing variants both with and without the division of the embedded compound (e.g. *standards of/for consumer protection* vs. *standards for the protection of consumers*). This, however, is obviously not the case.

### 7.9.2 Are the phrases competitors to the compounds?

To evaluate whether the syntactic phrases are used to the same extent as the respective compounds, the morphological and syntactic variants were compared quantitatively with the help of the respective usage frequencies from COCA. Table 18 displays the sample reduced to those 39 items for which semantically similar paraphrases were identified, including the respective token frequencies in brackets. Column 3 quantifies the relation between each three-noun compound and the most frequent of the alternatively used syntactic phrases.

**Table 18:** 3N and corresponding syntactic phrases with token frequencies.

| 3N | Types and tokens of syntactic phrases | Ratio |
| --- | --- | --- |
| *airport transfer* (36) | *transfers from the airport* (7) | 36: 7 |
| *bedroom window* (944) | *window(s) of my/his/her/your/their bedroom(s)* (22) *window(s) of the bedroom* (10) | 994: 22 |
| *birthday present* (1,040) | *present for my/your/his/her birthday* (6) *presents for the birthday* (1) | 1,040: 6 |
| *bone marrow transplant* (640) | *transplants of bone marrow* (1) | 640: 1 |
| *breast cancer survivor* (377) | *survivor(s) of breast cancer* (20) | 377: 20 |
| *campaign chairman* (508) | *chairman(/men) of the campaign* (25) *chairman of your/their/my/her campaign* (4) *chairman of his campaign* (3) *chairman of campaign* (1) *chairman on the campaign* (1) | 508: 25 |
| *car salesman* (589) | *salesman of cars* (1) | 589: 1 |
| *carbon dioxide emissions* (795) | *emission(s) of carbon dioxide* (188) | 795: 188 |
| *classroom guidance* (119) | *guidance in the classroom* (1) | 119: 1 |

**Table 18** (continued)

| 3N | Types and tokens of syntactic phrases | Ratio |
|---|---|---|
| college roommate (435) | roommate in college (45)<br>roommate from college (10)<br>roommate from the college (1)<br>roommates at college (1) | 435: 45 |
| community swimming pool (12) | swimming pool for the community (1) | 12: 1 |
| consumer affairs manager (8) | manager of consumer affairs (4) | 8: 4 |
| consumer protection office (19) | office(s) of consumer protection (9) | 19: 9 |
| control group participants (44) | participant(s) in the control group (22)<br>participants for the control group (1) | 44: 22 |
| credit card bills (427) | bill(s) for a credit card (2) | 427: 2 |
| death bed words (5) | words on her deathbed (1)<br>words from his deathbed (1) | 5: 2 |
| death row inmates (552) | inmates on death row (56)<br>inmates from death row (2)<br>inmates of death row (1) | 552: 56 |
| drinking water source (77) | source(s) of drinking water (110)<br>source(s) for drinking water (34) | 77: 110 |
| drug use abstinence (8) | abstinence from drug use (3) | 8: 3 |
| eyewitness account (401) | accounts of eyewitnesses (4) | 401: 4 |
| football player (3,077) | player(s) in football (26)<br>players at football (1) | 3,077: 26 |
| health care bill (299) | bill for health care (5) | 299: 5 |
| health insurance coverage (292) | coverage through the health insurance (6)<br>coverage in their health insurance (2)<br>coverage on the health insurance (1) | 292: 6 |
| heart disease risk (230) | risk of heart disease (689)<br>risk for heart disease (185) | 230: 689 |
| information system development (7) | development of an information system (1) | 7: 1 |
| internet service provider (486) | providers of internet service (1) | 486: 1 |
| missile defense system (594) | systems for missile defense (1)<br>system of missile defense (1) | 594: 1 |
| newspaper article (839) | article in the newspaper (26) | 839: 26 |

**Table 18** (continued)

| 3N | Types and tokens of syntactic phrases | Ratio |
|---|---|---|
| newspaper editor (596) | editor of the newspaper (53)<br>editor of a newspaper (17) | 596: 53 |
| newspaper reporter (500) | reporter for the/a newspaper (14)<br>reporter from the newspaper (2)<br>reporters from this newspaper (1) | 500: 14 |
| population growth rate (188) | growth rate of the population (4)<br>growth rate of a population (2) | 188: 4 |
| roller coaster ride (343) | ride on a roller coaster (9) | 343: 9 |
| stem cell research (1,152) | research on stem cells (29) | 1,152: 29 |
| sunflower seeds (634) | seeds of sunflowers (1) | 634: 1 |
| support network (568) | network(s) of support (85) | 568: 85 |
| television anchorwoman (4) | anchorwoman on television (1) | 4: 1 |
| trade union leader (59) | leaders of the trade union (3) | 59: 3 |
| war crimes trial (164) | trial(s) for war crimes (28)<br>trial on war crimes (1)<br>trial of war crimes (1) | 164: 28 |
| workplace safety (119) | safety in the workplace (11)<br>safety at the workplace (1) | 119: 11 |

The table shows that the token frequencies of the syntactic phrases are generally rather low. The phrase *leader(s) of the trade union*, for example, occurs only 3 times, while *safety at the workplace* occurs only once. This is rather surprising, as – purely introspectively – the phrase *safety at the workplace* is not marked in any way (as opposed to the phrase *player of football*, for example, which does sound marked). The only phrases that are actually used to a considerable degree are *emission(s) of carbon dioxide*, *source(s) of drinking water* and *risk of heart disease*. Only for a minority of the remaining phrases are the token frequencies high enough to categorize them at least as fairly frequent, as in the case of *roommates in college*, *networks of support* or *inmates on death row*. In those cases where there are several syntactic phrases for the same three-noun compound, generally only one of them is used to any degree, while the other ones are rather sporadic occurrences with extremely low token frequencies. Only in the cases of *drinking water source* and *heart disease risk* there are two syntactic phrases that are both used to some degree. Overall, the syntactic phrases must be said to be generally rather infrequent.

The ratios in column 3 show that in almost no case are the compound and its syntactic pendants used to the same or at least a similar degree. Only in the case of *control group participant* there is a corresponding paraphrase that qualifies token-wise as a competitor to the compound, being used at least half as much as the compound. In only two cases there is a syntactic phrase which is used more often than the compound, namely *risk of heart disease* for *heart disease risk* and *source(s) of drinking water* for *drinking water source*. In all other instances, the compound is indisputably used to a much greater extent than the respective syntactic equivalent.

This quantitative analysis indicates that although there are semantically equivalent syntactic variants of three-noun compounds, they do not seem to be used to a similar degree to the respective compounds but constitute fairly infrequent alternatives that cannot be classified as established forms of expression. It can thus be concluded that generally there is little onomasiological competition for the denotation of a particular concept through a morphological and a syntactical solution at the same time. Instead, the majority of three-noun compounds seem to be the only established way of expressing the concepts they denote.

### 7.9.3 Is there any systematicity in the usage of compounds and phrases?

In those cases where there is both a compound and a syntactic alternative to denote the same concept, is there any systematicity in their distribution that explains in which situations one variant is preferred to the other? Or are the compounds and their syntactic alternatives free variants that are used interchangeably?

In order to be able to investigate the alternation between compounds and their syntactic variants, only those items could be considered for which there was a syntactic solution that was actually used to some degree. Accordingly, the only word pairs considered were those in which there was a syntactic phrase that occurred at least 25 times. Therefore, the analysis could only be performed for a small set of 11 pairs, namely:
- *carbon dioxide emissions* vs. *emissions of carbon dioxide*
- *college roommates* vs. *roommate in college*
- *death row inmates* vs. *inmates on death row*
- *drinking water sources* vs. *sources of drinking water*
- *football player* vs. *player of football*
- *heart disease risk* vs. *risk of heart disease*
- *newspaper article* vs. *article in the newspaper*
- *newspaper editor* vs. *editor of the newspaper*
- *stem cell research* vs. *research on stem cells*

- *support networks* vs. *networks of support*
- *war crimes trial* vs. *trials for war crimes*

Obviously, this sample is too small for a representative investigation, which is why the following considerations merely constitute an exploratory analysis that aims to work out potential variables as a starting point for further, more extensive research with a larger database. Five variables that might be of influence were looked into, namely
(i) usage in different registers
(ii) pluralisation
(iii) adjectival modification
(iv) use of pronouns
(v) usage in headlines

Firstly, it is conceivable that the alternation between a compound and its syntactic alternative might be related to usage in different registers. It could be expected, for example, that one variant is used more frequently in written language, while the other one is preferred in the spoken register. In order to contrast the usage of each pair with regard to genres, the chart function of the online edition of COCA was employed. The distribution of the token frequencies of the compounds was contrasted with those of the phrases. However, the analysis of the usage in different genres did not yield any valuable insights, as for all word pairs in the sample the distribution of the compound was extremely similar to that of its syntactic variant. In no case was a significant difference detected. Therefore, the hypothesis of a functional division cannot be supported. Instead, the morphological and syntactic solutions seem to be highly interchangeable regarding their usage in different genres.

Based on the observation that some compounds in Table 18 are predominantly used in the singular, while some of the phrases are pluralised, it was suspected that pluralisation could be an aspect of influence. It is conceivable, for example, that one variant is generally used to express the singular, while the other one is preferably used in the plural, e.g. *control group participant* but *participants in the control group*. A comparison of the usage of the compounds and the phrases in the singular and the plural did not confirm this hypothesis. Both *control group participants* and *participants for the control group* occur almost exclusively in the plural. Only in the case of *drinking water source* is there a slight deviation in the behaviour of the compound and the phrase, as *drinking water source* occurs almost equally in the singular and the plural (33 times in the plural, 30 times in the singular), while *source(s) of drinking water* occurs more often in the singular (78 times) than in the plural (34 times). However, in all other cases, the compounds and their phrase behave the same way regarding singular and plural formation. Therefore, this aspect does not seem to be a variable that generally influences the choice of one variant over the other.

Another aspect of pluralisation that was expected to deliver a more plausible explanation for the alternating usage of compounds and phrases is the pluralisation of the embedded compound. As the plural formation in compounds is realized exclusively on the outermost element (e.g. *control group participants*), the paraphrase might be preferred in cases where the speaker wants to pluralise the embedded compound, e.g. *participants in the control groups*. However, only in the case of *stem cell research* was it found that the embedded compound in the paraphrase is predominantly pluralised (i.e. *research on stem cells*). For the other items in the sample, there was no noticeable usage of pluralisation for the embedded compound. Therefore, it cannot be confirmed that the usage of singular and plural forms has an influence on the alternation between compounds and their corresponding phrases.

A further aspect that was considered is the usage of adjectival modifiers. If premodifying adjectives are employed, it is conceivable that this prompts the use of the syntactic phrase rather than the compound, e.g. *the control group participants*, but *the youngest participants in the control group*. To investigate this situation, the words preceding the compounds and those preceding their corresponding syntactic phrases in COCA were contrasted. However, no patterns could be observed, as both the compounds and the phrases collocated with adjectives to a similar degree.

It was furthermore suspected that the usage of possessive pronouns correlates with the preference of the syntactic variant, e.g. *the participants of their control group* instead of *their control group participants*. None of the word pairs in the sample shows this alternation but it was observed for a few of the phrases that display very low token frequencies. For *birthday present*, for example, all but one phrasal formulation contain a pronoun, e.g. *present for my birthday* (3 tokens), *present for your birthday* (1), *present for his birthday* (1), *present for her birthday* (1). Obviously, however, the token frequencies are too low to confirm whether this tendency is true. Furthermore, it is disputable whether these variants are semantically fully equivalent to the compound variant, as *his birthday present* and *the present for his birthday* are not necessarily semantically identical, as the former could also denote 'the birthday present given by him'. Table 18 shows that for *bedroom window* as well, there are syntactic phrases that contain possessive pronouns. These variants can be assessed as semantically equal to the respective compound (cf. *his bedroom window* vs. *the window of his bedroom*). Again, however, the token frequencies of these syntactic variants are extremely low. The same is true for *deathbed words*, for which the only two paraphrases found are *words on her deathbed* and *words from his deathbed*, each occurring only once. Again, the token counts are too low to derive any representative conclusion.

A further hypothesis to explain the alternating usage could be that compounds are predominantly used in headlines in order to save space, while phrases tend to be found in running text. However, an investigation of the contexts around the compounds and their syntactic variants in COCA did not support this assumption at all. Almost none of the compounds were recorded in titles; instead, just like the phrases, they predominantly occurred in running text.

To sum up, this section has not managed to confirm any factors that could generally explain the alternating usage between compounds and their syntactic equivalents. It was partly possible to identify patterns for individual compound-phrase pairs, however, most of the token frequencies were too low to draw reliable conclusions. Due to the low number of items left to investigate and the low token frequencies of the syntactic variants, this aspect could not be explored sufficiently. Adding further material to the sample did not help form a clearer image but rather made it vaguer, as all further compounds that were examined showed a similar heterogeneous behaviour as has been reported above. This observation suggests that in the alternation between a compound and a corresponding syntactic phrase different factors might be at work for each compound-phrase pair.

### 7.9.4 Which three-noun compounds show variation?

Are there any reasons why some compounds show alternating use with syntactic solutions while others do not? Exploring this question is only possible for the small number of 39 items that have at least one alternative syntactic phrase. Obviously, this sample is too small to permit generalizations, which is why the following considerations must be seen merely as input for further research on this topic.

It is, firstly, conceivable that syntactic alternatives only exist for complex compounds with low token frequencies, as their formal side is less established, while those items that do not permit variation although there are semantically plausible forms are compounds which are highly established. The compound *football player*, for example, is strongly established, which is why a syntactic variant \**player of football* would sound marked. However, there are also frequent compounds for which syntactic variants were found, as is the case, for example, in *college roommates* (432 tokens), *newspaper editor* (596 tokens), *support network* (658 tokens) and *death row inmates* (552 tokens). Therefore, it cannot be confirmed that phrasal alternation occurs only for less established compounds, while conventionalized three-noun compounds lack alternative syntactic phrases.

It could furthermore be hypothesized that those compounds which show alternating use with syntactic phrases are those with a syntactic function, as they might have developed as shorter forms of syntactic expressions. To investigate whether this is true, a diachronic perspective that contrasts the usage of the compounds with their paraphrases over time would be highly interesting. An attempt has been made to do so; however, the token frequencies in the *Corpus of Historical American English* (COHA) for the syntactic phrases and the compounds are too low to be able to examine this hypothesis.

Thus, this section cannot provide an explanation for the question why only for some highly or partly compositional compounds an alternative use of syntactic phrases is found. Having merely considered but not empirically tested two variables, there is certainly room for further research on this question with regard not only to the variables mentioned here but also to other factors that could have an influence. The analysis of a much larger data set might help shed light on this issue.

### 7.9.5 Conclusion and discussion

The previous sections have shown that even though there are semantically equivalent syntactic alternatives for the majority of the tripartite compounds in the sample, these forms are used only to a limited degree. Based on this finding, it can explicitly be stated that complex compounds generally do not serve to replace longer, less economic, syntactic expressions. Rather, these results suggest that for the concepts denoted by three-noun compounds there seems to be no alternating use between a morphological process and a syntactic one. In this section only highly or partly compositional compounds were investigated. For all other items with lower degrees of compositionality, the use of alternative paraphrases can be excluded as by definition the paraphrases are not semantically equivalent to the respective compounds. Accordingly, the results found for partly and highly compositional compounds can be generalized for the phenomenon of three-noun compounds as a whole. These complex compounds can be claimed to be established ways of referring to the objects they denote. Even though many of them are partly or highly compositional, they are not just the preferred but, in most cases, the exclusive format for referring to the relevant concepts. They are conventionalized naming units which seem to block equivalent phrases.

It must be acknowledged that the queries performed to find syntactic phrases may still have been too exclusive. The queries ignored, for example, syntactic phrases that contain verbs. A more tolerant search for syntactic variants of the item *heart disease risk*, for example, that accepts other items than determiners and prepositions between the N3 and the embedded compound, delivers results such as *risk of developing heart disease, risk for developing heart disease, risk of getting heart disease* or *risk to develop heart disease*. Including syntactic phrases of this kind might yield different results. However, a more tolerant approach also has to face the discussion whether the instances found are semantically similar enough to the respective compounds: Is a *heart disease risk* the same as a *risk of developing/getting heart disease*? Do the phrases *research using stem cells* and *research involving stem cells* express the same content as *stem cell research*? As I would answer these questions in the negative, the queries were not extended to a more tolerant format.

The rather small number of syntactic phrases found was deemed to be surprising, just like their extremely low token frequencies. It would be interesting to involve the assessment of native speakers in answering the questions posed in this section, i.e. let them compare and evaluate the usage of complex compounds and their syntactic equivalents and perform an acceptability ranking for the syntactic alternatives.

The sample used for this study was too small to take into account potential differences between left- and right-branching compounds. This does not mean that this aspect is not expected to deliver interesting results when distinguishing the two branching patterns; on the contrary, it would be intriguing to see whether one of the two types of tripartite compounds allows for more variation when it comes to syntactic alternatives. Based on the observations made in Section 7.5, it could be expected that right-branching compounds show more alternation in their usage than left-branching ones.

## 7.10 Summary and conclusion

Chapter 7 has identified several characteristics concerning the meaning and use of three-noun compounds. It has shown that the majority of types of three-noun compounds are found in the lower frequency spectrum, which characterizes the word-formation process that combines three nouns as a productive tool to form new instances. At the same time, a large number of three-noun tokens go back to a set of items that can be considered strongly conventionalized in the English speech community. Investigating three-noun compounds regarding the registers in which they are encountered has shown that they are used in all areas of discourse covered by COCA. An examination of the semantic areas in which they find their field of denotation has demonstrated that they are not restricted to any particular fields but are used to denote concepts in a broad variety of semantic areas, including mundane areas of everyday life. They are a common part of everyday speech and are used to refer to entities and concepts in our everyday surroundings.

With regard to their meaning, three-noun compounds are predominantly determinative compounds in that what is denoted by the whole compound is a hyponym of the head. When it comes to their compositionality, tri-constituent compounds have been illustrated to occur along the entire range of semantic compositionality, with some being highly compositional, others containing a lexicalized embedded compound and thus being partly compositional, and only few being largely non-compositional. Based on the high number of highly or partly compositional compounds, it was investigated whether these compounds display alternating use with syntactic phrases. The contrast of the morphological and syntactic solutions demonstrated that three-noun compounds are generally not alternated with syntactic phrases. In those cases where there are semantically equivalent syntactic phrases, these are generally not used to the same degree as the respective compound and thus cannot be said to constitute established alternatives to the compounds. No generalizations could be drawn concerning a potential functional distribution between compounds and their corresponding syntactic phrase. Still, these results permit the claim that most three-noun compounds are established ways of referring that do not compete with syntactic alternatives.

This chapter has furthermore explored how homogeneous three-noun compounds are from a functional perspective. Contrasting the use of left-branching and right-branching compounds has shown that there are not only more instances of left-branching compounds but also that compounds with a complex modifier tend to be used more often than those with a complex head. An investigation of the complex heads has revealed that a large number of right-branching compounds are based on an embedded compound that is a highly established lexeme, such as *football*, *health care*, *network* or *baseball*. This, however, has shown to be just as true for left-branching compounds and is thus not necessarily attributable to the function of the head. Instead, it seems to be a general condition that three-noun compounds are preferably based on an established compound. Still, this is not an absolute requirement, as among both left-branching and right-branching compounds there are instances which are not based on a strongly established compound. A comparison of the modifiers in the two types of branching structures suggested that among right-branching compounds there are modifiers which contribute to the fact that the relevant compounds are less compound-like but have an appearance of syntactic phenomena, which renders some instances of right-branching compounds less typical instances of compounding.

In this portrait of semantic features of three-noun compounds, a distinction between left-branching and right-branching compounds could not be made for all the research questions examined. This is not because I believe the differences to be uninteresting but merely due to space and time restrictions. Aspects like the compositionality of three-noun compounds, their usage in different registers or the alternation with syntactic phrases could be subjected to further research that focuses on potential differences between left- and right-branching compounds.

Furthermore, this chapter has not been able to investigate the semantic relations that apply in three-noun compounds. It would certainly be intriguing to examine whether complex compounds employ the same set of semantic relations that are established in simple compounding. It would also be interesting to contrast the semantic relations found in left-branching compounds and in right-branching ones, as well as to analyse and contrast the set of semantic relations a particular compound employs in its function as modifier and those it employs in its function as head.

Part IV: **The formation of tri-constituent compounds**

# 8 Productivity in complex compounding

In the examples of tripartite nominal compounds used so far, it was quite remarkable that some embedded compounds like *football* or *health care* occurred in various three-noun compounds, while others like *body mass* or *world heritage* were only seldom encountered. Obviously, some two-noun compounds seem to be more available for the formation of complex compounds than others. This situation is captured through the concept of productivity. In this regard, there are several questions to be asked: Are there measurable differences between the productivity of two-noun compounds in forming more complex compounds? If so, which two-noun compounds are most commonly extended to complex compounds? And why do speakers use these compounds more productively than others? The answers to these questions are crucial to understanding why only certain tripartite compounds exist, as well as to retrace the processes that license polylexemic compounds.

To introduce the concept of productivity, Section 8.1 will present the theoretical background on the productivity of word-formation processes. Section 8.2 will examine whether there are two-word compounds that are used significantly more often for the formation of three-word compounds than others. Section 8.3 will investigate whether compounds show quantitative differences in their usage as heads and modifiers. In Section 8.4, the concept of productivity will be substantially enriched with a semantic approach to the phenomenon. Section 8.5 aims to explain the differences in compound productivity by identifying variables that distinguish productive compounds from less productive ones. Section 8.6 will highlight the cognitive relevance of those variables that show to be distinctive by outlining the neural processes involved in the formation of complex compounds. On this basis, Section 8.7 will illustrate how the knowledge about the productivity of two-noun compounds is represented in speakers' minds. Finally, Section 8.8 will demonstrate in how far the results gained throughout Chapter 8 can be used when it comes to predicting which kinds of tripartite compounds are likely to be formed in the future, followed by a summary and conclusions in Section 8.9.

## 8.1 The concept of morphological productivity

Productivity is quite a widespread phenomenon and there are different conceptions of the features it comprises. Accordingly, the notion of productivity is used quite inconsistently, with definitions not necessarily referring to the exact same phenomenon (Bauer 2001: 1; Barðdal 2008: 10–11; Bauer et al. 2019: 44). Detailed overviews of the most prominent approaches including their problems and intricacies can be found in Bauer (2001) and Plag (2003: 44–68).

The concept of productivity has almost exclusively been applied in the area of derivation, where it is a fundamental concept. Almost all linguists who approach affixation concern themselves with the number and kinds of bases that a particular affix can be used with. Moving away from an affixation-based understanding of productivity to a more general level, it is largely agreed on that synchronically oriented productivity is concerned with the question how extensively a word-formation pattern or process can be used to form words. Specifications on the newness of the words that are formed, their number and the requirement that their formation must be unintentional, are additional aspects that are found in earlier definitions but no longer find popular agreement and have been devalued by various linguists (cf. Gaeta and Ricca 2015: 842–843; Dal and Namer 2016: 70–73). In most current approaches, productivity is generally understood as the extent to which a word-formation pattern or process is used for the repeated formation of lexemes (cf. Bauer et al. 2019: 44).

Researchers in this area generally agree that productivity is a function of frequency. In this respect, however, there are different figures that are of interest, depending on the facet of productivity that is deemed most important. Some researchers focus on the number of possible formations of a pattern, others on the general size of a morphological category (i.e. the number of tokens or types it comprises) and still others are exclusively interested in the amount of *newly* formed items in a category. Accordingly, there are several measures of productivity, each covering slightly different aspects. The standard for the synchronic investigation of productivity are the corpus-based measures developed by Baayen (cf. Baayen and Lieber 1991; Baayen 1992, 1993, 2009). Summaries of his accounts on productivity can be found in Bauer (2001: 144–162, 2005) and Dal and Namer (2016), who also point out the deficits of these proposals.

Although in their definitions of productivity researchers tend to refer to productivity as the characteristic of a word-formation pattern or process, their works almost exclusively focus on affixes (cf. Bauer 2001, 2005; Plag 2006a; Baayen 2009). Plag (2003) and Schmid (2016) each dedicate a whole chapter to productivity in their books on word-formation but exclusively address affixes and do not consider – or at least mention – that this phenomenon could be relevant for compounds as well. Plag (2003: 44) even depicts productivity as an exclusively derivational phenomenon, defining it as "[t]he property of an affix to be used to coin new complex words". Bauer devotes a whole book to morphological productivity, asserting that "there are some word-formation processes which are non-affixal, but which may nevertheless be productive" (2001: 12). In this context, he mentions compounds that contain reduplication. He states that "[i]n order to avoid the unwanted implication that only affixation can be productive, we may thus prefer to assign productivity to morphological processes". Still, he does not make any further reference to the productivity of non-affixal patterns in the remainder of his book. It is only in Bauer et al. (2019) that Bauer finally addresses productivity in compounding. In this work, he builds on Tarasova (2013), a work that I regard as fundamental in research on compound productivity, as it is the first one to explicitly give attention to constituent productivity.

Constituent productivity is an aspect that is inherent to compounds and not relevant in derivation. A crucial difference between productivity in derivation and in compounding is that the elements whose productivity can be examined are of different kind, which impacts their availability. An affix is restricted in its location within the complex structure, as it is either a suffix or a prefix. As a consequence, it is predetermined in its function as modifier or as head. Compounding, however, employs lexemes, which are not determined concerning their positioning and can thus theoretically act both as modifiers and as heads, especially in the combination of nouns. Constituent productivity accordingly distinguishes a lexeme's productivity in the two different functions. Tarasova (2013) addresses the question of whether lexemes occur as heads and modifiers in compounds to the same degree, a question that will also be examined for complex compounds in this project (see Section 8.3).

Besides Tarasova's contribution, there are only a handful of researchers who have tackled productivity in compounding. When this project was initiated in 2016, research in this field was extremely scarce; this topic has only started to attract attention in very recent years. Two important works that examine productivity in simple compounds have been conducted at the IDS in Mannheim. Hein and Engelberg (2018) illustrate that semantically similar lexemes show differences in the extent to which they are used as heads in compounds. In this context, they provide a list of factors that can potentially influence the productivity of a lexeme to be used as a head constituent in compounds. Hein and Brunner (2019) address the question of why lexemes show differences in their productivity as a compound head and show that the morphological complexity of a lexeme has an impact on its usage. Bauer et al. (2019) build on Tarasova's work and notably look into semantic differences of lexemes in the head and modifier position, stressing the insight gained from Tarasova (2013) that a distinctive approach to productivity that looks into the behaviour of individual lexemes is crucial. Tarasova (2019) seems to simply be a condensed version of Tarasova (2013), presenting the very same data. Carstairs-McCarthy (2018) only seemingly relates productivity to compounding, as in his chapter "Productivity in compounding" he exclusively focuses on the semantic regularity of new formations and does not give a systematic account or a definition of his understanding of the concept of productivity. Studies that approach productivity in compounding from a diachronic perspective have been performed by Hilpert (2015), who examines the usage of English participle compounds, and Kopf (2018), who investigates the development of German N+N compounds under the influence of genitive constructions.

These works demonstrate why an elaboration of the concept of productivity in the area of compounding is long overdue. Although they partly work with German compounds and are limited to compounds consisting of two lexemes, the works by Tarasova and the IDS are an especially sound and valuable basis for the exploration of productivity in complex compounding. The present project will further contribute to transferring the phenomenon of productivity to the field of compounding, aiming to demonstrate how useful the respective insights are for the study of word-formation.

## 8.2 Are some compounds more productive than others?

Looking back at the 30 most frequent three-noun compounds on page 99 it is highly evident that some embedded compounds appear repeatedly. *Football*, for example, is found 7 times among these 30 items, just as *health care* and *basketball* occur in 4 different tripartite compounds. These 3 simple compounds already account for half of the 30 most common tripartite compounds. Obviously, there is a certain degree of repetitiveness among the embedded compounds that are used for the formation of tri-constituent compounds. Are three-noun compounds perhaps even based on a rather limited inventory of recurring two-noun compounds? This section is dedicated to investigating whether there are measurable differences in the degree to which two-word compounds are used to form tripartite compounds. If this is shown to be true, it will be intriguing to see how prevalent the productive compounds are among the whole set of three-noun compounds.

What is in focus conceptually is the *global* (or *realized*) *productivity* of two-noun compounds (Baayen and Lieber 1991; Baayen 1992, 1993, 2009: 904). Accordingly, what is of interest methodologically is the number of types of three-noun compounds formed by a particular two-noun compound. In order to determine these type frequencies, the embedded compounds of the tripartite compounds in the 3N database were extracted. They were identified through the branching tags, i.e. for tripartite compounds tagged as left-branching the embedded compound was taken to be the N1N2 sequence, while for those tagged as right-branching the N2N3 sequence was extracted. For each of these two-noun compounds, the number of times it occurs in a three-noun compound was calculated irrespective of the position (i.e. whether the compound acts as a head or as a modifier). This procedure delivers absolute values that can be used for a direct comparison and ranking of the two-word compounds with regard to their productivity.

The data collection in Chapter 4 had originally resulted in 57,741 types of three-noun compounds. The following calculations will be based on 57,606 items, subtracting those tripartite compounds that could not be directly assigned a clear status with regard to their branching pattern (cf. Section 5.2.3), as in these cases the embedded compounds could not be clearly identified. In 57,606 types of three-noun compounds there are potentially 57,606 different embedded two-noun compounds. However, the almost 60,000 embedded compounds are based on only 19,460 different types. Thus, on average, each two-noun compound is used for the formation of approximately three types of three-noun compounds. In fact, however, the spectrum of type frequencies among the two-noun compounds ranges widely: on the one end of the scale there are compounds that occur in only one type of three-noun compound; on the other end there are compounds that are used to form several hundred different types of three-noun compounds.

To give a qualitative insight into both ends, I will provide examples of both productive and less productive two-noun compounds. Table 19 displays the 34 two-noun compounds (2N) at the top of the productivity ranking, which is all items that produce more than 100 different three-noun compounds (3N).

**Table 19:** Most productive compounds based on types of 3N.

| 2N | Types of 3N | 2N | Types of 3N |
|---|---|---|---|
| network | 657 | taskforce | 154 |
| sidebar | 464 | workshop | 152 |
| health care m | 348 | railroad | 146 |
| baseball | 319 | community college | 145 |
| classroom | 316 | guidelines | 135 |
| football | 314 | law enforcement | 131 |
| weekend | 303 | bay area | 124 |
| newspaper | 297 | chairman | 124 |
| basketball | 249 | headquarter | 123 |
| household | 249 | workplace | 121 |
| airport | 221 | ice cream | 117 |
| website | 190 | landmark | 110 |
| air force | 170 | wartime | 109 |
| airline | 168 | warehouse | 106 |
| database | 165 | fundraising | 101 |
| aircraft | 157 | pipeline | 101 |
| lifetime | 155 | baseline | 100 |

The table shows that *network* is the most productive compound, forming more than 600 different three-noun compounds, such as *network television, network member, news network* or *support network*. With this high degree of productivity, *network* accounts for more than 1 percent of all types of three-noun compounds in the 3N database. The next item in the list, *sidebar*, is presumably slightly flawed. A look into the supposed complex compounds it forms (e.g. *sidebar reader, sidebar word, music sidebar, reading sidebar*), reveals that some of these presumable word-formation products are not meaningful but cases in which non-related words were joined during website crawling. These formations do not comply with the understanding of compounds as defined in Section 3.2, which is why not all instances of three-noun sequences produced by *sidebar* can be counted as compounds. Accordingly, the actual type count of compounds produced with *sidebar* must be assumed to be lower. As this error was only detected in the later stages of this project, it will remain part of the data. Besides this item, all other two-noun compounds in the table form a whole paradigm of tripartite compounds. The compounds that denote ball sports, for example, i.e. *football, basketball* and *baseball*, together form 882 different types of three-noun compounds, which is 1.5 percent of all types in the 3N database. Further very productive compounds are those in which *air* is used as a modifier (i.e. *aircraft, airline, air force* and *airport*), accounting for 716 types in total and thus for another 1.2 percent of complex compounds in the database. Other compounds that occur significantly more often than average are *health care, classroom, weekend* and *newspaper*, all found in around 300 types of three-noun compounds. All of these compounds are used extensively as input for further compounding, combining with further nouns in a highly repetitive fashion, and can thus be classified as extremely productive.

On the other end of the productivity scale are compounds that are found significantly less frequently in three-noun compounds. Table 20 displays exemplary two-noun compounds of medium productivity, i.e. compounds that are used for the formation of a considerable number of three-noun compounds, as well as items from the bottom of the productivity ranking with very low productivity, forming only few types of tripartite compounds.

**Table 20:** Compounds with lower degrees of productivity.

| 2N | Types of 3N | 2N | Types of 3N |
|---|---|---|---|
| credit card | 92 | keyword | 7 |
| birthday | 80 | roommate | 6 |
| rainbow | 75 | child safety | 6 |
| roadside | 67 | crossword | 5 |

**Table 20** (continued)

| 2N | Types of 3N | 2N | Types of 3N |
|---|---|---|---|
| cell phone | 66 | growth curve | 4 |
| court room | 64 | body mass | 3 |
| breast cancer | 63 | population growth | 4 |
| keyboard | 55 | fire protection | 4 |
| handbook | 46 | video cassette | 3 |
| taxpayer | 43 | internet service | 3 |
| death penalty | 41 | child rape | 2 |
| country music | 34 | infant mortality | 2 |
| data collection | 29 | energy storage | 2 |
| mountain bike | 27 | flood relief | 2 |
| child abuse | 27 | crisis pregnancy | 1 |
| music festival | 15 | industry research | 1 |
| sunflower | 12 | research paper | 1 |
| keynote | 10 | dustbin | 1 |
| world heritage | 10 | pain tolerance | 1 |

Some items on the left side of the table still account for a substantial number of complex compounds. *Credit card*, for example, is quite productive, forming more than 90 different three-noun compounds such as *company credit card, credit card bill, credit card payment* or *credit card interest*. *Death penalty* is less productive but still used in around 40 types of three-noun compounds like *death penalty abolition, death penalty defense, death penalty case, death penalty opponent* or *death penalty legislation*. The compounds on the right side of the table, by contrast, form very few tripartite compounds. *Child safety*, for example, merely occurs in *child safety seat, child safety worker* and *child safety lock*. *Body mass* is exclusively encountered in *body mass index, body mass loss* and *body mass reduction*. *Energy storage* is only found in *energy storage system, energy storage devices* and *energy storage capacity*. Some two-noun compounds are only ever used in one type of three-noun compound: *crisis pregnancy*, for example, only occurs in *crisis pregnancy center*; *research paper* only in *research paper assignment*; *dustbin* in *dustbin lid*; and *pain tolerance* exclusively in *pain tolerance scores*. These compounds can thus be said to be rather unproductive in forming complex compounds.

This comparison has demonstrated that two-noun compounds do not combine with further nouns to the same degree but that there are remarkable differences regarding their productivity: some seem to be readily available for becoming part of more complex constructions, while others barely engage in a further process of compounding. In order to be able to refer back to these differently productive compounds, I will use the categorization presented in Table 21, which is based on the number of three-noun compounds the respective two-noun compounds have formed:

**Table 21:** Categorization of 2N based on number of 3N formed.

| Categorization of 2N | Types of 3N |
|---|---|
| Extremely productive compounds | ≥ 100 |
| Highly productive compounds | 60–99 |
| Fairly productive compounds | 30–59 |
| Slightly productive compounds | 10–29 |
| Barely productive compounds | < 10 |

As to the terminology, all two-noun compounds that have given rise to at least 100 different types of three-noun compounds will be labelled as "extremely productive", those that occur in between 60 and 100 items as "highly productive", those that form between 30 and 60 different tripartite compounds as "fairly productive", those that are to be found in 10 to 30 types as "slightly productive" and those that occur in fewer than 10 different three-noun compounds as "barely productive".

To provide a qualitative insight into these different kinds of compounds, the following graphics will present one compound of each productivity category with the three-noun compounds it has formed. The concrete instances of complex compounds are displayed on the horizontal axis, while the corresponding token frequencies for each item are displayed on the vertical axis. For legibility, only the 20 most frequent types of three-noun compound per (two-noun) compound are presented. This means that for rather unproductive compounds all three-noun compounds they have formed are displayed, while for the more productive ones only an extract of the most frequent instantiations is shown. Extremely productive compounds are illustrated in Figure 16 (a) by *health care* (348 types of three-noun compounds), highly productive compounds in Figure 16 (b) by *credit card* (92 types), the category of fairly productive compounds is represented in Figure 16 (c) through *death penalty* (41 types), that of slightly productive compounds in Figure 16 (d) through *data collection* (29 types) and that of barely productive compounds in Figure 16 (e) through *roommate* (6 types).

The graphs strongly highlight that there are remarkable differences in the productivity of compounds. While there are extremely productive compounds such as *health care*, which are used extensively for the formation of a high number of complex compounds, there are also barely productive ones like *roommate*, which mainly form one fairly established instance and a few further sporadic three-noun compounds. The different behaviour of the compounds clearly illustrates why productivity cannot be considered an either-or category with two poles but should be understood as a cline that is organized as a continuum from more productive to less productive. Obviously, compounds feature quite different degrees of productivity, with some being highly productive in forming more complex compounds, while

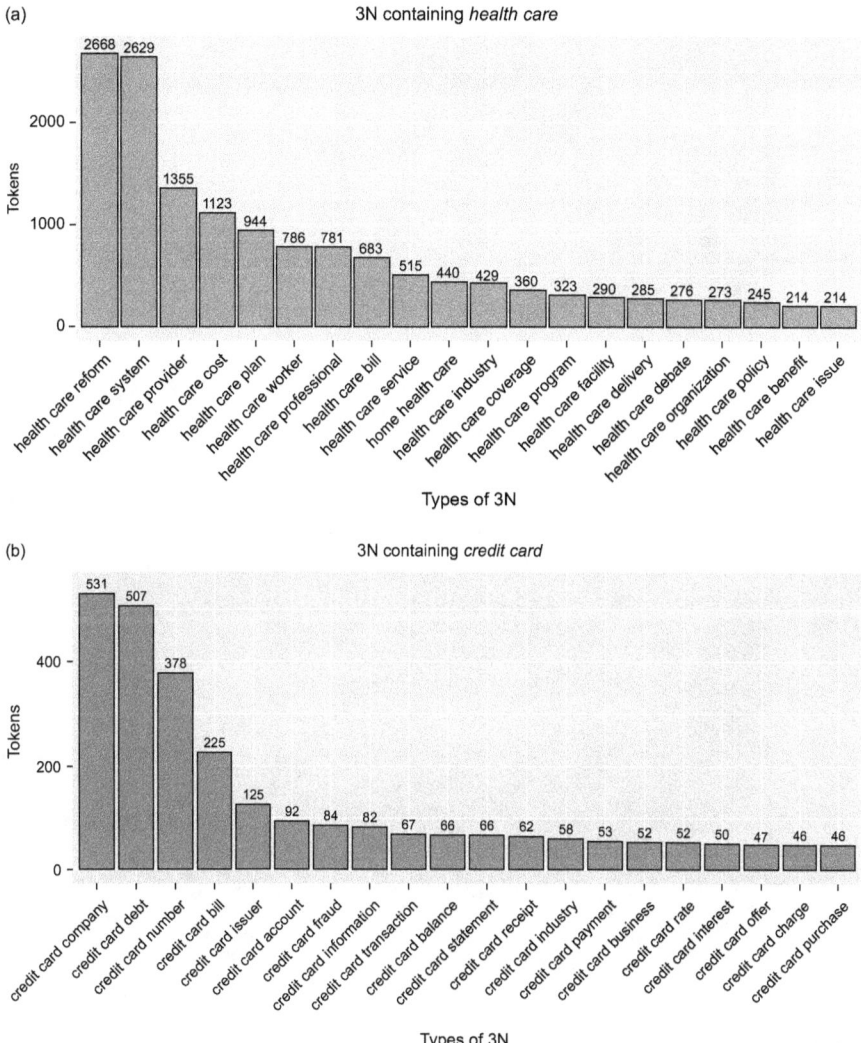

**Figure 16:** Examples of compounds with different degrees of productivity.

others barely lend themselves to recursive compound formation. The question that naturally arises is how these differences in productivity can be explained, an aspect that will be examined in Sections 8.5 and 8.6.

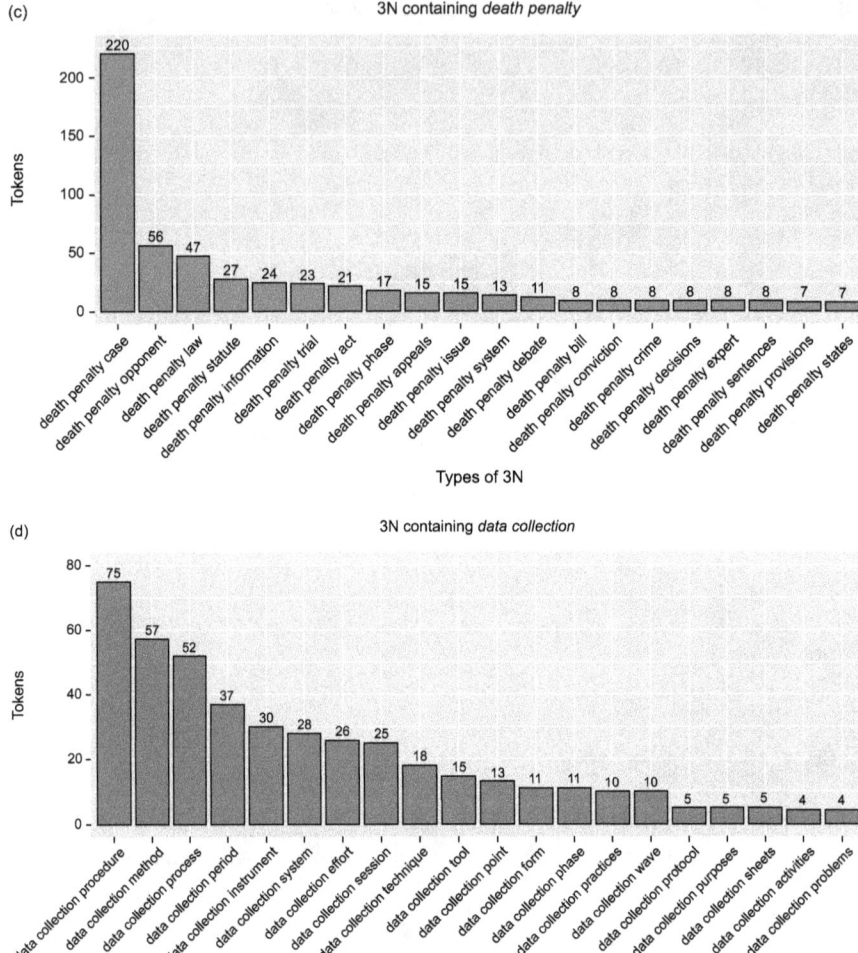

**Figure 16** (continued)

At this point, another question that was raised at the outset must be answered. Given that some compounds, such as *football*, for example, seem to be very common bases for tripartite compounds, accounting for hundreds of different types, does this imply that complex compounds are based on a rather limited, recurring set of two-noun compounds? To evaluate the prominence of the productive two-noun compounds among the set of three-noun compounds, Table 22 provides quantitative information on the different productivity categories that were established on page 152. It presents the number of two-noun compounds that fall into each of

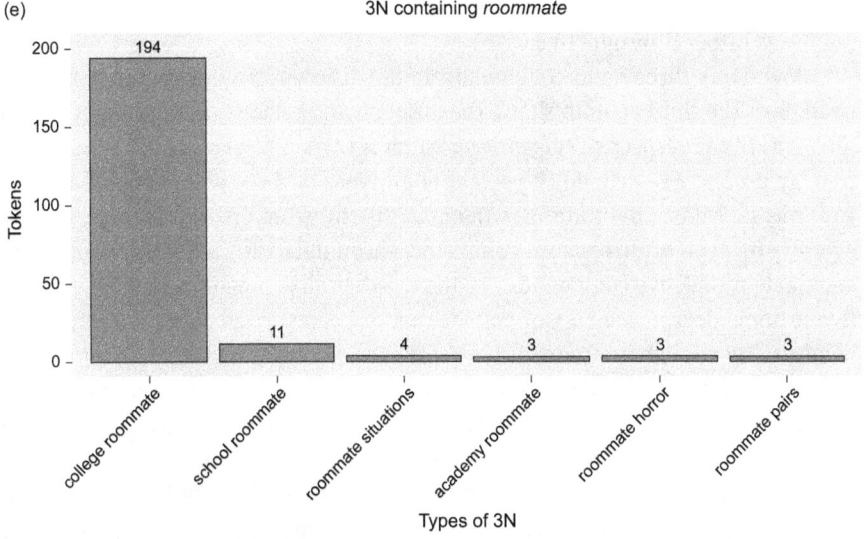

**Figure 16** (continued)

**Table 22:** Number of 3N formed by 2N of different productivity categories.

| 2N categorization | Number of 2N | 3N types | | 3N tokens | |
|---|---|---|---|---|---|
| | | total | % | total | % |
| Extremely productive compounds | 34 | 6,841 | 12 | 169,512 | 25 |
| Highly productive compounds | 39 | 2,904 | 5 | 56,178 | 8 |
| Fairly productive compounds | 144 | 5,856 | 10 | 86,170 | 13 |
| Slightly productive compounds | 623 | 9,837 | 17 | 118,570 | 17 |
| Barely productive compounds | 18,620 | 32,169 | 56 | 248,033 | 37 |

these categories (column 2), as well as the number of types (column 3) and tokens (column 4) of three-noun compounds the respective categories account for.

The table shows that the categories of the extremely and highly productive compounds are rather small. Only 34 two-noun compounds (those that were displayed on page 149) occur in more than 100 different types of three-noun compounds and can thus be classified as extremely productive. Almost the same number of compounds qualifies as highly productive. Another proportionally small number of 144 compounds are categorized as fairly productive and just above 600 items can be considered slightly productive. The overwhelming majority of embedded compounds belongs to the category of barely productive compounds that form fewer than ten types of three-noun compounds. Accordingly, the vast majority of two-word compounds that are used to form three-noun compounds is rather unproductive.

How many three-noun compounds do the different two-noun compounds account for? The third column shows the absolute and relative number of types that the items in the respective categories account for. The few compounds that are extremely productive occur in 12 percent of all types of three-noun compounds and can thus be said to be quite prevalent, as this suggests that on average at least every tenth type of three-noun compound encountered is based on one of these extremely productive compounds. Taking together all compounds that are productive to some degree, i.e. all compounds that are categorized as either extremely, highly, fairly or slightly productive, we envisage a comparatively small number of 840 two-noun compounds that account for 44 percent of all three-noun compounds, as opposed to 18,620 barely productive two-noun compounds which account for the remaining 56 percent. Still, type-wise there are more three-noun compounds that are based on a barely productive compound than those that are based on a compound that is productive to some degree. It can thus not be stated that the embedded compounds in three-noun compounds are dominated by a limited set of recurring two-noun compounds, as there is also an extremely high number of three-noun compounds that are based on a barely productive and thus less prevalent compound.

I will now proceed to the tokens. The fourth column in the table reports the number of absolute and relative tokens of three-noun compounds formed by the compounds of the different productivity categories. The two categories of extremely and highly productive compounds together, although consisting of 73 compounds only, form a similar number of tokens as the categories of fairly and slightly productive compounds together (which comprise 747 compounds), and the category of barely productive compounds by itself (with more than 18,000 compounds). This means that on average approximately every third token of three-noun compound encountered contains one of the 73 compounds that have been categorized as extremely or highly productive. Adding the category of fairly productive compounds to the extremely and highly productive ones, results in 217 two-noun compounds which make up 46 percent of all tokens of three-noun compounds. Accordingly, a comparatively small set of 217 two-noun compounds is to be found in almost every second three-noun compound. A look at the category of extremely productive compounds only is even more conclusive: these 34 compounds by themselves account for 25 percent of all tokens of three-noun compounds, which means that every fourth three-noun compound encountered is based on one of those two-noun compounds that were presented on page 149. Thus, token-wise these two-noun compounds can be said to be highly dominant as embedded compounds in tripartite compounds.

## 8.3 Are compounds used as heads and modifiers equally?

This section will attempt to further specify the productivity of two-noun compounds. In the previous section, the productivity of two-noun compounds was evaluated irrespective of their position – and thus function – within complex compounds, i.e. it was neglected whether a compound appears as N1N2 and thus acts as a modifier, or whether it is used in the position of N2N3 and thus acts as a head. Looking back at the concrete three-noun compounds in the Figures 16 (a)–(e), it becomes obvious that the majority of items are left-branching compounds. There are only very few instances of right-branching compounds, such as *home health care* and *college roommate*. Does this indicate that compounds do not occur as heads and modifiers in complex compounds to the same extent? Do they show different behaviour as a head than as a modifier, maybe occurring in one of the two positions exclusively?

The relevant concept for this research question is that of constituent productivity, an aspect that Tarasova (2013) investigates for simple compounds. For a sample of 50 nominal compounds, she compares the occurrences of their constituents as heads and modifiers and finds a negative correlation between the sizes of the modifier and head families, i.e. the more often a noun occurs as a head in a compound, the less often it occurs as a modifier. From these results she concludes that "any given noun is used more productively either as a modifier or as the head of the compounded structure" (Tarasova 2019: 61). In a paper dedicated to the processing of compounds, Baayen (2010) finds in a study of 2,200 simple compounds that about 27 percent of all compound constituents occur both as a head and as a modifier, 32 percent only as a head and 41 percent only as a modifier. These studies suggest that lexemes do not occur in the two positions in a compound to the same degree but show a prevalence for one of them. This situation is not surprising, as it is reasonable to assume that the semantic properties of a word make it suitable for a particular function. It is conceivable that some concepts are more suitable in the role of the modifier than in that of the head and vice versa, which is why it will be interesting to contrast the usage of compounds in these two functions. Although the studies mentioned examine the constituent productivity of simple words, work with a considerably smaller set of items and might be better controlled for noise, I expect to find the same situation for two-word compounds that are used to form more complex compounds, hypothesizing that compounds show a different degree of productivity as modifier than as head.

To investigate this matter, the type frequencies of the 19,460 embedded compounds in the 3N database were distinguished for the occurrences in the two different functions. For each of these compounds the constituent family sizes were calculated, which include:

- The modifier family size (ModFamSize): number of 3N in which the compound occurs in the position N1N2, i.e. as a modifier
- The head family size (HeadFamSize): number of 3N in which the compound occurs in the position N2N3, i.e. as a head

Contrasting the two constituent family sizes for each compound allows a comparison of the extent to which a compound acts as a head and as a modifier. To examine whether there is a statistically relevant correlation between a compound's modifier family size and its head family size, a Spearman's correlation was calculated. The correlation coefficient amounts to −0.496, with a significant p-value ($p < 0.005$), i.e. there is a negative correlation of medium strength between the constituent family sizes: the higher one family size is, the lower the other family size. This result suggests that those compounds that are productive in one position will be less productive in the other, which is in agreement with Tarasova's finding for simple words. Figure 17 displays the relation between the constituent family sizes for each of the 19,460 compounds in a scatterplot. The vertical and the horizontal axes represent the modifier and head family size respectively. The bottom left corner, where most of the data points are to be found, is displayed in more detail at the top of the diagram.

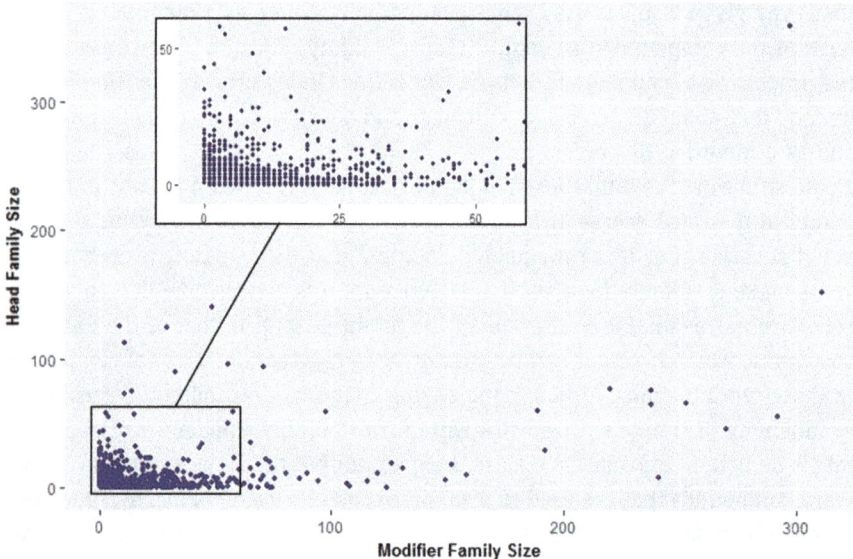

**Figure 17:** Relationship between constituent family sizes.

From a purely descriptive perspective, there seems to be little systematic connection between the two variables of head family size and modifier family size. The data points are quite dispersed, with some compounds featuring high numbers for their modifier families but low ones for the head families, and vice versa. Looking more closely at the enlarged section, which zooms in on the accumulation of items for which both constituent family sizes are lower than 60, does not yield a clearer picture, as the data points are scattered in all directions. The descriptive analysis thus does not fully support the results gained in the statistical analysis. To find the reason for this discrepancy, the data was further scrutinized.

What can be seen in the scatterplot is that there are compounds that have head family sizes or modifier family sizes of zero. Accordingly, the extent to which compounds exclusively occur as heads or modifiers was determined. Figure 18 displays the proportions for the compounds' preferences to be used only as a head, only as a modifier or in both functions.

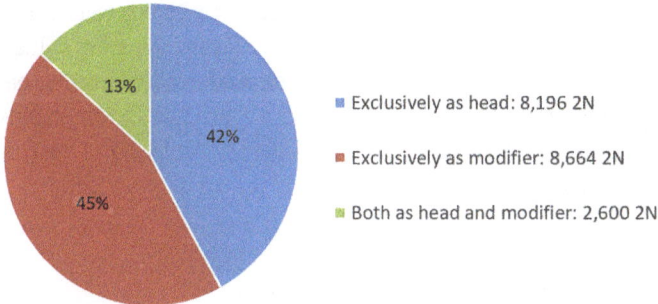

**Figure 18:** Distribution of compounds on functions in 3N.

Of the 19,460 embedded compounds in the 3N database, 8,196 have a modifier family size of 0, which means they occur exclusively as a head. Almost the same number of 8,664 compounds has a head family size of 0 and thus acts exclusively as a modifier. Accordingly, an overwhelming sum of 16,860 compounds, i.e. 87 percent of all compounds, occurs in one of the two positions exclusively, while only a minority of 2,600 compounds is used in both the head and modifier function. These results are quantitatively not fully in line with those found in Baayen's (2010) study, with a much smaller proportion of items occurring both as head and modifier in my data set. Nevertheless, the figures suggest the same trend, namely that compounds do not seem to occur in both positions alike but tend to be used in only one of the two positions. These results seem to suggest that compounds are not more productive in one position than in the other (as Tarasova had suggested) but that the majority of compounds tend to exclusively occur in one position and thus are suitable either as a head or as a modifier in complex compounds.

However, a further look at the data indicates that even this claim cannot be confirmed. Out of the 16,860 seemingly position-bound compounds that appear in one position exclusively, 75 percent occur only once in this particular position, i.e. have an overall productivity of 1. These compounds clearly *can* only occur in one position and will thus automatically have a correlation coefficient of −1 for the relationship between their family sizes, as one of the family sizes is 0 and the other one is 1. Therefore, the correlation coefficient yielded in the statistical analysis is not very informative and conclusive if it is predominantly based on items that only occur once. Drawing the conclusion that the respective compounds can exclusively be used in that particular position is deceptive, as this could only be stated if there were more than one occurrence per compound, which is only given for a minority of data points.

Based on the assumption that the correlation coefficient might be flawed by the high number of items with an overall productivity of 1, the correlations were calculated for 3 different subsets of (i) barely productive compounds (forming fewer than 10 three-noun compounds), (ii) compounds with medium productivity (forming between 10 and 100 three-noun compounds) and (iii) extremely productive compounds (forming more than 100 three-noun compounds). The following table shows the correlation coefficient for the constituent family sizes yielded for the different subsets:

**Table 23:** Correlation coefficients for different productivity subsets.

| Overall | Sample (i) PROD < 10 | Sample (ii) PROD > 10 < 100 | Sample (iii) PROD > 100 |
|---|---|---|---|
| −0.496* | −0.629* | −0.335* | −0.111 |

The subsets in the table receive quite different results for the correlation between the modifier family sizes and the head family sizes. The higher the overall productivity of the compounds, the less strongly the effect is pronounced: fairly unproductive compounds show a much stronger negative correlation than highly productive compounds, for which the correlation is close to non-existent. Does this indicate that compounds behave differently in this respect depending on their overall productivity? This would suggest that compounds that are not very productive preferably occur in one of the two positions, while more productive compounds are productive in both positions. Tarasova does point out that "the degree of preference for being used in one position differs for different nouns and ranges from absolute (100%) to low (≥51%), which allows for the suggestion that morphological productivity of an element in one position is gradient" (2019: 62). I assume that this preference might be related to the overall productivity (i.e. overall type frequency) of a compound, with those cases with an absolute preference for one position having a low productivity in the first place. To verify this assumption, a closer examination of the actual behaviour of compounds with different degrees of overall productivity is required.

For this, the group of more productive compounds will be examined first. Table 24 displays the 20 most productive compounds in terms of global productivity, specified with information on how the total type frequencies are distributed on the modifier (MOD) and head (HEAD) families. The last column presents the ratio between the modifier and head family.

**Table 24:** Head and modifier family sizes for most productive compounds.

| 2N | 3N TYPES | MOD | HEAD | RATIO |
|---|---|---|---|---|
| network | 657 | 297 | 360 | 1 : 1 |
| sidebar | 464 | 311 | 153 | 2 : 1 |
| health care | 348 | 292 | 56 | 5 : 1 |
| baseball | 319 | 253 | 66 | 4 : 1 |
| classroom | 316 | 270 | 46 | 6 : 1 |
| football | 314 | 238 | 76 | 3 : 1 |
| weekend | 303 | 238 | 65 | 4 : 1 |
| newspaper | 297 | 220 | 77 | 3 : 1 |
| basketball | 249 | 189 | 60 | 3 : 1 |
| household | 249 | 241 | 8 | 30 : 1 |
| airport | 221 | 192 | 29 | 7 : 1 |
| website | 190 | 49 | 141 | 1 : 3 |
| air force | 170 | 152 | 18 | 8 : 1 |
| airline | 168 | 158 | 10 | 16 : 1 |
| database | 165 | 71 | 94 | 1 : 1 |
| aircraft | 157 | 98 | 59 | 2 : 1 |
| lifetime | 155 | 149 | 6 | 25 : 1 |
| taskforce | 154 | 29 | 125 | 1 : 4 |
| workshop | 152 | 56 | 96 | 1 : 2 |
| railroad | 146 | 131 | 15 | 26 : 1 |

The direct comparison of head and modifier family sizes shows that generally there is a clear discrepancy in the distribution of the two different functions. The compound *football*, for example, appears as a modifier in 238 three-noun compounds; when used as a head it is only found in 76 formations. Its head family size is clearly significantly smaller than its modifier family size. Accordingly, the compound *football* can be said to be more productive as a modifier. The same seems to be true for the majority of compounds in the table. They do not tend to be used as heads and modifiers to the same degree but show a preference for being used in either of the two functions. In most cases, the respective compound is more productive as a modifier than as a head. Still, there are also compounds in which the head family size outweighs the size of the modifier family, i.e. which are more productive as a head than as a modifier, such as *network, website, taskforce* and *workshop*. Despite these preferences, the figures show that it is clearly not true that these compounds are productive in one position only; most of them are fairly productive in the other position as well.

To gain an insight into the behaviour of less productive compounds, Table 25 displays how the total number of three-noun compounds formed by compounds with medium and low productivity are distributed in the modifier (MOD) and head (HEAD) families.

**Table 25:** Head and modifier family sizes for less productive compounds.

| 2N | 3N TYPES | MOD | HEAD | RATIO |
|---|---|---|---|---|
| credit card | 92 | 81 | 11 | 7 : 1 |
| birthday | 80 | 71 | 9 | 8 : 1 |
| rainbow | 75 | 73 | 2 | 13 : 1 |
| roadside | 67 | 66 | 1 | 66 : 1 |
| cell phone | 66 | 66 | 0 | 66 : 0 |
| court room | 64 | 60 | 4 | 15 : 1 |
| breast cancer | 63 | 57 | 6 | 10 : 1 |
| keyboard | 55 | 45 | 10 | 5 : 1 |
| handbook | 46 | 2 | 44 | 1 : 22 |
| taxpayer | 43 | 40 | 3 | 13 : 1 |
| country music | 34 | 32 | 2 | 16 : 1 |
| data collection | 29 | 24 | 5 | 5 : 1 |
| mountain bike | 27 | 26 | 1 | 26 : 1 |
| child abuse | 27 | 25 | 2 | 13 : 1 |
| music festival | 16 | 2 | 14 | 1 : 7 |
| keynote | 10 | 8 | 2 | 4 : 1 |
| keyword | 7 | 6 | 1 | 6 : 1 |
| child safety | 6 | 6 | 0 | 6 : 0 |
| roommate | 6 | 3 | 3 | 1 : 1 |
| crossword | 5 | 5 | 0 | 5 : 0 |
| growth curve | 4 | 3 | 1 | 3 : 1 |
| body mass | 4 | 4 | 0 | 4 : 0 |
| fire protection | 4 | 4 | 0 | 4 : 0 |
| video cassette | 3 | 3 | 0 | 3 : 0 |
| internet service | 3 | 2 | 1 | 2 : 1 |
| energy storage | 3 | 3 | 0 | 3 : 0 |

**Table 25** (continued)

| 2N | 3N TYPES | MOD | HEAD | RATIO |
|---|---|---|---|---|
| infant mortality | 2 | 2 | 0 | 2 : 0 |
| discourse analysis | 1 | 1 | 0 | 1 : 0 |
| crisis pregnancy | 1 | 1 | 0 | 1 : 0 |
| research paper | 1 | 1 | 0 | 1 : 0 |
| dust bin | 1 | 1 | 0 | 1 : 0 |
| pain tolerance | 1 | 1 | 0 | 1 : 0 |

The table shows that for the majority of items there is a noticeable difference between the sizes of the modifier family and that of the head family. This suggests that less productive compounds as well have a tendency to occur more frequently in one of the two positions. At the same time, it cannot be confirmed that less productive compounds are used in one position exclusively, as the majority of compounds displayed in the table occur at least a few times in the respective other position.

Based on these observations, it can be claimed that highly productive compounds are generally productive in both positions (even if not to the same degree). Although it cannot be confirmed that compounds occur in one position exclusively, it is definitely true that they show a preference for being used in one of the two functions. The compound *football*, for example, produces complex compounds both acting as a modifier (e.g. *football game, football player, football coach, football match*) and as a head (e.g. *college football, night football, quality football*) and can thus be said to be productive in both functions. At the same time, with a modifier family size of 238 and a head family size of 76, it shows a clear preference for being used as a modifier. *Handbook*, by contrast, has a modifier family size of 2 and a head family size of 44. It thus mainly acts as a head, forming complex compounds such as *activities handbook, agriculture handbook, employee handbook, engineer handbook* or *member handbook*, but seldom works as a modifier in more complex compounds, only producing *handbook series* and *handbook magazine*.

What do these results entail for the quality of those compounds that occur as modifiers and those that occur as heads? Are the most productive modifier compounds the same ones as those that are used most commonly as heads? To answer this question, Table 26 displays the 20 compounds that are most productive as modifiers (left side) and those that are most productive as heads (right side). For both categories the occurrences in the respective other function are also given.

A comparison of the two inventories of compounds shows that there is a high degree of overlap between the compounds that are most productive as modifiers and those that are most productive as heads. 8 compounds are encountered in

**Table 26:** Most productive modifiers (left) and heads (right).

| 2N | MOD | HEAD | 2N | HEAD | MOD |
|---|---|---|---|---|---|
| sidebar | 311 | 153 | sidebar | 311 | 153 |
| network | 297 | 360 | network | 297 | 360 |
| health care | 292 | 56 | health care | 292 | 56 |
| classroom | 270 | 46 | baseball | 253 | 66 |
| baseball | 253 | 66 | football | 238 | 76 |
| household | 241 | 8 | weekend | 238 | 65 |
| weekend | 238 | 65 | newspaper | 220 | 77 |
| football | 238 | 76 | basketball | 189 | 60 |
| newspaper | 220 | 77 | aircraft | 98 | 59 |
| airport | 192 | 29 | database | 71 | 94 |
| basketball | 189 | 60 | ice cream | 58 | 59 |
| airline | 158 | 10 | workshop | 56 | 96 |
| air force | 152 | 18 | website | 49 | 141 |
| lifetime | 149 | 6 | headquarter | 33 | 90 |
| railroad | 131 | 15 | taskforce | 29 | 125 |
| community college | 126 | 19 | newsletter | 15 | 57 |
| bay area | 124 | 0 | framework | 14 | 75 |
| workplace | 116 | 5 | chairman | 11 | 113 |
| wartime | 108 | 1 | parking lot | 11 | 73 |
| landmark | 107 | 103 | standpoint | 3 | 58 |

both tables: *sidebar, network, health care, baseball, weekend, football, newspaper* and *basketball* are among both the most frequent modifiers and the most frequent heads. This observation suggests that those compounds that are used as modifiers and those that are used as heads are not completely different items. At the same time, there are compounds that are overwhelmingly found in one function only (e.g. *wartime, standpoint* or *lifetime*).

It is noticeable in Table 26 that while the most productive modifier compounds are always more productive as modifiers than as heads, this is not true for the most productive head compounds: of the most frequent head compounds, 8 out of 20 are still more productive when used as modifier than when used as head. A look at the previous tables that contrast the head and modifier family sizes furthermore indicates that there seem to be more cases in which the modifier family outweighs that of the head family, rather than the other way round. Does this mean that compounds are generally more productive as modifiers than as heads? It was quantified earlier that in total there are more instances of left-branching compounds, i.e. three-noun compounds in which the embedded compound occurs in the modifier position. Is this situation attributable to the fact that there are more types of two-noun compounds that form left-branching compounds than two-noun compounds that form right-branching ones? Or does it rather indicate that each individual two-noun compound tends to form more left-branching compounds than right-branching ones?

To answer these questions, two aspects are relevant: firstly, the number of (two-noun) compounds that produce more left-branching compounds than right-branching ones, and, secondly, the average number of left- and right-branching items formed per two-noun compound. Table 27 displays the relevant figures for the first question. It contrasts the number of compounds that are more productive as modifiers than as heads to those that are more productive as heads than as modifiers and to those that occur as heads and modifiers equally:

**Table 27:** Comparison of constituent family sizes for embedded compounds.

| Relationship of family sizes | Number of 2N | % |
|---|---|---|
| ModFamSize > HeadFamSize | 9,876 | 50.75 |
| HeadFamSize < ModFamSize | 8,765 | 45.04 |
| HeadFamSize = ModFamSize | 819 | 4.21 |

The table shows that only a minority of compounds have equal head and modifier family sizes and thus occurs in both positions to the same exact degree. Half of all compounds show a larger modifier family size than head family size, which means that the majority of compounds are used more productively as modifier than as head. The compounds whose head family size outweighs that of the modifier, i.e. those that are more productive as heads than modifiers, is only slightly lower. These figures confirm that there are indeed more compounds that are more productive as modifiers than as heads; however, the difference is not significant. Can this relation fully account for the quantitative discrepancy between the number of left- and right-branching compounds? Or does each two-noun compound also tend to form more left-branching instances of three-noun compounds than right-branching ones? Table 28 displays the figures relevant for answering this question:[19]

The table shows that, on average, each two-noun compound produces more than six left-branching compounds but fewer than four right-branching ones.

---

[19] What is done here might feel similar to what was examined in Section 7.3, when it was determined whether left-branching compounds tend to have higher token frequencies than right-branching ones. There, however, the items were not related to the same types of embedded compounds, which is why this account is more thorough.

**Table 28:** Average number of 3N formed per 2N.

| BP | Number of 3N per 2N |
|---|---|
| LEFT-BRANCHING | 6.44 |
| RIGHT-BRANCHING | 3.95 |

Consequently, it can be claimed that two-noun compounds generally tend to form fewer right-branching items than left-branching ones.

Based on these results, it can be concluded that both the facts that (i) there are more compounds which form left-branching compounds than such which form right-branching ones and that (ii) each individual compound tends to form more left-branching than right-branching items contribute to the situation that there are more three-noun compounds with a left-branching structure than such with a right-branching one.

To summarize, this section has shown that
(i) compounds do not occur as heads and modifiers to the same degree but generally show a preference for one of the two positions
(ii) compounds that are productive to some degree generally occur in both positions to some extent
(iii) it cannot be confirmed that compounds that are more productive as heads are necessarily less productive as modifiers or vice versa
(iv) those compounds that are used as modifiers are not completely different items than those compounds that are used as heads
(v) there are more compounds that form left-branching three-noun compounds than right-branching ones
(vi) on average, each compound forms more left- than right-branching instances of three-noun compounds

The observations made so far in Chapter 8 allow to refine the concept of compound productivity. It has been shown that compounds can differ greatly in the extent to which they lend themselves to the formation of more complex compounds. Not only are some compounds more productive than others, as was demonstrated in Section 8.2, but the present section has furthermore revealed that the productivity of compounds is also determined by the function in which they are used. Therefore, it can be claimed that productivity in polylexemic compounding is not just lexeme- but also position-based. This entails that we must not only consider the productivity of a compound in general, i.e. state that the compound *football*, for example, is extremely productive in forming more complex compounds, but rather specify a compound's productivity in the function of modifier or head. Accordingly, the description of productivity in three-noun compounding should refer to specific patterns of the format *'football* + N' or 'N + *football'*. When I address patterns in tri-constituent compounding in the remainder of this work, I will be referring to a specific compound in a concrete function. Based on the observations made, finally a definition can be established that encompasses the concept of productivity in three-noun compounding: Productivity is understood to be the degree to which a pattern that employs a particular compound in a specific function (i.e. modifier or head) is used for the formation of three-noun compounds.

## 8.4 Can productivity be specified semantically?

While the previous sections have approached productivity exclusively from a quantitative perspective, this section will demonstrate that an additional examination of semantic aspects permits a more fine-grained description of productivity. Instead of focusing on the number of three-noun compounds that a particular pattern has produced, i.e. the number of nouns a compound has combined with in a particular function, I will investigate the semantic diversity of the nouns that have been used in a pattern. The pattern *'football* + N', for instance, was shown to be extremely productive, forming several hundreds of three-noun compounds by combining with a high number of heads. Is it possible to identify semantic subcategories among the set of head nouns that permit further specifying the productivity of this pattern?

In order to investigate the semantic diversity of the outer nouns in exemplary patterns, I made use of the methodology of word embeddings combined with a PCA and t-SNE procedure (cf. Maaten and Hinton 2008; Turney and Pantel 2010; Levshina 2015). These tools produce maps that locate the input words in a semantic space and thus display the semantic distance between the relevant words. A similar technique has been applied by Hilpert (2018) in his study on participles, in which he examines how densely the semantic space of particular participles is populated. In this project, word embeddings will be applied to give an insight into the semantic field covered by the outer nouns occurring in patterns that produce three-noun compounds. The tool developed for this purpose converts the outer nouns that occur in a particular patters into more-dimensional vectors with the help of the library "spaCy", which is based on the Ontonote5 corpus, run on Python. Using the PCA and the t-SNE procedure, the multiple dimensions are flattened to two dimensions in order to be able to present them in an image. The resulting graphic typographically locates the input items. The spatial distance between them mirrors their semantic proximity: words that are displayed close to each other can be assumed to be semantically similar, while words that are more distant are rather different with regard to their meaning.

In the following, I will present exemplary illustrations produced with the help of this application for patterns with different degrees of quantitative productivity. Each picture displays the outer nouns that occur in a particular pattern based on data from the 3N database. The size of the nouns mirrors the token frequency of the respective three-noun compound in which these nouns are used. All graphics have been run with 250 iterations. The illustrations have been colour-coded manually to highlight areas that I have assessed as being semantically related. These fields are not intended to present clearly delineated categories but are merely an attempt to identify semantic clusters.

The first illustration is provided for the pattern *'football* + N' in Figure 19. Denoting a sport, the compound *football* opens a relatively broad semantic frame with a wide range of concepts that can be denoted in this frame and can thus act as a head. The graphic on the following page locates all 238 outer nouns that *football* combines with as a modifier across the semantic space.

The graphic shows that the most prominent heads that are used with *football* are *player, game, team, coach, league* and *field*. Generally speaking, there is a great degree of semantic variability among the head nouns that occur in the pattern *'football* + N'. They cover a wide range of concepts, including *injury* and *captain*, but also *management* and *factory*, reflecting the richness of the frame FOOTBALL. Despite this semantic diversity, the map permits identifying clusters within the semantic range covered by the head nouns, which have been marked in different colours. The most prominent of these clusters can be related to the following areas:

– AGENTS /PEOPLE (highlighted in purple):
  *men, man, guy, jock, dad, wife, widow, kids, player, captain, hooligans, outsiders, scout, observers, supporters, leaders, members, alumni, coach, athletes, fanatic, fan, watchers, referee*
– EQUIPMENT/CLOTHING (LIGHT blue):
  *shoes, pants, jersey, jacket, helmet, uniform, pads, gear, equipment*
– COMPETITION (red):
  *trophies, bowl, tournament, championship, victory, champion, rivalry, competition, awards, final, title, match, record, scholarship, fight, league*
– FAME (brown):
  *giants, lore, legend, hero, talent, prowess, genius, prodigy, fame, stardom, star*
– MANIA (brown):
  *immortality, gods, folly, glory, mania, fan, fanatic*
– NUMERICS (grey):
  *scores, rankings, rating, numbers, statistics*

8.4 Can productivity be specified semantically? — 169

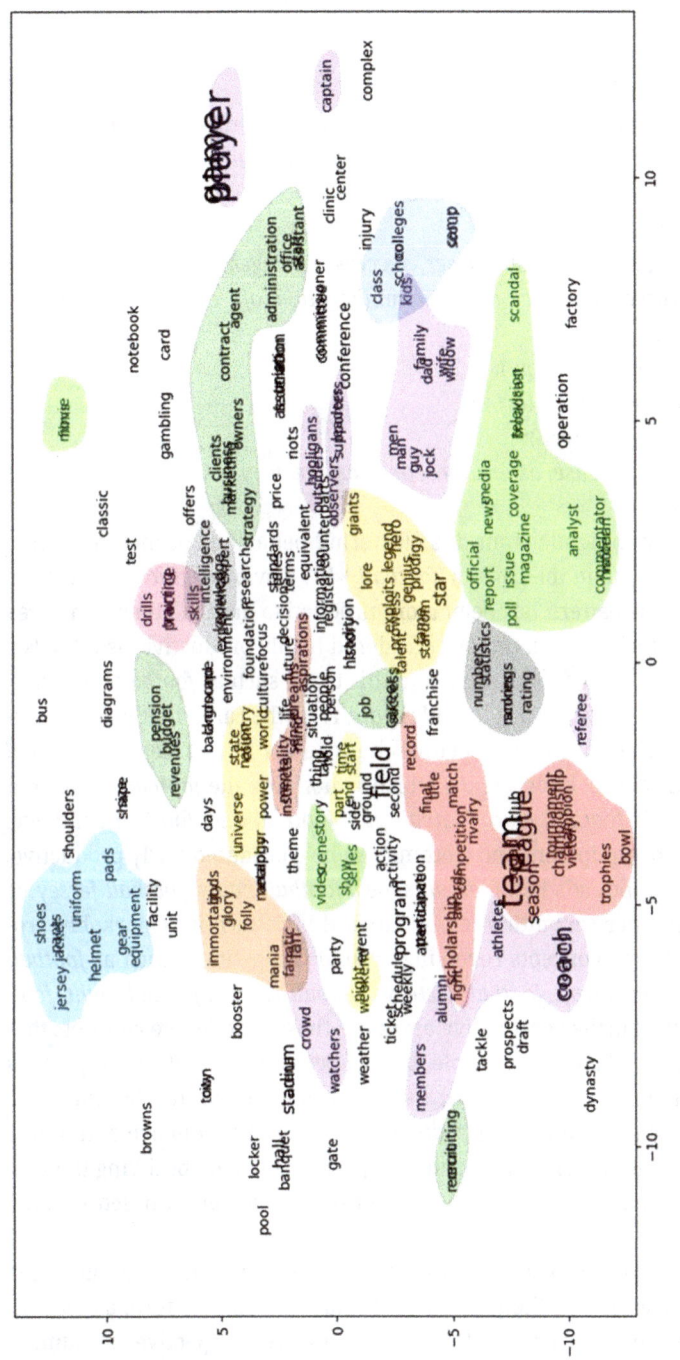

**Figure 19:** Semantic map of head nouns in the pattern 'football + N'.

- LOCAL DIMENSIONS (beige):
  *universe, state, nation, country, world*
- MEDIA COVERAGE (light green):
  *official, report, news, media, poll, issue, magazine, coverage, television, broadcast, scandal, analyst, commentator, historian, writer, movie, films, video, scene, story, show, series*
- FOOTBALL AS A JOB (dark green):
  *pension, budget, revenues, job, career, success, management, clients, business, marketing, strategy, contract, agent, administration, office, staff, assistant, recruit, recruiting*
- TIME-RELATED CONCEPTS (yellow):
  *night, weekend, end, time, start*
- MIND-RELATED CONCEPTS (red):
  *mentality, instincts, sense, aspirations, dreams, strategy*

What inferences can be made from this clustering behaviour of the nouns that take the function of head in the pattern '*football* + N'? Obviously, there are semantic areas in which this pattern has been more productive than in others. The area of media coverage, for example, can be considered highly productive, as it holds a considerable number of instances related to this topic, such as *football magazine, football scandal, football movie* or *football report*. A further area that is fairly productive is that of different kinds of people that can act in this field, as *football* provides a wide framework for agents, which is not only the *football player* but also the *football wife, football man, football guy, football dad, football child*, etc. Similarly, the area of equipment and clothing can be considered fairly productive, holding complex compounds like *football shoes, football pants, football jersey* or *football helmet*. Another semantic area in which this pattern is remarkably productive is that denoting concepts revolving around competition, such as *football trophies, football tournament, football victory, football rivalry, football fight, football competition*, etc. Further productive areas are those that denote concepts that relate to *football* as a job, as for example *football pension, football career, football contract* or *football recruiting*. Clearly, the semantic map illustrates that there are semantic areas in which the pattern '*football* + N' is more productive and others where it is less productive. This approach thus permits further specifying the productivity of this pattern in addition to a quantitative evaluation based on type frequencies.

The next illustration in Figure 20 displays the semantic distribution of the outer nouns that are used in the pattern '*weekend* + N'. This pattern, as well, licenses a great wealth of formations from a quantitative perspective, accounting for 238 different three-noun compounds.

8.4 Can productivity be specified semantically? — 171

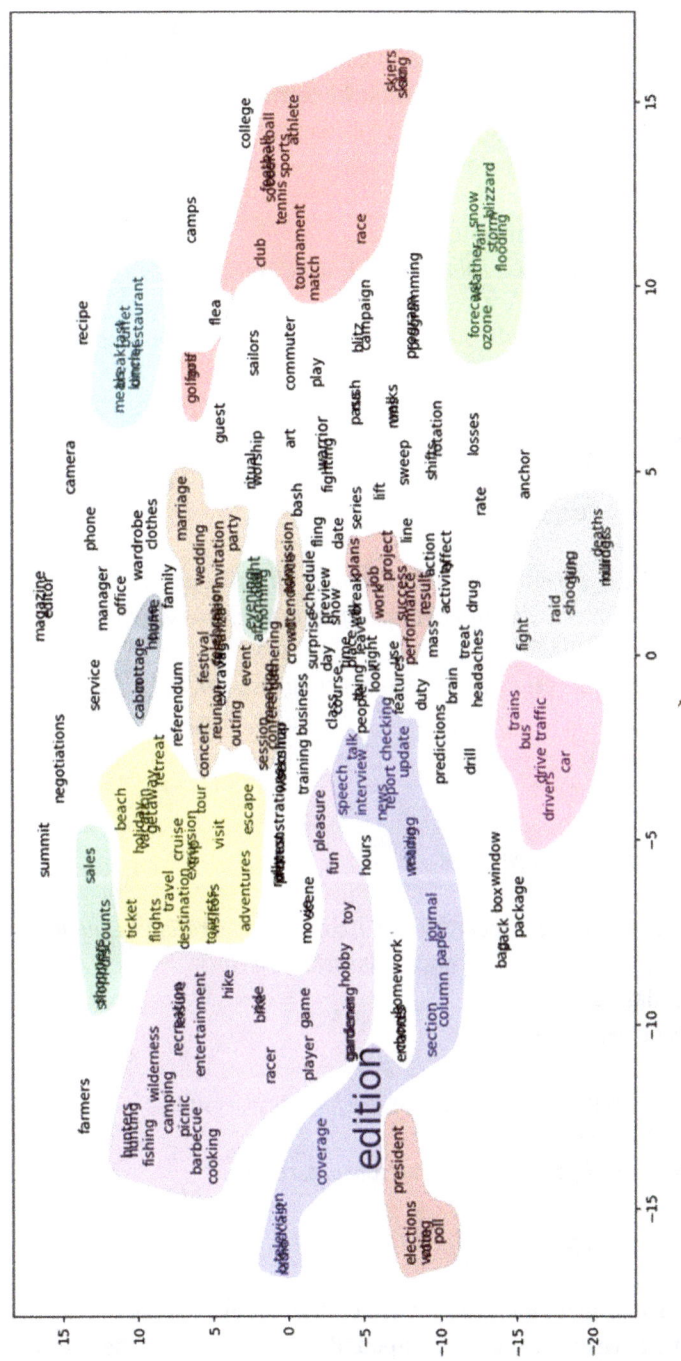

**Figure 20:** Semantic map of head nouns in the pattern 'weekend + N'.

The figure shows that the semantic range covered by the slot-fillers in this pattern is relatively broad. The nouns cover a variety of concepts that are part of the frame WEEKEND, ranging from *weekend blizzard, weekend elections* and *weekend beach* to *weekend traffic*. Still, there are various areas where accumulations can be recognized among the head nouns, which can be related to the following fields:

- WEATHER PHENOMENA (highlighted in green):
  *forecast, ozone, weather, snow, rain, blizzard, storm, flooding*
- SPORTS (red):
  *golf, club, football, basketball, soccer, tennis, sports, athlete, tournament, match, race, skiers, ski, skiing*
- ACTIVITIES AND LEISURE TIME (purple):
  *hunters, hunting, fishing, wilderness, camping, picnic, barbecue, cooking, recreation, leisure, entertainment, hike, bike, ride, racer, player, game, hobby, gardening, toy, fun, pleasure*
- NEWS COVERAGE (blue):
  *television, broadcast, coverage, edition, section, column, journal, paper, writing, reading, news, report, update, checking, speech, talk, interview*
- TRAVELLING/HOLIDAY (yellow):
  *beach, holiday, vacation, getaway, retreat, ticket, flights, travel, cruise, destination, excursion, trip, tourists, visitors, visit, adventures, escape*
- TRANSPORTATION (pink):
  *trains, bus, drive, drivers, car, traffic*
- POLITICS (red):
  *poll, elections, voting, president, vote*
- EVENTS (brown):
  *marriage, wedding, invitation, party, festival, concert, celebration, reunion, session, event, festivities, guest, attendance, admission, meeting*
- PLACES TO STAY (dark grey):
  *cabin, cottage, home, house*
- WORK (red):
  *job, work, plans, meeting, project, success, performance, result*
- FOOD (turquoise):
  *meals, breakfast, lunch, dinner, buffet, restaurant, recipe*
- CONFLICTS (grey):
  *fight, raid, shooting, gun, deaths, killings, murders*

Clearly, there are some semantic areas in which the pattern '*weekend* + N' has produced more instances of tripartite compounds than in others. The areas of news coverage, activities and leisure time, for example, host a high number of three-noun compounds formed with this pattern, just as well as the areas denoting concepts related to travelling and events taking place at the weekend. It can thus reasonably be claimed that the pattern *'weekend* + N' shows different degrees of productivity in the various semantic areas.

The next example is a considerably less productive pattern, namely *'birthday* + N', which has produced 71 types of three-noun compounds. Figure 21 is an illustration of the nouns that occur as heads in this pattern.

Although the number of words in this map is comparatively small, it is possible to identify clusters in the semantic frame opened by *birthday*. They can be related to the following concepts:
- FOOD (highlighted in pink):
  *luncheon, cake, dessert, dinner, lunch, tea, picnic, feast, supper, meal*
- EVENTS (yellow):
  *event, party, gala, concert, fete, festival, celebration, parade, anniversary, festivities*
- CLOTHES (orange):
  *hat, suit, dress*
- TIME (green):
  *year, month, week, weekend, time*
- PERSONS (purple):
  *boy, girl, baby, child*
- DECORATION (blue):
  *flowers, candle, decorations*

Based on this clustering, it can be claimed that nouns that denote different types of food are comparatively productive in the pattern *'birthday* + N', as well as nouns denoting different kinds of events. As the objects that can be given as a present on a birthday are quite diverse (e.g. *money, bike, card, book, ball*), the majority of the remaining head nouns is semantically less strongly connected.

The last pattern that will be examined is that of *'roadside* + N'. The graphic in Figure 22 displays the 66 different nouns that have been employed as heads in this pattern.

A large proportion of the outer nouns that are used in this pattern can be grouped into semantic areas. The different clusters that can be identified in this semantic map denote aspects that can be related to the following areas:
- LANDSCAPE (marked in green):
  *weed, grass, vegetation, trees, flowers, landscape*
- ESTABLISHMENTS FOR SLEEPING/EATING AND GOODS SOLD (purple):
  *tavern, inns, shop, café, bar, restaurant, diners, coffee, food, fruit, motel, hotel*

**174** — 8 Productivity in complex compounding

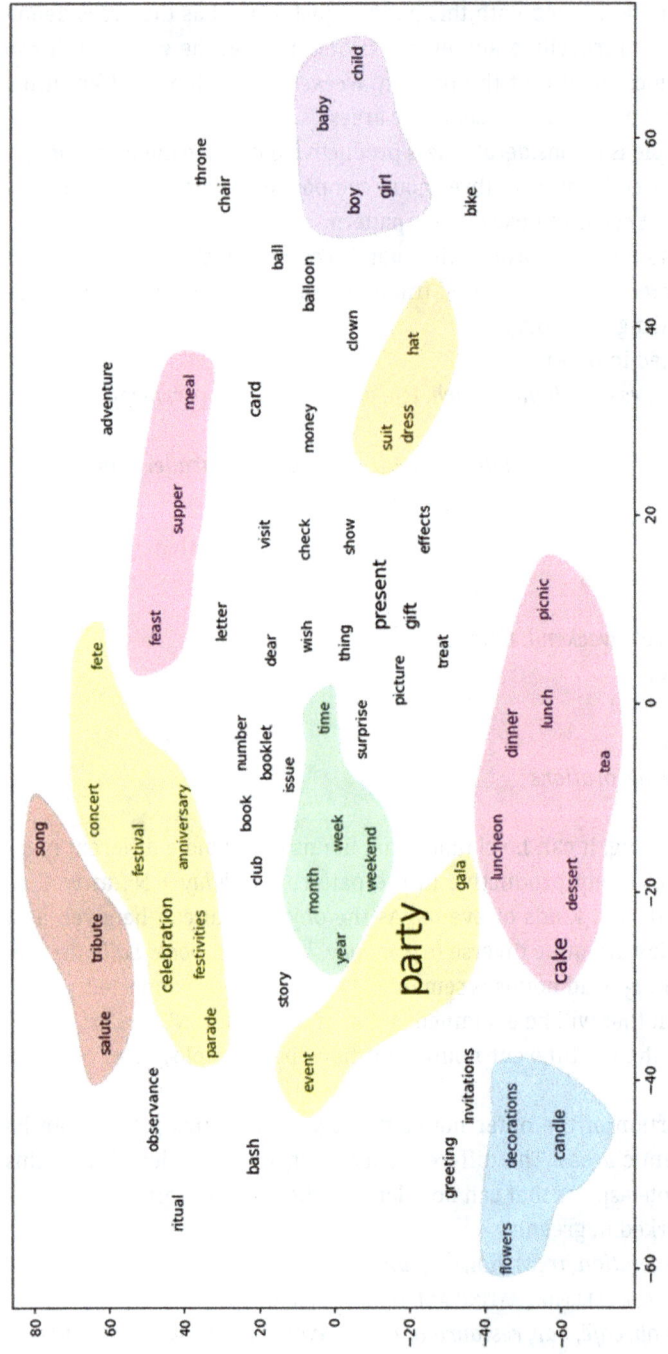

**Figure 21:** Semantic map of head nouns in the pattern 'birthday + N'.

8.4 Can productivity be specified semantically? — 175

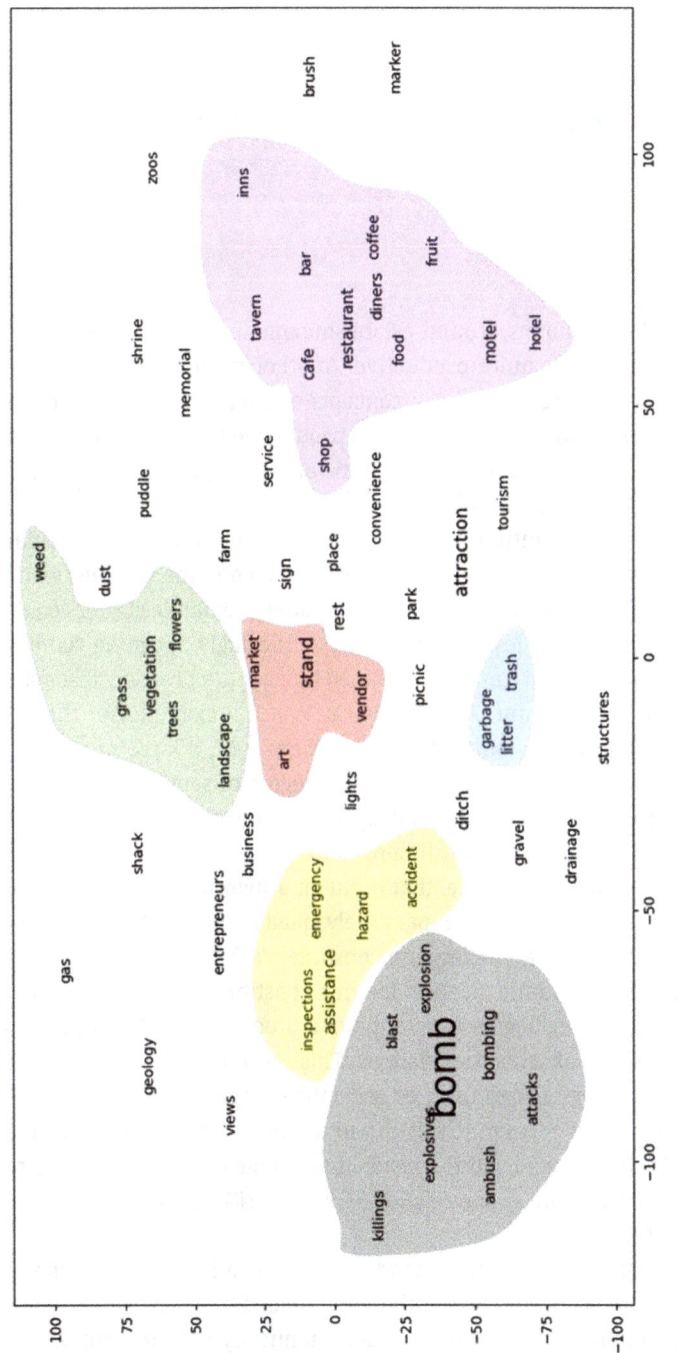

**Figure 22:** Semantic map of head nouns in the pattern '*roadside* + N'.

- STANDS (red):
  *market, stand, vendor, art*
- ATTACKS (grey):
  *killings, blast, explosives, explosion, bomb, bombing, ambush, attacks*
- CAR PROBLEMS (yellow):
  *accident, hazard, emergency, assistance*
- LEFTOVERS (blue):
  *garbage, litter, trash*

The concentration of head nouns around establishments for sleeping and eating indicates that this category is quite productive. Another productive category is presented by nouns revolving around the concepts of explosion and landscape. This observation demonstrates that even for less productive patterns it is possible to specify their productivity to particular semantic areas in which these patterns are used more productively than in others.

This insight into the semantic range filled by the head nouns in particular patterns has demonstrated that the semantic similarity among the slot-fillers of a pattern can vary greatly. At the same time, for each pattern semantic clusters could be identified that are more and less strongly filled. Accordingly, it can be claimed that the productivity of a pattern can be determined much more precisely if semantic aspects are taken into account. As demonstrated at the examples of the extremely productive patterns *'football* + N' and *'weekend* + N', a large number of outer nouns does not necessarily impede a certain degree of semantic coherence among these items. This insight is not fully unexpected. Tarasova (2013) investigates the semantic relations of compound constituents and finds that compounds whose constituents have large family sizes (i.e. that occur in a high number of different compounds) still tend to instantiate a comparatively small set of semantic relations. She arrives at the conclusion that the larger a constituent's family size is, the more dominant is one specific semantic relation for this constituent in different compounds. Accordingly, a higher degree of quantitative productivity does not necessarily entail a wider range of semantic relations. This result can be understood to be supported by the findings gained here, as semantically similar head nouns can be expected to hold a similar semantic relation to the modifier compound. In the pattern *'football* + N', for example, all the heads that denote clothes are related to the compound *football* by means of the relation FOR PLAYING, which expresses the purpose of these items.

Before I can conclude this section, I intend to give insight into a further aspect of semantic productivity. With the help of the word embedding application, I also compared the semantic maps for patterns with semantically similar compounds, namely *'football* + N', *'basketball* + N', *'baseball* + N' and *'volleyball* + N'. These patterns have quite different degrees of quantitative productivity: while *football* forms 238 types of three-noun compounds, *baseball* forms 253 items, volleyball 37 and *basketball* 189. A comparison of the heads these compounds are used with shows that they tend to combine with similar nouns. All four patterns, for example, feature clusters for persons, locations and equipment among their head nouns. This indicates that while semantically similar words might not have the same degree of quantitative productivity, they tend to have a similar semantic productivity. This impression is in line with the results of Hein and Engelberg (2018). They investigate the heads of German compounds and find that the semantic proximity of nouns does not necessarily lead to a similar degree of productivity but instead to comparable patterns of compounding.

To summarize, this section has enriched the concept of productivity by adding a semantic perspective to the predominantly quantitative approaches to this phenomenon. It has demonstrated that there are valuable insights to be gained on the productivity of the patterns that give rise to three-noun compounds by not just looking at the number of items they form, but by further specifying the semantic areas in which these patterns are more and less productive. This way, a more adequate description of the productivity of a word-formation pattern can be provided. The insights of this section are relevant beyond the present research question and will be drawn on again in Section 8.8.

## 8.5 What distinguishes productive compounds from unproductive ones?

Section 8.2 has shown that compounds differ greatly in their productivity in forming more complex compounds. What are the principles that govern this different behaviour? This section will be dedicated to exploring in what aspects productive compounds differ from less productive ones by investigating variables that might give rise to differences in compound productivity.

The prerequisite of productivity is of course an onomasiological demand, as the motivation for the formation of new items is mostly concept-driven, motivated by speakers perceiving a gap in the lexicon. This language-external factor is understood as a crucial basis for speakers to make productive use of compounds in the first place. On these grounds, this section will test for linguistic criteria that can explain why some compounds are more suitable for the formation of complex compounds than others.

I will draw on variables that have been reported to be influential in previous studies that investigate the productivity of base words in derivation or the productivity of lexemes in simple compounds. Hein and Engelberg (2018), for example, have compared a small sample of German colour compounds and report an influence of the frequency of a lexeme on its productivity as a head in these compounds: frequent words are used more productively as compound heads than infrequent ones. Hein and Engelberg furthermore provide a sound and detailed compilation of potential factors that might have an influence on the degree to which words are employed in compounds (2018: 42). Building on this, Hein and Brunner (2019) investigate the role of morphological complexity in compound productivity, finding that simple words are used more often as heads in German compounds than derivatives or compounds themselves. Krott et al. (1999) examine what kinds of words act as bases in derivation and compounding in Dutch. Their study reports similar results: shorter words (measured in number of phonemes or morphemes) and more frequently used words serve more often as input for further word-formation processes.

The following subsections will investigate whether these variables hold true for productivity in complex compounding. Section 8.5.1 will test whether the length and morphological complexity of a compound is related to its productivity. Section 8.5.2 will examine to what extent a compound's frequency has an influence on its usage in tri-constituent compounds. In Section 8.5.3, an additional potential variable will be explored that is not based on the literature but is suspected to be influential when it comes to the productivity of compounds as opposed to that of simple words, namely the association strength that holds between the components of a compound.

The data used to test these variables was exported from the 3N database and the offline database of COCA. As compounds with different degrees of productivity needed to be contrasted, a random sample of 150 two-noun compounds was drawn from the list of items that act as embedded compounds in the 3N database. Not all figures required for the operationalization of the three criteria were available in the 3N database, which is why the offline database of COCA was additionally used for the extraction of the relevant figures. In order to receive coherent figures, the productivity values (i.e. the number of types formed by a particular two-noun compound) were calculated from COCA's offline data as well, which entails that the type frequencies in the following sections will not be in accordance with those shown in previous sections but will be considerably higher, as the type frequencies used so far are based on the n-gram set, which is smaller than COCA's offline database.

### 8.5.1 Formal complexity

This section will examine the formal complexity as a potential factor of influence for a compound's degree of productivity. It will contrast more and less productive compounds regarding their length and morphological constituents. If the results of the studies cited above are transferrable to compounds, productive compounds should be shorter and contain fewer morphological constituents than less productive ones. In order to test this expectation, the morphophonological and morphosyntactic properties of the 150 compounds in the sample were determined. Their length and morphological complexity were operationalized analogously to what was done in Section 6.1 in terms of syllables and morphemes. Productivity again was measured through the number of types of three-noun compounds formed by a particular two-noun compound. Figure 23 displays a scatterplot for the sample items, relating the productivity of a compound to its number of syllables on the one hand (left side) and to its number of morphological constituents on the other (right side).

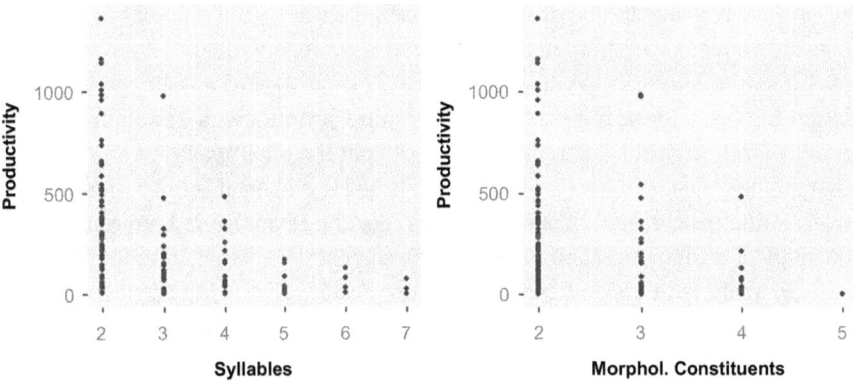

**Figure 23:** Relationship between productivity and formal complexity.

The left picture shows that compounds with a large number of syllables yield low productivity scores, while those compounds with high productivity scores mostly tend to consist of two syllables. A similar situation is found for the relation between productivity and the number of morphemes in the right picture, as items with a higher number of morphological constituents are concentrated in lower productivity areas, while those compounds with high productivity values tend to consist of two morphemes only. Adding up these two observations suggests that compounds with high productivity values are those that consist of two morphemes and two syllables only, i.e. compounds that are composed of two monomorphemic and monosyllabic nouns, while compounds in lower productivity areas tend to be longer and more complex. Consequently, from a purely descriptive perspective, the impression is confirmed that compounds with a low degree of formal complexity are more productive in forming tri-constituent compounds.

Of course, the two variables of length and morphological complexity are not independent of each other: the more complex a word is, the more likely it is to be longer, i.e. to have more syllables. A statistical evaluation of the data confirms that there is a significant positive relation between these two variables (rho = 0.61, p < 0.005), which affirms that those compounds that comprise more syllables also have more morphological constituents. A qualitative look at the data shows that there are barely any short compounds with a comparatively high number of morphological constituents (e.g. *growth curve, strength training, newsmaker*), while there are quite some long compounds with a comparatively low degree of morphological complexity (e.g. *emergency room, teacher education, video cassette, carbon dioxide, pollution control, internet service, energy conservation*). This suggests that increasing length is a corollary of increasing morphological complexity, rendering morphological complexity the more dominant factor.

A statistical evaluation of the relationship between productivity and morphological complexity with a Spearman's correlation test delivers a result of rho = −0.32, with a significant p-value (p < 0.005). This means there is a negative correlation between these two variables: the more productive a compound is, the fewer morphological constituents it has, or – put the other way round – the more morphological constituents a compound has, the less likely it is to be used productively. Still, this correlation is rather weak. For the relationship between the productivity of a compound and its length, the correlation coefficient amounts to rho = −0.57, again with a significant p-value (p < 0.005). This result suggests that the more syllables a compound has, the less productive it is. Based on the stronger correlation efficient yielded for the relation between length and productivity as compared to morphological complexity and productivity, a compound's length seems to be the more decisive predictor for its productivity. Considering that it was reported above that there are barely short compounds which are morphologically complex but long compounds which are morphologically simple, this suggests that if the length of a compound increases, this has a negative influence on its productivity only if the increasing length comes with further morphemes. Long compounds that are still relatively uncomplex from a morphological perspective can still be productive, as can be seen at the examples of *air quality, carbon dioxide* or *death penalty*, each of which can be categorized as a fairly productive compound.

It can thus be concluded that the higher a compound's number of syllables and morphological constituents, the lower its productivity. This result is in line with the studies cited above, confirming the general trend that shorter and morphologically less complex lexemes are used more often as input for further word-formation processes. This result, however, does not imply that unproductive compounds are automatically long and complex. A look back at Figure 23 shows that the relation does not necessarily work both ways: compounds with low productivity values can consist of two morphologically simple and monosyllabic nouns. Obviously, not all compounds that are short and morphologically simple are automatically used productively, presumably because there is no onomasiological demand to denote concepts in the semantic frame of these compounds. Nevertheless, since long and morphologically highly complex compounds are clearly not very productive, being short and containing two morphemes only seems to be a beneficial condition for compounds to be used productively.

As correlation does not necessarily express causation, it cannot be claimed at this point that the morphological complexity and length of a compound actually have an influence on a compound's productivity; it can merely be stated that those compounds that are used productively are those that show a minimum degree of formal complexity. It will, however, be argued in the next section why these features can be assumed to be cognitively relevant and might thus not just be a symptom of productive elements but rather a cause for their productivity.

### 8.5.2 Frequency

As reported on page 178, previous studies find that higher-frequency words tend to occur more often as input in word-formation processes than lower-frequency ones. Research on the processing of complex words has confirmed this tendency, explaining that complex words that are used frequently have a processing advantage over lower-frequency complex words (Bertram et al. 2000; Jong et al. 2000). Of course, the frequency of a word is not independent of the two variables examined in the previous section. Simple and short words are used more frequently than longer, morphologically complex words, as they are easier to produce and recognize (Zipf 1935; Krott et al. 1999; Baayen 2005: 250–252). Accordingly, I expect to find a correlation between a compound's degree of productivity and its frequency.

To verify this expectation, a Python-script was programmed that searches the offline version of COCA for the occurrences of the 150 compounds in the sample. Importantly, the tokens counted for the compound frequencies are not the overall occurrences of the respective compounds but only the occurrences of the compounds by themselves, as otherwise the two variables would work with dependent figures. Thus, what will be referred to as "compound frequency" is not the total frequency of a compound, as it does not include its occurrences as an embedded compound in complex compounds, but only those occurrences where the compound is not followed or preceded by further nouns.

The scatterplot in Figure 24 displays the relation between a compound's frequency and its productivity in forming three-noun compounds, based on logarithmic transformation of the data.

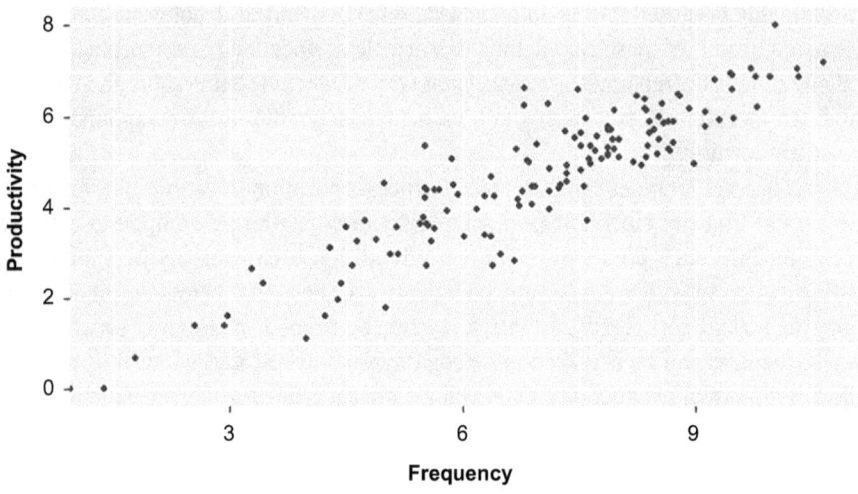

**Figure 24:** Relationship between productivity and frequency.

The graph quite clearly portrays a linear dependency for the two variables: the higher the frequency of a compound, the higher its degree of productivity. There are no items in the sample that are frequent but unproductive, or items that are highly productive but infrequent. A statistical evaluation via a Spearman's test delivers a correlation coefficient of rho = 0.88 with a significant p-value ($p < 0.005$). These figures confirm that there is a strong positive correlation between productivity and compound frequency: the more frequently a compound is used, the more likely it is to be employed as a base for complex compounds, while infrequent compounds are unlikely to be utilized for further compound formation.

However, it must be pointed out that based on these results it cannot be claimed that all compounds that are used frequently will be productive in forming three-noun compounds. Obviously, the 3N database only contains two-noun compounds that have formed at least one complex compound. It does not contain two-noun compounds that have never been combined with any other noun. Therefore, it is possible that there are highly frequent two-noun compounds that are fully unproductive and that are consequently not part of the database. Accordingly, the conclusion needs to be formulated more carefully, as strictly speaking it can only be stated that those compounds that are infrequent are not productive, and that those compounds that are highly productive must be frequent. For the sake of simplicity, in the remainder of this work I will claim that compounds that are used more frequently are more productive; however, this includes the reservation that I am referring only to those compounds that have acted as embedded compounds in a three-noun compound.

Based on the high degree of correlation, the frequency of a compound seems to be a strong predictor for its productivity. One reason for the explanatory power of this variable is presumably found in the connection between word frequency and the extra-linguistic world. It was pointed out at the beginning of Section 8.5 that productivity is co-determined by socio-cultural needs. The frequency of a word is a good mirror of the extra-linguistic relevance of the concept it describes, as frequent words can be assumed to represent salient concepts. The relevance of a concept in the extra-linguistic world has an impact on the productivity of the respective word, as it creates the possibility of naming further instances in the semantic frame denoted by that word. Salient ontological concepts can be assumed to open up a broader frame of roles for protagonists, ideas, objects or circumstances to be named within that frame than less salient concepts. The compound *health care*, for example, is much more frequent than *body mass*, which entails that it describes a more salient concept. Accordingly, in the semantic frame related to this concept there is more room for fillers in the form of heads or modifiers. *Health care* opens up quite a broad semantic frame with many different roles to be named, e.g. the people who provide it or the financial aspects related to providing it. In the semantic frame of *body mass*, by contrast, there are fewer roles to be named due to the lower salience of the concept it describes. If one day the activities and referents related to the concept of *body mass* should increase, this might trigger the productivity of this compound. Before contenting myself with frequency as a valid explanation for compound productivity, I would like to bring into play another factor that could potentially be even more influential when it comes to explaining the productivity of compounds.

### 8.5.3 Association strength

The variables examined so far are those that have been suggested in the literature and are based on studies that test the productivity of simple words. As the present study is concerned with the productivity of compounds, I aim to test a further variable that has not been used in productivity studies so far, guided by a qualitative analysis of the compounds in the sample. In contrasting compounds with different degrees of productivity, there are some aspects that are striking, which I will outline briefly before conceptualizing the different features with a measurable criterion.

The first noticeable aspect when comparing compounds that rank high in productivity with those that rank rather low is that the former are overwhelmingly spelt as one orthographic unit (e.g. *birthday, basketball, network*), while less productive compounds tend to consist of two orthographic words (e.g. *pain tolerance, research paper, flood relief*). As previously discussed, compound spelling is not necessarily reliable in English (cf. Section 6.3). Still, I claim that in the majority of compounds that have been shown to be productive, no native speaker would hesitate to spell them as one orthographic unit, while the majority of unproductive ones would probably never be realized in this format. This goes along with the impression that the formal side of more productive compounds seems more conventionalized, as they cannot be substituted with an equivalent phrase, while this is possible for some at least of the unproductive ones (cf. *child safety: safety of the child; pain tolerance: tolerance of pain*; versus *football:* \**ball for foot, network:* \**work in nets*). The same is true for the semantic side: while the meaning of less productive compounds tend to be highly compositional, most of the productive compounds are lexicalized to some degree (e.g. a *football* is not any ball played with the foot, while *child safety* is largely synonymous with 'the safety of a child'). As a corollary of these aspects, more productive compounds are those that are highly likely to be found in a dictionary. It is generally agreed that listedness is not necessarily an informative criterion in compounding (Di Sciullo and Williams 1990: 14; Bauer 1998: 68); however, in addition to capturing lexicalization and thus reflecting the need to explain the meaning of a word, a dictionary entry hints at the socio-cultural need for a concept.

To summarize these observations, those compounds that are more productive tend to fulfil more of the attributes of typical compounds: they are lexicalized to some degree, spelt as one unit and are semantically different from the combination of their components. By contrast, unproductive ones are overwhelmingly spelt as two orthographic words and tend to be both formally and semantically replaceable by a paraphrase. These differences are of course not categorical, as can be seen in the cases of *health care*, a productive compound that is not spelt as an orthographic unit, and *keyword*, which represents a typical compound judging from its formal and semantic features but is not very productive. Still, these commonalities are too striking to go unnoticed. It is, of course, conceivable that these attributes are merely by-products of high frequency and thus might not be independent of the variable of frequency tested in the previous section. Still, it is the goal of this section to examine whether a higher degree of compound typicality can be turned into a testable criterion that is able to account for compound productivity more reliably than bare compound frequency.

In the search for a concept that encompasses the attributes listed above, I have come to focus on the fact that more typical compounds are both formally and semantically more of a unit than less typical ones, featuring more proximity between their components. The proximity between *foot* and *ball* in *football*, for example, is felt to be stronger than that between *witness* and *protection* in *witness protection*. Based on this background, I hypothesize that the bonds between the elements of a compound are stronger in productive compounds than in less productive ones. To test this hypothesis, first the bonds that hold between compound constituents will be measured in Section 8.5.3.1, before the relation to productivity can be tested in Section 8.5.3.2.

### 8.5.3.1 Measuring the proximity between compound constituents

In linguistics, the bonds between the components of multi-word units are focused on most prominently in the area of collocations. In collocation research, the joint occurrence of words is commonly assessed through association measures, which quantify the amount of "glue" between linguistic items, as Evert (2005: 20) nicely describes. The resulting association scores mirror the strength with which a sequence of words is connected. Evert points out that not all forms of joint appearance are statistically significant: a high absolute frequency of a word pair does not automatically mean that the bond between the elements is remarkably strong. If the constituents of a frequent multi-word unit occur very frequently themselves, their joint occurrence might not be very remarkable. For this reason, proposals on association strength do not employ frequency-based measures but prefer statistical measurements that take into account the individual frequencies of the constituents. Thus, if two words that are frequent independently also co-occur together frequently, this co-occurrence will be treated as less important than the co-occurrence of words that mainly occur together but are only infrequently used by themselves (cf. Evert 2005: 20–21). Based on the occurrences of the constituents outside of the combination, statistical association measures calculate an expected frequency for the multi-word unit, which is related to its actual observed frequency. Setting these figures in relation to the occurrences of other potential sequences with the same form, permits normalizing the frequencies and thus evaluating the statistical significance of the co-occurrence.

This procedure has to my knowledge never been applied to measure the association strength between the constituents of compounds, although it seems to be fully suitable for this purpose. The next sections will explain how association measures were used to assess the different degrees of proximity between the constituents of the 150 compounds in the sample. As the selection of the relevant usage frequencies turned out to be highly complex and entailed many decisions, it will be presented in greater detail.

#### 8.5.3.1.1 Data and search details

In order to measure the association strength of the compounds, co-occurrence data needed to be obtained for the 150 items in the sample. As the relevant figures could not be extracted from the 3N database, COCA's offline database was employed. The usage frequencies required from the corpus for each compound in the sample are the following:
- frequency of the bigram (e.g. frequency of the combination *health care*)

- frequency of the first word without the second word (e.g. occurrences of *health* without being followed by *care*)
- frequency of the second word without the first one (e.g. occurrences of *care* without being preceded by *health*)

These usage frequencies are required for the arrangement of a 2x2 contingency table. To normalize these absolute frequencies, they need to be set in relation to the remaining noun-bigrams of the corpus, i.e. the number of noun-noun sequences not containing the bigram or any of the noun constituents. Table 29 illustrates the contingency table for the example of *health care*:

**Table 29:** Contingency table for *health care*.

|  | N2 | Not N2 |
|---|---|---|
| **N1** | (i) Bigram<br>i.e. *health care* | (ii) N1 without N2<br>i.e. *health* not followed by *care* |
| **Not N1** | (iii) N2 without N1<br>i.e. *care* not preceded by *health* | (iv) Other noun-noun combinations<br>i.e. noun-noun sequences which contain neither *health* nor *care* |

The relevant frequencies for measuring the association strength of the compound *health care* are (i) all occurrences of the sequence *health care* in the singular, the plural and different spellings, (ii) all occurrences of *health* not followed by *care*, as well as (iii) all occurrences of *care* not preceded by *health*. The fourth figure (iv) is the remaining number of noun-noun combinations in the corpus, i.e. all sequences of two nouns that contain neither the word *health* nor the word *care*.

The respective usage frequencies were extracted from COCA's offline database with the help of a self-programmed Python-script. The input for the code was the list of 150 sample compounds in the singular and with separate spelling, i.e. in the orthographic format N N, e.g. *health care*. The code was run in Python 3.5 and accessed the "text" directory as well as the "word_lemma_PoS" directory from COCA's offline data set. The output file is a text document listing the required usage frequencies per two-noun sequence for the fields (i) to (iii). The number of noun-noun sequences relevant for field (iv) was calculated on the basis of the 2-gram dataset. Before the usage frequencies computed by the code could be evaluated statistically, extensive manual refinement was necessary due to various issues that will be presented in the following section.

### 8.5.3.1.2 Searching for frequencies of compound constituents

Collecting usage frequencies for compounds requires more effort than acquiring usage frequencies for collocations, as determining the frequencies of the compound constituents outside the bigram for fields (ii) and (iii) presents a major issue. Generally, these frequencies are yielded through a simple calculation, as they consist of the overall frequency of the respective word minus the tokens of the bigram. Accordingly, in collocations and other kinds of multi-word units, the individual word can be searched for and the bigram tokens need to be subtracted from the overall frequency of that word. This procedure works just as well for compounds whose constituents solely occur in open spelt compounds. Determining the figure for field (ii) for the compound *health care*, for instance, requires a simple query for the lexeme *health*. This query delivers the overall frequency of *health* from which the bigram frequency of *health care* must be subtracted. The query for *health* will contain all occurrences of *health*, including those where *health* appears as part of other compounds (e.g. *health insurance, health problems, health benefits*). The problem is posed by lexemes that also occur in compounds that are spelt as one orthographic unit. In determining the figure for field (ii) for the compound *football*, for example, simply searching for *foot* in order to determine its overall frequency would lack all occurrences in which *foot* is used in solid spelt compounds (e.g. *footprint, footstep, footwork*). However, in order to be able to determine how significant the occurrence of *ball* after *foot* is, it is vital to know how many times *foot* is followed by a noun that is not *ball*, including those instances in which it combines with other nouns in solid spelt compounds.

This insight has methodological implications, as a code that is written to search for words, i.e. units defined through spaces before and after, produces wrong word frequencies. To explain the impact of this aspect, I will demonstrate the word-based frequency search for the first constituent of *basketball*. A search for the word *basket* yields a token frequency of 9,820. This number only accounts for the usage of *basket* in isolation and does not include its occurrences in solid spelt compounds like *basketball*. In some cases, this discrepancy might be negligibly small; for *basket*, however, it is substantial, as in *basketball* alone it is found 22,004 times. Using these flawed numbers to determine the field (ii) for the contingency table to calculate the association strength of *basketball* would entail subtracting the bigram frequency from the alleged overall frequency of *basket*, i.e. 9,820 minus 22,004, which would result in a negative frequency. For this reason, contrary to the procedure used in acquiring frequencies for the constituents of collocations, a word-based search is not an adequate approach for calculating the frequencies of compound constituents.

Accordingly, a different methodology is required that can detect lexemes that occur in solid spelt compounds. This is severely complicated by the fact that the constituents of compounds are not tagged as such in COCA (cf. Section 4.2.2), which is why they can only be detected through a string-based search. A search for strings results in different kinds of issues. While the results in word-based searches are too narrow, the results in a search for strings are too extensive and thus require substantial manual screening.[20] A script that searches for words as parts of other words with a string-based procedure obviously lists all words that contain a particular string as a potential instance of that string. This is especially problematic for short words and/or words with several senses. In a search for instances of the word *line*, for example (in order to determine the single word frequency for field (iii) for the compound *baseline*), the script yields an extreme number of results, identifying more than 500 different instances that supposedly contain the word *line*, such as *vaseline, lineage, matriline, masculine, manliness* and *discipline*. All of these matches are obviously false positives that are not related to the word in question and thus need to be sorted out manually as their frequencies must not be added to the word frequency of *line*. Despite the enormous amount of manual inspection entailed in a string-based search, this procedure guarantees more precise single word frequencies for the cells of the contingency table than a word-based search and is thus deemed the more suitable approach.

There is another intricacy that renders the precise calculation of word frequencies of compound constituents difficult. This aspect is not caused by string-based searching but would also occur in a word-based search. Even in cases where the instances found by the code contain the noun searched for and yield actual compounds in which the constituent is contained, it can be hard to decide which occurrences should be accepted as an instance of the respective lexeme. To continue with the example of *line*, compare the following compounds in which the script finds the constituent *line*: *guideline, airline, gasoline, headline, outline, hotline, deadline*. Are all of these compounds instantiations of the word *line*, i.e. should their token frequencies be counted in the overall frequency of *line*? While the sorting of false positives portrayed in the previous paragraph is merely an issue of effort, these cases, where semantic nuances are in focus, are obviously more complex to solve. In the decision-making process about which of the compounds listed by the script should be counted as an instantiation of the respective word, the OED was consulted to determine whether the compound constituent could be categorized as polysemous or homonymous to the word in question. In the case of polysemy, the respective words were counted as instances and their frequencies were added to the overall frequency of the respective word. In those cases where the OED was not

---

**20** The option of having the code search for strings that are at the same time identified as nouns was rejected based on the experiences described in Section 4.2.2.

helpful, the decision was based on the assessment of the relatedness between the meaning of the word and that of the compound constituent.

The decision making is especially difficult for nouns that have several senses or vague and unspecific meanings, such as *base* or *board*. In the case of *baseball*, for example, can all compounds containing *base* as a constituent, such as *database* or *baseline*, be categorized as an instantiation of *base*? Obviously, in many cases the meanings of compound constituents are not discrete and clearly delineable, which makes it hard to evaluate which formal instances are tokens of the same type and thus which frequencies need to be included or excluded. This kind of individual decision-making renders the procedure impractical and makes the results subjective and debatable.

### 8.5.3.1.3 Results and discussion

Once accurate usage frequencies had been obtained for all items in the sample, the statistical significance of the co-occurrence data could be evaluated. The methods most commonly used for the statistical analysis of the co-occurrence data are the $G^2$-test from the log-likelihood test, T-scores and Z-scores. In this project, the $G^2$-test was employed. Evert (2005: 137) points out that the log-likelihood test does not actually measure the effect size of the association. Accordingly, if it is used as an indication of association strength, its results must be interpreted relatively. The scores thus allow comparing the compounds in the sample with regard to the association strength between their constituents: higher values indicate a higher degree of association strength, i.e. a stronger bond between the components, while lower values indicate a comparatively weaker bond between the constituents of the respective compound.

Table 30 gives an insight into the association scores for exemplary compounds. To ensure visibility, the results are only displayed for a part of the

**Table 30:** Association scores for exemplary compounds.

|    | Compound    | Association score |
|----|-------------|-------------------|
| 1  | network     | 464,323           |
| 2  | health care | 379,530           |
| 3  | newspaper   | 342,194           |
| 4  | weekend     | 260,239           |
| 5  | baseball    | 242,312           |
| 6  | classroom   | 230,054           |
| 7  | football    | 210,044           |
| 8  | bedroom     | 152,410           |
| 9  | credit card | 102,104           |
| 10 | birthday    | 100,754           |

**Table 30** (continued)

|    | Compound            | Association score |
|----|---------------------|-------------------|
| 11 | health food         | 1,481             |
| 12 | money market        | 1,221             |
| 13 | air defense         | 1,181             |
| 14 | home loan           | 1,118             |
| 15 | career counselling  | 1,113             |
| 16 | teacher certification | 1,014           |
| 17 | growth curve        | 633               |
| 18 | wartime             | 547               |
| 19 | energy storage      | 517               |
| 20 | crisis pregnancy    | 304               |

sample, namely for ten compounds with comparatively high association scores (items 1 to 10), followed by ten items with low scores (items 11 to 20).

The table shows that compounds differ greatly regarding the strength with which their components are connected. There are compounds like *network, health care* and *newspaper*, for example, which show a relatively high association strength. This means that their components are quite strongly connected. By contrast, in compounds with low association scores, such as *crisis pregnancy* or *energy storage*, the strength of association between the constituents is considerably weaker. These results confirm that there are measurable differences in the strength of the bonds that hold between the components of compounds. Having quantified the association strength of the compounds in the sample, it is of interest whether these different degrees of proximity can account for differences in productivity.

#### 8.5.3.2 Relation between association strength and productivity

Are those compounds that show a higher association strength between their constituents more productive in forming three-noun compounds? At this point, one might raise the question of whether the measurements of productivity and association strength are independent in the first place, as both work with the occurrences of the two-noun compound in three-noun compounds. To clarify, association strength uses the overall frequency of a compound for the first field of the contingency table. This bigram frequency includes those occurrences in more complex formations, i.e. also the tokens in three-noun compounds. Productivity, only encompasses the number of types of three-noun compounds in which a compound occurs but not the tokens, which is why these two variables are not directly related. It can be assumed that compounds that form more types of three-noun compounds also account for more tokens. However, as there are also compounds that form few types but yield relatively high token frequencies, this connection is not necessarily a given.

Figure 25 is a visual presentation of the relationship between the association strength in a compound and its productivity in forming three-noun compounds for the 150 items in the sample, with logarithmic transformation of the data.

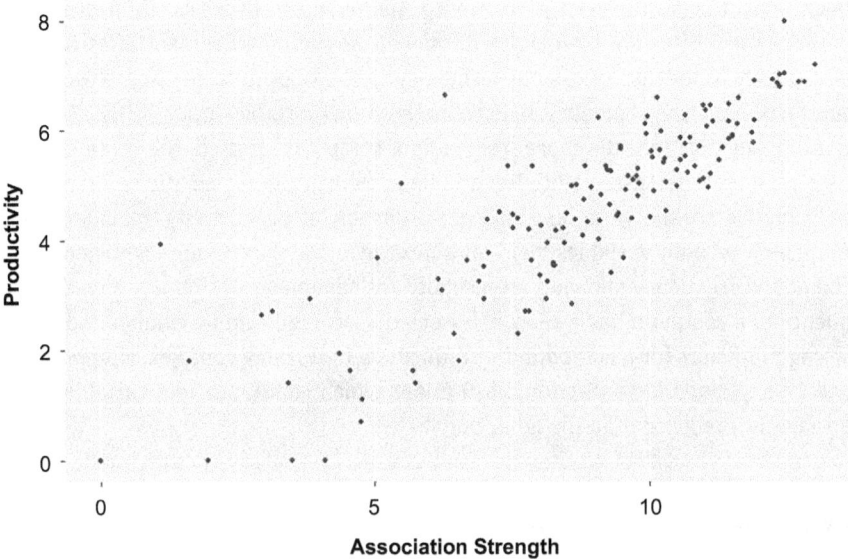

**Figure 25:** Relationship between productivity and association strength.

From a purely descriptive perspective, the plot indicates that the two variables tend to correlate positively: there seems to be a tendency for stronger association scores to be in accordance with higher degrees of productivity. The plot thus suggests that there is a general tendency for compounds that feature a stronger bond between their components to be more productive in forming tri-constituent compounds, whereas compounds whose components are only weakly connected are less productive. This effect seems to be stronger for higher values than for lower ones, as the productivity values of items with lower association scores are quite dispersed.

To test this relation statistically, the data was analysed with a Spearman's test, which yields a correlation coefficient of rho = 0.86 with a significant p-value ($p < 0.005$). As expected, there is a strong correlation between the variables of productivity and association strength, which confirms that the degree to which a combination of two nouns is associated as a unit correlates with its tendency to become part of more complex sequences. It is clearly visible that this correlation becomes stronger the higher the association strength of the compounds is: while the 25 items with the lowest association strength yield a correlation coefficient of rho = 0.37 only, compounds with higher association scores show a linear increase in productivity.

It was addressed earlier that a strong bond between the constituents of a compound might be a side-effect of frequency. Methodologically, association strength is definitely a function of compound frequency, as the measurement of association strength includes the compound frequency in the bigram frequency. Needless to say, there is a strong correlation between these two variables (rho = 0.94). This relationship suggests that the more frequently a compound is used, the more strongly its components are associated. Nevertheless, contrary to expectations, association strength has not shown to be a stronger predictor for productivity than compound frequency, as both variables yield an almost identical correlation coefficient, with compound frequency showing an insignificant advantage. Therefore, both the frequency of a compound as well as its association strength can be claimed to be very strong predictors for a compound's productivity in forming complex compounds. It will be explained later (Section 8.6.4) under which conditions one variable might be a better predictor than the other one.

### 8.5.4 Summary and implications

Section 8.5 has been dedicated to the task of finding differences between productive compounds and less productive ones. In this context, it has identified several linguistic features that have been shown to be distinctive: productive compounds tend to be rather short words that comprise two syllables only, consist of two morphologically simple words, are used frequently by themselves and have measurably stronger bonds between their constituents. By contrast, compounds with low productivity values could be characterized as being longer in terms of syllables, containing more than two morphological constituents, being used less frequently and showing weaker bonds between their components.

Accordingly, the productivity in compounds reveals a correlational system in which word length, morphological complexity, frequency and association strength are interrelated. The reasoning behind this connection is understood as follows: compounds that are short and consist of morphologically simple constituents are used more frequently. The frequency with which a combination of two nouns is used influences the degree to which its components are associated as a unit. The following section will provide an explanation for the connection between the variables of frequency, association strength and productivity in the formation of three-noun compounds by looking into the cognitive implications of these aspects.

## 8.6 Why are some compounds used more productively than others?

The previous section has revealed that those compounds which are used productively for the formation of three-noun compounds are ones which occur frequently by themselves and, probably as a consequence, show a high degree of association strength between their components. How exactly does the frequency of a compound contribute to the growth of the bond between its components? And how do these two aspects promote the availability of a compound to become part of more complex sequences? In order to answer these questions, the users of these linguistic signs need to be included. Obviously, it is the speakers who choose which compounds they use for the formation of more complex compounds, which implies that the variables examined must have a cognitive impact that leads speakers to use some compounds rather than others. It is the aim of this section to outline to what extent the frequency of a compound and the bonds between its components have cognitive relevance that benefits its productivity.

To do so, I will draw on the ideas of cognitive and usage-based approaches to language, which model linguistic knowledge in the form of a network in which linguistic elements are systematically connected (Langacker 1987a, 1991; Croft 2001; Goldberg 2006; Booij 2010; Bybee 2010). In cognitive linguistic theory, the organization of this network is described through the idea of *entrenchment*, which explains how the use of language shapes the cognitive network. The theoretical basis of this concept will be described in Section 8.6.1. Section 8.6.2 will explain how this phenomenon can be grasped methodologically by the utilization of corpus data. On this basis, Section 8.6.3 will outline in what ways entrenchment affects more complex linguistic structures in general and compounds more specifically. Building on this, Section 8.6.4 will explain the causal relationship between the frequency of a compound, its degree of association strength and its productive use in forming three-noun compounds. Section 8.6.5 will point out implications of these results and discuss critical aspects involved in approaching the concept of entrenchment through corpus data.

### 8.6.1 The idea of entrenchment

The concept of entrenchment builds on the premise that language is based on the same fundamental psychological learning mechanisms that are vital for the development of other human skills and abilities. It encompasses several cognitive processes that are seen as driving forces in the organization of both the linguistic and the non-linguistic cognitive network, such as association, chunking, statistical learning, memory consolidation, schematization, categorization, routinization and automatization (Langacker 1987a: 65–73; Schmid 2007: 117, 2017b: 437–439). These processes are sensitive to frequency, which means that their repeated employment is a crucial factor in their development. This section will show in what ways the usage frequency of linguistic items impacts the cognitive processes that shape the way in which language is stored in the human brain.

The idea of entrenchment goes back to Langacker (1987a, 1991) and Bybee (1987), but has been further developed by Langacker (2008) and Schmid (2007, 2015, 2017b, 2020). In its basic tenets, the concept of entrenchment is based on the assumption that each token of linguistic behaviour experienced leaves a trace in a speaker's memory (Langacker 1987a: 59; Bybee 2006, 2007, 2010; Vaan et al. 2007). While the first exposure to a linguistic element results in the creation of a mental representation, encountering instantiations of this linguistic element repeatedly will carve it deeper into the long-term memory. Accordingly, its representation is increasingly strengthened, which means that its activation is facilitated. Furthermore, its formation and processing is continuously routinized, taking place in an automated way without conscious monitoring (cf. Hartsuiker and Moors 2017; Schmid 2017a: 13–16).

Entrenchment processes work both ways: linguistic elements which are encountered frequently become more strongly entrenched, while a lack of repetition results in a weakening of the degree of entrenchment and thus a reduction of the strength of representation (Langacker 1987a: 59). Linguistic elements can thus become gradually more or less entrenched over time, which is why entrenchment must not be conceived of as an either-or concept but as a gradual, scalar phenomenon (Langacker 1987a: 59; Schmid 2007: 118).[21] The increase of entrenchment is not completely linear, but the effects described are stronger in the beginning than in later exposures (Schmid 2008: 21), which means that the first encounters with a linguistic element will have a stronger impact than later encounters. Based on these processes, the concept of entrenchment conceptualizes the cognitive and neural effects of frequency. Accordingly, it does not just account for the fact that different speakers have different mental representations for the same linguistic element, but also for differences in the representation of linguistic elements in the mind of an individual.

While most usage-based approaches understand entrenchment as processes that operate on constructions (e.g. Langacker 1987a; Croft 2001; Goldberg 2003), this project will be working with a more extended understanding of entrenchment as

---

[21] Note that the term *entrenchment* describes both the cognitive processes and their output (Schmid 2017a: 10).

developed by Schmid (2020). In Schmid's account of entrenchment, this phenomenon is still understood as the "continual reorganization of linguistic knowledge caused by repeated usage activities in usage events" (Schmid 2020: 205). However, this reorganization process is depicted in a more dynamic way, as linguistic knowledge is understood as being exclusively available in the form of associations instead of individually represented entities. There are four kinds of associations that are relevant for the linguistic elements in the cognitive network (Schmid 2020: 5):
– symbolic associations: link forms and meanings
– syntagmatic associations: link sequences of forms and meanings
– paradigmatic associations: link competing forms and meanings
– pragmatic associations: link forms and meanings to context

It is these associations on which the mechanism of routinization operates (cf. Schmid 2015: 11–13, 2017c: 439–445, 2020: 226–234). This entails that "speakers do not entrench utterance types but they entrench the pattern of associations that become active while they process utterance types" (Schmid 2020: 206). This understanding of entrenchment suggests that for any linguistic element the four types of associations are routinized to different degrees, depending on how often language users have been exposed to relevant tokens or have actively used them in communication. Strongly developed associations entail that the respective elements are processed in a highly routinized and thus highly automated way. Furthermore, strongly entrenched elements share more prominent associations with other items in the network and thus serve as stronger attractors in the associative network than those elements which are less strongly entrenched.

Exemplifications of entrenchment that make use of established expressions are somewhat unsatisfying, which is why I want draw on a neologism that has been spreading among the younger speech community in the last years to illustrate the process of entrenchment. Imagine that a speaker who is not familiar with the verb *ghost* is confronted with the following utterances in different usage situations (examples 3–6 taken from COCA, examples 1–2 invented for purpose of demonstration):
(1) *If she doesn't fancy the guys, she simply ghosts them.*
(2) *Why would she ghost you after texting for two weeks?*
(3) *And then I know how to ghost them without them being offended.*
(4) *Why did you ghost me like that?*
(5) *I couldn't just ghost my boyfriend.*
(6) *If she does decide to keep it, you better not ghost her.*

In the first encounters with instances of the verb *ghost*, the speaker derives a hypothesis about the meaning of this word based on their knowledge of the existence of *ghost* as a noun and on the situational context. The speaker will probably arrive at the understanding that ghosting describes the action of disappearing or creating distance to another person and will thus create a symbolic association that links this meaning with the form. If the speaker is exposed to further situations in which the verb *ghost* is used, they will notice that these instances share crucial aspects of form and meaning, and might thus foster their hypothesized meaning or change it slightly (e.g. realize that *ghosting* is primarily used in the context of social media platforms). Accordingly, the symbolic association that connects the form *ghost* to the meaning 'stop having written contact with a person without explicitly communicating this intention' is fostered over the different usage events.

Not only is the symbolic association negotiated and continuously strengthened, but the speaker also recognizes the commonalities in the combinatorial and functional tendencies which anchor the verb in the situational co- and context in the different usage events and thus develops syntagmatic and pragmatic associations. Furthermore, paradigmatic associations to other words in the associative network are developed, e.g. to semantically competing verbs such as *block* or *unfriend*. Whenever a further instantiation of the verb *ghost* is encountered, these associations are activated and routinized and thus make *ghost* an increasingly strong attractor in the cognitive network. These processes explain why for many members of the speech community the use of the verb *ghost* by now requires only little cognitive effort. Considering that ghosting is a recurrent subject in the discourse revolving around social media, it probably constitutes a fairly entrenched concept in the mind of an average speaker of the age group between around 15 and 30.

Empirical evidence of the cognitive impact of frequency comes from various areas of research (cf. Blumenthal-Dramé 2017: 135–139; Schmid 2017a: 13–15). There are numerous studies working with lexical decision tasks, reading-time experiments, priming, eye-tracking or fMRI, which evaluate processing times in order to grasp the effects of frequency on the brain. These studies can prove that processing ease correlates with the frequency of the input items, i.e. higher-frequency items are recognized, accessed and activated faster and processed with greater speed and less effort (cf. Forster and Chambers 1973; Dell 1990; Jurafsky et al. 2001; Hauk and Pulvermüller 2004; Vaan et al. 2007; Arnon and Snider 2010; Blumenthal-Dramé 2012). In psycholinguistics, this phenomenon is described by the metaphor of resting activation: frequently used words are constantly activated, i.e. retrieved from the network, and are thus in a more active waiting position to be retrieved (Plag 2003: 49). In the proposal suggested here, advantages in processing time can be explained through (i) the stronger syntagmatic and paradigmatic associations a linguistic element holds with other items in the network, which result in quicker activation, (ii) its stronger pragmatic associations, which trigger their expectancy in a certain context and thus entail quicker activation, and (iii) the routinization of the symbolic association, which reduces its processing time.

As Stefanowitsch and Flach (2017: 101–102) point out, based on the fact that entrenchment is a cognitive phenomenon, quite commonly psycholinguistic methods are seen as the only adequate way to measure it (cf. Blumenthal-Dramé 2012). It has, however, become a common alternative to approach entrenchment by means of corpus-based measurements. To what extent are corpora justified in providing information about a cognitive concept? The next section will provide the link between corpus data and entrenchment and will argue that using corpus data to operationalize entrenchment is not a second-choice proposal but a perfectly adequate method of approaching this phenomenon.

### 8.6.2 Approaching entrenchment through corpus data

Considering that entrenchment is a function of frequency, corpora are an obvious choice for its operationalization. In fact, corpus-based approaches to entrenchment have gained more and more prominence in the last decades. Based on Schmid's claim that "frequency in text instantiates entrenchment in the cognitive system" (2000: 39), referred to as the *corpus-to-cognition-principle*, studies that work with corpus data make use of token frequencies to evaluate how strongly linguistic elements are entrenched. Why, however, is it legitimate to make statements about processes in an individual's mind based on corpus data? To answer this question, we need to scrutinize the corpus-to-cognition-principle and disclose the connections that bridge the gap between cognition and corpus data. Figure 26 depicts the triangle that relates entrenchment, corpora and a third component, namely *conventionalization*. Conventionalization can be understood as the establishment, exchange and re-adaption of linguistic conventions in a speech community (Schmid 2020: 2).

The figure illustrates that the connection between corpus data and entrenchment is an indirect one, symbolized by the dotted line, taking a detour via conventionalization. While the connection between corpus data and conventionalization might be obvious to some degree, the link between entrenchment and conventionalization is less so. How is the cognition of the individual speaker connected to the aggregate of many speakers? It is the aim of this section to reveal the relationship between corpus and cognition by making explicit the links between conventionalization and entrenchment on the one hand, and between corpora and conventionalization on the other.

First the link between corpora and conventionalization needs to be explained. For this, we must recall the role of corpora in Cognitive Linguistics: provided that the corpus employed is a large enough sample of a particular language and that it

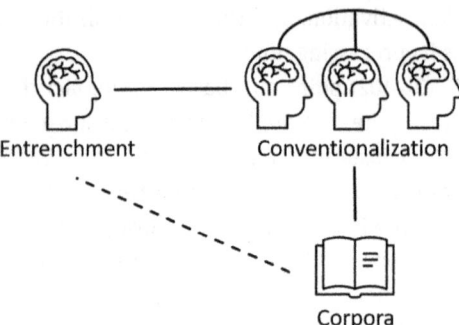

**Figure 26:** Relationship between corpus data and entrenchment.

contains data from a broad area of usage events from multiple individuals and sources, the language in a corpus can be seen as representative of a given language. Therefore, the extent to which a linguistic element occurs in that corpus can be taken to reflect the relative degree to which it is used in the relevant speech community. Accordingly, linguistic elements with very high token frequencies can be considered strongly established and diffused in the relevant speech community. Consequently, what is measured by frequency counts in corpora is strictly speaking the degree of conventionalization of an utterance type, i.e. its utilization in a speech community.

How does this relate to the language experience of the individual speaker? The connection between the conventionalization of linguistic elements and the representation of linguistic structures in an individual's mind can be provided by the *Entrenchment and Conventionalization Model* (EC-Model) developed by Schmid (2014, 2015, 2020). The EC-Model is an integral approach that aims at explaining the dynamic nature of language, based on the usage-based tenet that the structure of the linguistic system is shaped by language use. The model connects the cognitive processes taking place in the mind of an individual speaker with the socio-pragmatic processes that operate among the speech community, arguing that the language system is formed by the interaction between the processes of entrenchment and conventionalization. The model also integrates, links and explains a large number of forces that operate on the linguistic system, which cannot be addressed here. For more information on these forces and the full version of the model, the reader is referred to Schmid (2015, 2020). The aspect of the model that is most relevant here is the exchange between the cognitive processes operating in the individual speakers' minds and the processes taking place in the speech community, which is illustrated in Figure 27 in a simplified version of the EC-Model (adapted from Schmid 2020: 4).

## 8.6 Why are some compounds used more productively than others?

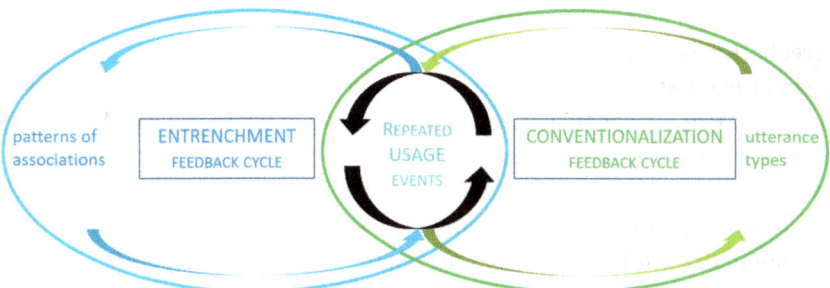

**Figure 27:** The Entrenchment and Conventionalization Model.

The process of entrenchment is represented through the blue circle on the left side, while that of conventionalization is illustrated through the green circle on the right.

The arrows in the circles illustrate that entrenchment and conventionalization are processes which are constantly in motion. The networks in the minds of speakers are constantly reorganized, just as the structure of the linguistic system that is maintained through its speakers is developing continuously. The interface between these two processes is displayed in the middle of the model and is provided by usage events: it is those situations in which speakers interact through language which constitute the driving force for the processes of conventionalization and entrenchment (Schmid 2020: 15–19). Those linguistic elements that are salient in usage events due to their recurrent use find their way into both the cognitive entrenchment system and the social conventionalization system.

To retrace the interaction, let us start on the side of entrenchment. When individuals are exposed to language in usage events, a particular pattern of associations linked to the linguistic elements encountered is activated. Thus, for aspects which are recurrent, the respective pattern of associations become increasingly routinized. Entrenched associations can be activated more easily and effortlessly than less entrenched ones, which makes the respective linguistic elements more likely to be chosen ahead of competitors in usage events (Schmid 2020: 205–234).

Besides feeding into the intra-individual process of entrenchment, the aspects that occur repeatedly in usage events also stream into the inter-individual process of conventionalization. If the same or similar linguistic elements or structures are used recurrently in the speech community, they become established as utterance types which are diffused in the whole or parts of the speech community. The more often they are used, the more strongly they become part of the tacit norms of that language (cf. Schmid 2020: 92–94; for the role of usage events as input for and output of the linguistic system see also Barlow and Kemmer 2000: ix). Conventionalized utterance types are in turn more likely to license further usage events.

Accordingly, entrenchment and conventionalization can each be understood as feedback loops which are kept in motion through usage events that contain recurrent features. These feedback cycles lead to a continuous exchange, adoption and updating of the utterance types that are widespread in a speech community and the associations that are entrenched in the individuals' minds. In this way, the EC-Model connects the cognition of the individual speaker with the aggregate of many speakers and thus provides the link between entrenchment and conventionalization (for a detailed description see Schmid 2020). Against this backdrop, the connection between corpus data and cognition can be comprehended: corpus data do not just reflect which utterance types are conventionalized in a speech community but can also be used as an approximation to the entrenchment of the relevant associations in the minds of individuals.

Similarly, in other accounts outside this framework that explicate the relation between corpus data and cognition, the role of the corpus is modelled as both the input of what becomes entrenched and the output of what is entrenched (cf. Stefanowitsch and Flach 2017: 102–105). In the "corpus-as-output view", it is reasoned that the extent to which utterance types are found in the corpus mirrors the ease with which they are produced, and thus the degree to which they are entrenched in the minds of individuals (Stefanowitsch and Flach 2017: 102–103). Schmid (2020: 217), however, points out that this is only partly adequate. Due to the fact that the data in a corpus are the collective product of many speakers, it is not fully legitimate to make inferences about the entrenchment of linguistic items in the individuals' minds, as this would require a corpus that contains the linguistic output of an individual speaker – which to my knowledge does not at present exist. In the "corpus-as-input view", it is argued that the data in a corpus are a close model of the utterance types that the members of a speech community are exposed to, and which consequently become familiar and routinized elements in the minds of individuals (Stefanowitsch and Flach 2017: 103). On these grounds, the data in a representative corpus can serve as an indication of which elements might be entrenched to what degree in the mind of an average speaker of the respective speech community.

Nevertheless, the relationship between corpus data and cognition must not be simplified, as there are several aspects that need to be treated with some reserve, which is why the corpus-to-cognition-principle has been subject to discussion (cf. Schmid 2010; Blumenthal-Dramé 2012: 28–44). Firstly, equating the degree to which utterance types are widespread in the speech community with the degree to which these linguistic elements are entrenched in the mind of an individual is of course a generalization. There are certainly interindividual differences among the members of a speech community regarding their language experience. Not all the words that are used frequently in the speech community will automatically be entrenched in each language user's mind. Concepts in political discourse, for instance, might be generally highly diffused within a speech community, but there might still be speakers who are very seldom exposed to them. Vice versa, there are utterance types which display a fairly low diffusion among the speech community but are strongly entrenched concepts in the minds of some individuals, as is demonstrated by Schmid (2014: 249) with the example "How can I help you today?", a sentence exclusively but intensely used by telephone counsellors or sales assistants (cf. also Schmid 2008: 8; Blumenthal-Dramé 2017). Similarly, there is a German wheelchair basketball community whose members use the expression *Geher* ('walker') constantly to refer to players who are able to walk. This expression can be assumed to be quite strongly entrenched in the minds of players and visitors. It is, however, not used outside of this environment and is thus not established in the German speech community. Accordingly, it must be acknowledged that there are differences between the language experience of individuals and the discourse within the speech community, which is why drawing inferences from the degree of conventionalization of an utterance type to its degree of entrenchment can only be a generalization for an average member of the relevant speech community.

If the relationship between conventionalization and entrenchment must be treated with some reserve, this is even truer for the relationship between corpora and entrenchment. There is certainly no perfect correlation between what is found in the corpus and what is entrenched in a language user's mind. Firstly, sometimes there is a discrepancy between the frequency with which speakers encounter a concept and the extent to which they verbalize it. Normal speakers of English, for example, can be expected to be commonly exposed to the concept of *toilet paper roll*. Still, in COCA this complex compound is only found 38 times, as speakers might not necessarily talk about this concept as much as they encounter it. Although the concept of *toilet paper roll* might be fairly entrenched in the minds of language users, this is not mirrored to the same degree in the corpus. Secondly, there are concepts which are encountered frequently but their forms are not part of the data typically collected for corpora, especially if they are generally not part of an utterance, i.e. embedded in a written or spoken instance of speech production. This could be the case for the complex lexemes *sea food salad* or *airport café*, for example. Each of these compounds describes a fairly common concept, still they have vanishingly small frequencies of 38 and 4 tokens respectively in the corpus, which is probably due to the fact that menus and signs at the airport usually do not find their way into corpora. Accordingly, there are concepts and forms which are encountered more often and are thus more strongly entrenched than is reflected by the token frequencies in the corpus. Vice versa, there are also data in the corpus that will never find their way into the cognition of speakers. Section 4.2.1 demonstrated that corpora contain a considerable amount of noise that does not represent linguistic material that language users are actually exposed to. These objections show that corpora are not a perfect reflection of the utterance types and concepts that are experienced by language users. Nevertheless, these kinds of accidental gaps do not devalue the usefulness of corpora in approaching the phenomenon of entrenchment, as corpora still provide a very close model of the linguistic experience of an idealized average member of the speech community.

In this context, Blumenthal-Dramé (2012: 27–65) criticizes that corpus-based approaches make generalizations about language users that are only weakly representative of the cognitive states of an individual. However, Stefanowitsch and Flach point out that similar constraints also apply to psycholinguistic studies:

> It is true that a given linguistic corpus is not typically representative of the input, let alone the output of a particular individual. However, this does not constitute an argument against using corpora in the study of cognition because the same is true of experimental measures, which are also averaged across groups of subjects. As in a balanced corpus, these subjects are assumed to be, but never actually shown to be, representative of the speech community. Thus, experiments, like corpora, measure the average entrenchment of a structure in the mind of a typical member of the speech community (Stefanowitsch and Flach 2017: 122).

Therefore, corpus-based approaches can be claimed to be just as adequate an approach to entrenchment as psycholinguistic experiments. Both methods target the same phenomenon but start at different ends: while psycholinguistic experiments draw their conclusions from the processing speed, i.e. the effects of entrenchment, corpus-based measures make use of token frequencies, which can be seen as both the cause of what becomes entrenched in the minds of individuals as well as the result of what is entrenched in the minds of individuals (see corpus-as-input/corpus-as-output views cited above). Accordingly, these two approaches and methodologies are rather to be seen as different ways of accessing entrenchment that can and should complement each other (cf. Stefanowitsch and Flach 2017: 121–122).

While corpus-based proposals are generally a valid measure for approaching entrenchment, there are some constraints that must be addressed with regard to its operationalization. It has been explained that entrenchment is a function of frequency, which is why generally token frequencies are used to assess the entrenchment of a linguistic element. This relationship must not be simplified, since firstly, frequency itself is not the only factor that governs entrenchment. There are several other forces that have an influence on what becomes entrenched in the cognitive network (cf. Schmid 2020: 216–226). Accordingly, corpus-based approaches are necessarily reductionist in their attempt to capture entrenchment exclusively through token frequencies. However, considering that repetition is the most important factor influencing entrenchment (Schmid 2020: 216–218), operationalizing it through frequency still permits a very close approximation.

Secondly, an operationalization based on frequency can only be upheld as long as the methodological apparatus is discriminating enough regarding the figures that are used. This aspect is mostly what has been the target of criticism of the corpus-to-cognition-principle. It would be too simplistic to claim that bare token frequencies in texts can be used to assess entrenchment. Discussions in this field (Schmid 2010; Blumenthal-Dramé 2012; Schmid and Küchenhoff 2013) have led to the agreement that several kinds of frequencies need to be taken into account, depending on the complexity (and schematicity) of the linguistic element in question. Absolute token frequencies can be equated with entrenchment only in the case of simple, monomorphemic words (Stefanowitsch and Flach 2017: 105–120; Schmid 2020: 52). In the case of more complex linguistic units, additional figures are required, which is why Stefanowitsch and Flach (2017: 108) have coined the notion of *usage intensity* as a general term for the different kinds of relevant frequencies; a convention that I will adopt here. Before expanding on this, I first need to detail in what ways complex sequences are affected by entrenchment processes.

### 8.6.3 Entrenchment processes on complex elements

Section 8.6.1 has explained that entrenchment strengthens the pattern of associations that are activated in the processing of utterance types and thus creates more and less strong attractors in the cognitive network. When it comes to complex words and multi-word sequences, what is particularly relevant is the strengthening of the syntagmatic associations between the individual constituents. In this section, I will first present the way in which the entrenchment of complex linguistic elements has conventionally been approached (Section 8.6.3.1), before introducing a more holistic proposal for this phenomenon. This concept will then be applied to compounds with the aim of explaining how entrenchment processes affect their cognitive representation (Section 8.6.3.2). It has been foreshadowed in the previous section that corpus-based approaches to the entrenchment of complex linguistic elements require different facets of frequency, an issue that will be dealt with in Section 8.6.3.3. These sections will prepare the ground for an explanation why the entrenchment of compounds is a decisive factor in their productivity.

#### 8.6.3.1 The notion of chunk

The different degrees of syntagmatic entrenchment that hold between the constituents of complex sequences are generally referred to as degrees of *chunking*. The notion of *chunking* focuses on the growing strength with which the components of a complex word or multi-word expression are connected by continuous entrenchment as a result of repeated exposure. In principle, this proposal is compatible with the present approach; what is problematic, however, is the related notion of *chunk*. It describes the idea that complex words or multi-word sequences which are used extensively might reach an endpoint of the chunking process and be cognitively stored as one holistic unit (Blumenthal-Dramé 2012, 2017; Schmid 2015: 12, 14, 19; Langacker 2017). A sequence that is categorized as a chunk is understood as an autonomous unit that has emancipated itself from its constituents and is perceived as a single gestalt (Langacker 1987a: 59; Gobet 2017). Accordingly, chunks are no longer generated at the moment of use but are stored, processed and activated holistically and in an automated way, requiring no on-line-processing nor conscious monitoring (Smet and Cuyckens 2007: 188; Langacker 2008: 16; Hartsuiker and Moors 2017; Schmid 2017a: 11–12).

Determining whether a complex linguistic element is cognitively stored as a unit is not straightforward. As reported in the previous section, many of the psycholinguistic experiments that investigate the effects of entrenchment make use of the processing time in order to draw conclusions about the entrenchment of the linguistic elements at question. In the case of complex linguistic elements, quite commonly fast processing is equated with chunk status (Blumenthal-Dramé 2012: 47–48; 2017: 133). This, however, is not justified, as most studies just assume but cannot prove that the quick processing of complex sequences is due to holistic storage (cf. Blumenthal-Dramé 2012: 47–50, 2017: 133–137). "Rather, most results are equally compatible with the weaker alternative interpretation that higher frequency strings are simply assembled with greater efficiency as a result of greater association strengths between morphemes" (Blumenthal-Dramé 2017: 147). Experiments which specifically test for chunk status are comparatively rare as they are laborious and costly (cf. Blumenthal-Dramé 2012: 50–52, 2017: 139–141; Schmid 2017a: 16–18). Accordingly, it is to some extent obscure which complex sequences are stored as an entity, which is why in case of doubt it is more accurate to merely talk of strong syntagmatic associations or a high degree of chunking instead of postulating chunk status (cf. Schmid 2017c: 441–443).

These remarks on the empirical investigation of chunks prepare the way for another point of criticism, namely that the notion of chunk is imprecise when it comes to the relationship between strong syntagmatic entrenchment, holistic processing, storage as a unit and the role of the individual constituents. As Blumenthal-Dramé (2012, 2017) points out, a maximum degree of syntagmatic entrenchment – and thus a maximum degree of chunking – does not necessarily entail that the respective sequence is stored as a cognitive unit.[22] There are reasons that might prevent holistic storage, such as the length of a sequence. Even if they are not stored as one unit, complex words and multi-word sequences with a high degree of syntagmatic entrenchment can be units of processing, which means they are processed holistically without being computed online via their constituents. Idioms, for example, are chunks in the sense of processing units; however, this does not mean they must be cognitively stored as one unit. Accordingly, the notion of chunk is not subtle enough when it comes to differentiating between units of processing and units of storage. Furthermore, even if complex linguistic elements are units of storage and/or processing, this does not mean that their constituents are automatically backgrounded to such degree that they are not accessed during processing.

Moreover, the notion of chunk suggests that there must be a threshold from which point onwards items are categorized as chunks, and it furthermore conveys the impression that there is a categorical distinction between chunks and items which are not chunks, which somewhat undermines the conception that entrenchment is a gradual process. Accordingly, proposals that replace the notion of chunk by the idea that there are items with an extremely high degree of chunking are more compatible with the dynamic nature of entrenchment.

### 8.6.3.2 The syntagmatic-strengthening principle

A more fine-grained proposal regarding the entrenchment of complex words and multi-word sequences is provided by the syntagmatic-strengthening principle as developed by Schmid (2020: 235–240). It makes similar predictions to those that have been presented in the previous section under the notion of chunking; however, it takes into account that in the entrenchment of complex linguistic elements not only syntagmatic associations are affected but also all other types of associations. Furthermore, it explicitly expounds the changing role of the constituents in the course of chunking. According to the syntagmatic-strengthening principle, the strengthening of the syntagmatic associations of a complex sequence

---

[22] There are linguists who claim that non-compositional items, such as idioms, have to be stored due to their arbitrary form-meaning association, see, for example, Schmid (2008: 24); Herbst (2010: 136). In these cases, it seems that processing and storage are wrongfully treated as the same thing or scholars are too incautious in their usage of the notion "stored". It has been pointed out above that in many instances it cannot be proved whether a complex linguistic item is actually stored as one unit. Obviously, the meaning of idioms is idiomatic, which means they have a symbolic association of their own and their meaning needs to be stored, i.e. they are processing units, which is why they are accessed as a whole. This, however, does not automatically mean they are stored holistically.

stimulates the other kinds of associations in the following ways (Schmid 2020: 235–237):
(i) the symbolic association between the form and meaning of the sequence as a whole is routinized
(ii) the paradigmatic associations that link the whole sequence to competing (not necessarily complex) linguistic items are fostered
(iii) the syntagmatic associations that link the whole sequence to preceding or following linguistic items are fostered
(iv) the pragmatic associations affecting the usage of the sequence are strengthened

Parallel to the routinization of the associations of the sequence as a whole, the individual associations of the constituents are weakened. More precisely, this involves the following processes:
(i) a weakening of the symbolic association that holds between the forms and meanings of each of the individual constituents
(ii) a reduction of the paradigmatic associations that link the individual constituents to related items in the associative network
(iii) a reduction of the syntagmatic associations that link the individual constituents to preceding of following linguistic items
(iv) the fading of the pragmatic associations related to the use of the individual constituents

Accordingly, the stronger the syntagmatic association between the constituents of a complex word or multi-word unit becomes, the less salient are the associations that connect their components in the associative network, while the associations of the complex sequence as an entity are fostered. This leads to "the sequence as a whole [being] experienced as a unit that has emancipated itself from the parts and is subserved by its own pattern of associations" (Schmid 2020: 236). This idea is highly similar to that of the gestalt-like unit of a chunk, however, instead of suggesting a categorical change in the quality of the representation of complex sequences, this conceptualization of entrenchment is based on the interplay between the differently routinized patterns of associations of the sequence as a whole and its constituents. These more or less strongly entrenched associations account for both the way in which the respective items are processed and the way in which they are stored, which is why this proposal is wary of distinguishing between processing and storage.

How can the different degrees to which the associations are routinized be determined? As Schmid (2020: 239–240) outlines, there are various aspects that can influence the strength of the syntagmatic associations between the components of lexically specific utterance types (and thus the strength of the associations of the whole over the constituents' associations):

- ABSOLUTE FREQUENCY of the complex sequence:
  syntagmatic associations between repeatedly processed strings will be stronger than between less frequently processed strings
- RELATIVE FREQUENCY of the complex sequence compared to the individual frequencies of the constituents:
  if the utterance type is used frequently but the constituents themselves only occur rarely outside the combination, the syntagmatic association is higher than in cases where the constituents themselves occur frequently in numerous other contexts
- PRAGMATIC ASSOCIATIONS of the utterance type as an entity:
  sequences which are linked to specific situations, functions or illocutions will show stronger effects of syntagmatic strengthening: instances of formulaic language, such as *Good morning* or *Excuse me?*, for example, have strong pragmatic associations and thus a higher degree of syntagmatic strengthening
- degree of COMPOSITIONALITY of an utterance type:
  idiomatic expressions require the development of a symbolic association of their own, which is why their components are more strongly backgrounded than those of compositional sequences

Against this background, I will outline the predictions that the syntagmatic-strengthening principle makes for compounds, drawing on Schmid (2020: 243–245). In this context, I will prepare the way for understanding why different usage intensities are relevant for measuring the entrenchment of compounds. In the case of compounds that are opaque or have only a minimum degree of compositionality, such as *butterfly*, *ponytail* or *hotdog*, the symbolic association that links the form as a whole with the particular meaning is quite strongly developed. In the case of *hotdog*, for example, the symbolic association provides the meaning 'food in the form of a sausage in a bun'. The symbolic associations of its constituents have strongly faded, as the meanings of 'hot' or 'dog' are generally not associated with *hotdog*. Therefore, the compound *hotdog* is paradigmatically connected to other words describing food, such as *hamburger* or *bread*, instead of words connected to its components *dog* (e.g. *cat*) or *hot* (e.g. *warm*). Similarly, it is syntagmatically connected to words like *eat*, and thus independent of the syntagmatic relations of its constituents (such as *lovely*, *barking*, etc.). Furthermore, the compound has developed its own pragmatic associations that are independent of those of the constituents, as the concept of *hotdog* is pragmatically situated in different contexts than the concepts of *hot* and *dog*. Accordingly, the compound *hotdog* can be argued to constitute a unit that is fully emancipated from its parts and to be characterized by syntagmatic associations that are strengthened to such degree that this compound is presumably perceived as one unit by native speakers instead of a complex sequence that is composed of two individual words.

By contrast, in the case of highly compositional compounds such as *mortality rate*, for instance, the individual constituents with their symbolic associations are highly present, which is why also their pragmatic, paradigmatic and syntagmatic associations are still intact. *Mortality*, for example, might paradigmatically be strongly related to *death* or *life*, and *rate* to *number* or *figures*. The fact that the associations of the constituents are relatively prominent has an influence on the strength of the syntagmatic relation that holds within the compound. This presumably entails that a compositional compound that is used to the same degree as an opaque one has developed weaker syntagmatic associations. In order for the syntagmatic, paradigmatic, symbolic and pragmatic associations of the compound as a whole to be more prominent than those of its components, the compound needs to be used very frequently and/or needs to be used relatively frequently compared to the use of its constituents.

Apart from compounds from the two ends along the scale of compositionality (cf. Section 7.8), there are items which are not fully compositional but still transparent, such as *weekend, bedroom* or *barman*. As their meaning cannot be fully derived from their constituents, these compounds have developed their own symbolic associations and, consequently, also syntagmatic, pragmatic and paradigmatic associations in the cognitive network. Nevertheless, even if they have developed fairly routinized patterns of associations which are largely independent from those of their constituents, their constituents have not fully faded but are merely backgrounded. The extent to which these compounds are emancipated from their constituents depends on their degree of compositionality and their transparency (which can vary greatly as has been shown in Section 7.8). As a consequence, in the case of non-compositional, transparent compounds, the relevance of their constituents for their syntagmatic strengthening must be assumed to vary along a scale that correlates with the compound's degree of compositionality.

In this context, it must be pointed out that this depiction is simplified, as it assigns a similar status to both constituents. However, as pointed out by Langacker (1987a: 465), the components of a compound can have differing degrees of salience, which he demonstrates at the example of *screwdriver*. Clearly, in this compound the first constituent is more salient than the second one, which is why it must be assumed that the associations of *screw* are more strongly intact than those of *driver*, which are more strongly backgrounded. Accordingly, if generalized statements are made about compound constituents in the following sections, this is intended to express the general tendency that affects the constituents and does not mean to suggest that both constituents result in the same status.

### 8.6.3.3 Approaching syntagmatic entrenchment through usage intensity

It has been propounded in Section 8.6.1 that the entrenchment of complex sequences is related to frequencies of different forms, summarized under the notion of *usage intensity*. Based on the explanations in the previous section, it can be reasoned which frequencies are relevant in approximating the syntagmatic strength that holds between the constituents of compounds.

It has been suggested that in opaque compounds the paradigmatic relations between the compound and its constituents are presumably almost non-existent. Accordingly, in assessing the entrenchment of opaque compounds, the frequencies of the constituents can be considered largely irrelevant. Therefore, it can be reasoned that the degree of entrenchment of opaque compounds can be evaluated by means of their absolute frequency, i.e. identically to that of simple words.

In highly compositional compounds, the constituents are fairly prominent, which is why the degree to which they are used has an influence on the syntagmatic associations that exist within the compound. If a compound's constituents occur frequently in other compounds, this will lead to a lower degree of syntagmatic strength between the constituents of this compound. If, however, the constituents of a compositional compound are not used frequently by themselves or in other compounds, while the compound itself is used frequently, this compound stands a high chance to have developed a strong syntagmatic association. Accordingly, in order to assess the degree of syntagmatic entrenchment of a compositional compound, the relation between the frequency of the compound and that of its constituents needs to be assessed. Therefore, what is methodologically relevant is the relative compound frequency, i.e. its frequency in relation to the frequencies of its constituents.[23]

For compounds that are not highly compositional, it depends on their degree of compositionality whether absolute or relative compound frequency is a better approximation to their degree of syntagmatic entrenchment.

Accordingly, there are different frequencies that are relevant for approaching the entrenchment of compounds: the absolute compound frequency in the case of opaque and strongly lexicalized compounds; and the relative compound frequency in the case of more compositional compounds. As it is not straightforward to determine for which kinds of non-compositional compounds which of the two measurements might be more adequate, and since furthermore the number of fully opaque compounds is comparatively low (cf. Section 7.8), the most

---

[23] The same principle is commonly applied in derivation, where the relative frequency of a complex word is taken as an indication of whether the relevant word might be decomposed, with the difference that what is relevant in derivation is the frequency of the base only, not that of the affix (cf. Hay 2001: 1044; Haspelmath 2010: 116).

suitable approach seems to be an inclusive one that takes into account the relation between the absolute frequency of the compound and that of its constituents for all compounds. In order to be able to derive conclusions from the relative frequency of a compound to its degree of entrenchment, statistical measures need to be employed that assess the significance of the co-occurrence of a compound's constituents by relating it to other relevant co-occurrences of two lexemes. In this context, Stefanowitsch and Flach (2017: 115) suggest the $G^2$-test, which statistically evaluates the relation between the observed frequency of a complex sequence and its expected frequency. The outcome of this measurement are concrete scores that have no absolute validity but a relative one and thus can be used to compare word combinations with regard to their degree of syntagmatic entrenchment: items with a high score in the $G^2$-test can be assumed to show more strongly routinized syntagmatic associations (and accordingly more strongly developed symbolic, pragmatic, syntagmatic and paradigmatic associations as well), while those with low values must be assumed to have less strongly developed syntagmatic associations and thus to be rather loosely connected.

The attentive reader will have realized that the measurement that has just been described is exactly what has been applied in Section 8.5.3 to quantify the strength of the association that holds between the constituents of a compound. A compound's association strength thus can be said to equal its degree of entrenchment in the mind of an average speaker. This means that those compounds that yielded high association scores are stronger attractors in the associative network and their associations can be assumed to be more strongly routinized than for those compounds with low association scores. The next section will explain the implications of this insight.

### 8.6.4 Relevance of entrenchment for compound productivity

To remind the reader: the concept of entrenchment was introduced as a means of explaining why some two-noun compounds are used more productively to form more complex compounds than others. It is the aim of this section to merge the pieces of information gained so far into a puzzle by outlining in what way a compound's degree of entrenchment is relevant for its productivity.

Based on the explanations given in the previous sections, the constituents of compounds show different degrees of association strength and thus different degrees of syntagmatic entrenchment. These degrees have been quantified in Section 8.5.3. Accordingly, the compounds *football, health care, newspaper* or *credit card*, for example, can be assumed to show highly routinized associations. Those compounds with high association scores which are furthermore lexicalized to some degree, such as *football*, *website*, *weekend* or *birthday*, for example, have quite strongly emancipated themselves from their constituents and can be assumed to be learned as holistic units, which are probably not perceived as sequences of two individual, separate words any more by members of the English speech community. By contrast, those compounds with low association scores, like *energy storage* or *crisis pregnancy*, are only weakly interconnected in the associative network. The syntagmatic association between their constituents is rather weak, just like the pragmatic, syntagmatic and paradigmatic associations of the compound as a whole. Accordingly, also their symbolic associations are less prominent than those of their constituents, which is why these compounds must be assumed to be computed online via their constituents instead of constituting units of processing.

When we recall the effects of entrenchment, the connection between a compound's degree of entrenchment and its productivity becomes obvious. Entrenched compounds are firstly stronger attractors in the cognitive network, which means they are more easily and quickly accessible, which is why they are more likely to be chosen for further compound formation. Furthermore, they show more strongly routinized associations, which is why their processing and formation happens in an automated fashion. Accordingly, those compounds which yielded higher scores in Section 8.5.3.1.3 can be assumed to be processed more quickly and effortlessly than those with low association scores, which must be assumed to require comparatively more effort for processing. This reasoning permits making predictions about the cognitive effort required for using compounds with differing degrees of entrenchment to form more complex compounds: not only are compounds which are strongly entrenched more easily accessible, but the necessity of online processing is also reduced to a minimum. The cognitive effort of combining them with another noun can be assumed to be relatively low. Weakly entrenched compounds, by contrast, are less easily available as they are less strongly connected in the associative network and their processing is less routinized, which is why they are less likely to be used as input for a further word-formation process. This connection explains why those compounds with higher association scores have proved to be more productive.

Before we can content ourselves with this outcome, there is another point to be made. It has been explained that in the literature that discusses the entrenchment of complex linguistic units, it is argued that it is not merely joint occurrence as provided by bare token frequencies that accounts for their degree of entrenchment, but what is decisive is the statistically relevant co-occurrence of their constituents. In view of this, how can the fact be explained that in Section 8.5.3.2 bare compound frequency turned out to be a slightly better predictor for productivity than association strength? The crux of this matter is presumably the heterogeneity among the compounds when it comes to their compositionality. The suitability of the measure depends on the different status the constituents play in compounds with different degrees of compositionality (cf. Section 8.6.3.2). This result thus supports Stefanowitsch and Flach's assumption that "the more the multi-word expression behaves like a simple unit (i.e. the less likely it is that speakers recognize or are aware of its constituent parts), the better frequency will predict its degree of entrenchment, and the more the multi-word expression behaves like a complex unit, the better probability- and/or association-based measures will do" (Stefanowitsch and Flach 2017: 116–117). Therefore, it can be concluded that in the case of opaque or lexicalized compounds bare token frequency seems to be a better predictor of their degree of entrenchment, while for more compositional compounds statistical measures are a more suitable approximation to their syntagmatic entrenchment.

### 8.6.5 Conclusion and discussion

This section has introduced the idea of entrenchment in order to explain why not only the association strength between the components of a compound but also its frequency have a strong explanatory power for its degree of productivity. It has been argued that based on their usage intensity, compounds show different degrees of entrenchment. Strongly entrenched compounds provide advantages both in processing and activation: they are more easily accessible as they are more prominent attractors in the cognitive network, and they show more strongly routinized associations, which is why the cognitive effort required for their processing is comparatively low. These aspects have an influence on the availability of these compounds for forming more complex compounds: the more strongly entrenched a two-noun compound's associations are, the more easily it can be used to form tri-constituent constructions, or conversely, if a compound's associations are not strongly entrenched, it is unlikely to be used repeatedly as input for the formation of more complex compounds. Thus, entrenchment is not necessarily a precondition for having complex compounds but definitely for the productive formation of complex compounds.

A major implication that can be drawn from these results is that in strongly entrenched two-noun compounds which are furthermore lexicalized to some degree, such as *football*, *network* or *birthday*, the constituents are backgrounded to such an extent that native speakers might not even perceive them as consisting of two words. These compounds are basically ready-made items which are available in the long-term memory of speakers as prepacked units. Accordingly, it can be argued that those three-noun compounds which are based on a strongly entrenched and lexicalized two-noun compound are pseudo-tri-constituent. Although these cases formally constitute a composition of three parts, based on the embedded compound's highly routinized associations and the emancipation from its constituents it can be argued that both semantically and formally it is only two lexemes which are combined. These complex compounds are exactly those instances which one might be surprised to find in the category of tri-constituent compounds in the first place.

It is important to note that the relation between entrenchment and productivity is not valid both ways. Only compounds that are entrenched to a certain degree will be productively available for the formation of more complex compounds. This means that a productive two-noun compound will always be entrenched to some degree, whereas the opposite is not necessarily true. There are compounds with a high degree of entrenchment which are still not very productive in forming complex compounds, such as *keyword*, for example. The factor of influence that is potentially at work here is the extra-linguistic relevance of respective roles in the semantic frame of these words. Obviously, there is currently no onomasiological need to denote further agents or circumstances within the semantic frame surrounding the concept of the word *keyword*.

This section has furthermore argued why corpora are an adequate tool for approaching entrenchment. Still, in the operationalization of a cognitive concept by corpus data criticism must be taken into account. It is, of course, debatable to what degree the measurement applied is transferable to the cognitive status of compounds in the minds of individuals, as it is impossible to control the language exposure that the members of a speech community have – not to speak of the exposure to the selected sample. The results of this project are based on the assumption that there is a relatively high degree of overlap between the occurrences of words in the corpus and the linguistic experience of an average language user. This seems justified considering that COCA is a large enough corpus that is not specialized as regards subject and contains both spoken and written language. Besides, operationalizing entrenchment by means of corpus data is still seen to be the most efficient measurement to date if faced with more laborious alternatives like eye-tracking, which are harder to interpret and highly susceptible to disruption through other variables. Nevertheless, it would be desirable to complement the results of this section with psychological measurements.

Further criticism that can be raised is that the figures employed in calculating usage intensity have not been distinguished according to their use in specific situations and functions. In order to improve the operationalization of entrenchment, more distinctive token counts would be required that take into account features of the concrete speech situations. As has been mentioned earlier, there are several other determinants that can have an impact on entrenchment (cf. Schmid 2015, 2017a: 20–22, 2020). However, as frequency is the main determinant for the phenomenon of entrenchment, the focus adopted in this work (and in corpus-based approaches to entrenchment in general) seems justifiable.

Nevertheless, I want to address a potentially mundane but methodologically very important issue related to the determination of usage frequencies for the operationalization of entrenchment by means of corpus data. This point was not relevant for the data collection in this project as it concerns the entrenchment of single words, but it came up in determining the usage frequencies for compounds. Counting the token frequencies of a word in order to determine its entrenchment is not as trivial as might be assumed. If we deal with semantically vague, unspecific, polysemous or even homonymous items, simply using the token frequency of the relevant word in the corpus clearly is not sufficient. Instead, considerable manual refinement that is sensible to homonymous and polysemous words is necessary in order to determine the correct usage frequency and thus the degree of entrenchment of a word. Besides this quite obvious remark, however, it seems quite nebulous which instances of a word contribute to its entrenchment, especially if a word also occurs as part of word-formation products. Does a pre- or suffixed lexeme contribute to the entrenchment of its base, i.e. do the instances of *action*, *activity* and *reaction* contribute to the entrenchment of *act*? Is the participle form *based* still related strongly enough to the lexeme *base* to contribute to its entrenchment? What about the occurrences of *base* in *database* or *basement* – do they contribute to the entrenchment of *base*? Or, in determining how strongly entrenched the word *line* is, do we count its instantiations in *guideline*, *airline*, *gasoline*, *headline*, *outline*, *hotline* and *deadline*? In those compounds that are lexicalized to some degree, the paradigmatic relation to the constituent *line* and its symbolic association might be weakened to some degree – nevertheless, it has also been argued that speakers are not blinded to the constituents of non-compositional compounds. So, do these compounds contribute to the entrenchment of *line*?

To further illustrate this issue, here are some examples of compounded and derived forms in which the word *board* is used: *cardboard, keyboard, boarding, onboard, billboard, headboard, boardroom, cupboard, snowboard, surfboard, soundboard, boarding-house, keyboard, wash-board, flakeboard, boardwalk*. Which of them foster the entrenchment of the word *board*? What about cases of verb-noun conversion, such as *cost*, for example: Does the use of the verb contribute to the entrenchment of the noun? To conclude this questioning, the point I want to make is that to my knowledge there has so far been no account of corpus-based entrenchment that is precise enough when it comes to the question of which tokens are to be counted as an instantiation of a word in order to measure its entrenchment. Stefanowitsch and Flach (2017: 109) quite vaguely state that "[i]n at least some cases, different forms derived from the same stem presumably contribute jointly to the entrenchment of the stem". Considering that it is argued that each encounter with a word has a cognitive impact, a clearer idea is required to decide which instantiations of a token contribute to its entrenchment in order to guarantee the use of adequate usage frequencies in the employment of corpus data to measure entrenchment.

## 8.7 How is knowledge of compound productivity stored cognitively?

The previous section has argued that more and less productive compounds are cognitively represented in the form of more and less strongly routinized patterns of associations. The compound *football*, for example, is highly productive and is thus characterized through strongly routinized associations in the cognitive network. Section 8.3 has also demonstrated that productivity is not just lexeme-dependent but also position-dependent, as compounds behave differently as heads than as modifiers. Speakers form, for example, considerably more complex compounds with the pattern '*football* + N' than with 'N + *football*'. How do speakers "know" which patterns they can use productively? It has furthermore been shown in Section 8.4 that there is a semantic component to productivity, as the outer nouns in the different patterns form semantic clusters. Do speakers have knowledge of these more and less productive areas? For two-noun compounds, Bauer et al. (2019: 51) point out that "[o]ur knowledge of the way a noun is used in compounds is expected to be based on our previous experience with this noun as an element of a compound". Accordingly, speakers have a tacit knowledge of the use of an item as part of a compound, based on previous encounters with this item. How is this knowledge about the use of the different patterns that give rise to three-noun compounds stored in the minds of speakers? It is the aim of this section to outline in what form productivity is represented in the cognitive network.

The previous section 8.6 has already given an insight into the organization of the cognitive network through the explanation of the different kinds of associations that hold between and among linguistic elements. It has focused on the question of how the exposure to similar utterance types affects the associative network. This section will demonstrate that speakers also establish associations between less similar utterance types, which is the foundation of their knowledge about productivity. To explain the underlying cognitive mechanisms, I will draw on the process of schematization. Section 8.7.1 will outline the concept of schematization, while Section 8.7.2 will apply this mechanism to complex compounds. In these sections, following Schmid (2020), I will be employing the concept of schematization in a way that slightly deviates from the established way of framing it, which is why Section 8.7.3 will deliver the pieces of information that those readers who work with mainstream constructionist approaches to schematization might feel to be missing.

### 8.7.1 Schematization over variable patterns

In the processing of similar linguistic input experienced in different usage events, speakers derive generalizations concerning these usage events based on the similarities they perceive. Generalization requires abstraction away from concrete uses and thus involves the process of schematization. If items in the linguistic input are highly similar, such as the same word or different word forms of the same lexeme, the detection of similarities is quite straightforward, which is why in these cases the process of schematization is an unnoticed side mechanism (Schmid 2020: 227–228). The effect of generalization and thus schematization becomes more prominent if the linguistic input shows more variability. This section will explain how speakers react to utterance types that show systematic variation. For this, I will first present the conventional understanding of the concept of schematization before introducing a more current proposal concerning this phenomenon.

The idea that speakers derive knowledge about the use of patterns based on input that varies systematically has conventionally been captured through the concept of schemata. In mainstream construction grammarian approaches, it is argued that in processing events in which similar but systematically different linguistic elements are repeated, speakers recognize the commonalities between these linguistic elements. Based on the summed similarity of the different instances, they gradually derive generalizations from the lexically specific items, which are caught in the form of schematic representations. These representations contain variable, unspecific placeholders as a result of the categorization of the input items and are stored in the form of schemata, which are symbolic units, i.e. associations of form and meaning (Langacker 1987a: 492; Barlow and Kemmer 2000: ix; Goldberg 2006; Abbot-Smith and Tomasello 2006; Booij 2010: 51–93). Besides form and meaning, schemata store information about situational and functional characteristics that become part of the knowledge about the use of the relevant linguistic element. These schemata can have different levels of abstractness, varying on a scale of schematicity from fully abstract schemata which consist of unspecific placeholders only, through schemata that are partly lexically filled, to lexically specific constructs (cf. the illustration of degrees of schematicity by Stefanowitsch and Flach 2017: 106). The less semantically similar the elements are that have occurred in the variable slots of a pattern, the more abstract is the resulting schematic representation (Blumenthal-Dramé 2017: 142).

Schemata are thus patterns of experience which, if they are activated repeatedly, become subject to entrenchment processes which strengthen their form-meaning association (Langacker 2009: 2; Schmid 2015: 15, 2017a, 2017c). Unlike concrete instantiations of linguistic elements, which are understood to become more entrenched by identical processing events (*token entrenchment*), schemata are strengthened by similar processing events, i.e. by the encounter of different instantiations of a particular pattern (*type entrenchment*) (Croft 2001: 28; Croft and Cruse 2004: 308–312; Langacker 2008: 234; Stefanowitsch and Flach 2017: 118). Accordingly, the entrenchment of a schema correlates with its productivity as measured by type frequency. This is a self-enforcing cycle, as the more deeply entrenched a schema is, the more likely it is to be activated to create novel units, while at the same time the repeated exposure to similar instantiations will foster the schema, which again licenses the production of new formations. Accordingly, if speakers have developed a schema that is entrenched to some degree, it enables them to produce, process and interpret novel structures based on this schema more easily.

This account of linguistic knowledge is not fully consistent with the idea of entrenchment as a dynamic process, since in part it makes categorical distinctions (Schmid 2020: 233–234), which is why Schmid (2020) has developed an approach that permits a more flexible conception of linguistic knowledge. It builds on the previously presented idea that linguistic knowledge is available in the form of associations only. Accordingly, Schmid's proposal objects to the idea of schemata and representations and replaces them with an idea that is more compatible with the depiction of the cognitive network as a dynamic organism. In his approach, the function of schemata is taken over by patterns of associations that are routinized to differing degrees. This approach accounts for the same effects that have been described for schema-based approaches (i.e. that there are structures which are cognitively more available than others), but does so in a more dynamic conception of the phenomenon, as it stresses that this process is a continuum instead of involving different stages (cf. Schmid 2020: 233). Importantly, it does not distinguish between token and type entrenchment but argues that the processes that are at work in the recognition of similar processing events are the same ones for highly similar or identical utterance types and such utterance types which display a less obvious kind of similarity. If a similarity is recognized between different processing events, then the associations reflecting this similarity are routinized (Schmid 2020: 227–228). Accordingly, the distinction made in conventional approaches between type and token entrenchment is reframed as a continuum, as the very same processes of routinization and schematization are at work whenever processing events are identified as sharing similarities.

Before exemplifying this process, let me point out a further aspect in which this proposal is superior to conventional ones. It has been explained that schema-based approaches assume the existence of a schema as soon as there is productive use of a pattern. For constructions whose constituents do not display high constituent familiarity, i.e. which are not part of a productive paradigm, it is assumed that speakers have not developed any kind of schematic representation. If speakers form new instances with an unproductive pattern, this is explained to happen through the process of analogy, which means that the new expression is derived directly from a specific one which serves as a model (cf. Booij 2010: 88–93). Thus, when new expressions are formed by analogy, they are modelled on concrete words, while schemata are assumed to operate on more abstract levels. Supporters of such a proposal find themselves confronted with the need to explain where the "line" between analogical formations and schemata is. Schmid's approach works without this distinction and instead postulates a continuum of differently routinized syntagmatic associations between the fixed and the variable elements in a pattern (cf. Schmid 2020: 231, 288). In his proposal, new formations are produced in analogy to existing formations on the basis of paradigmatic extension.

Schmid (2020: 227) demonstrates the mechanisms of his proposal with the utterance types of *take a chance, take a breath, take a decision* and *take a nap*, which are obviously partially similar and partially different, but in a systematic way. As Schmid (2020: 232) points out, "[s]tatistical learning operating over syntagmatic associations registers and routinizes syntagmatic tendencies, while statistical learning over paradigmatic associations detects and routinizes the similarities and differences between them". Accordingly, speakers will recognize that these utterance types share a structural similarity and will identify *take* as an identical recurrent element based on the perceptual similarity. They will furthermore observe the analogical role taken by the nouns following it, which are thus paradigmatic competitors in the syntagmatic combination with *take*. The pattern of associations which represents the commonalities between the instances *take a chance, take a breath, take a decision* and *take a nap* will become increasingly routinized by repeated processing events of the pattern 'take a N'. Thus, knowledge about the use of this pattern, namely that *take* can be combined with various nouns, is cognitively represented by the different strengths of the syntagmatic associations between *take* and each of these nouns.

The strength of this knowledge, i.e. the degree to which a pattern that captures the interaction of syntagmatic and paradigmatic associations is routinized and thus develops its own symbolic association, depends on the extent of variability of the fixed and the variable elements, as well as the number of competitors in the variable position (Schmid 2020: 231–232). The higher the variability among the slot-fillers in a pattern, the less likely is the pattern to yield a schema-like representation that has a symbolic association of its own, as a high degree of variability means that there is no perceptual similarity but only relational similarities, which are obviously harder to detect.

Having presented the general background on the cognitive representation of productive patterns, the next section will apply this framework to the phenomenon of three-noun compounds in order to show how the knowledge of the use of the different patterns that give rise to these complex compounds is represented in the cognitive network.

### 8.7.2 Schematization in the formation of complex compounds

The various aspects related to the productivity of two-word compounds that have been examined throughout Chapter 8 have helped collect pieces of information about the working mechanism of the word-formation pattern in which compounds are combined with further nouns. The different insights gained will now be used to make suggestions about what the cognitive representations employed in the formation of three-noun compounds might look like.

It has been shown that there are two-noun compounds that occur repeatedly as an embedded compound in more complex compounds in a particular function, i.e. either as head or modifier. Accordingly, in the relevant processing events in which the respective tripartite compounds occur, speakers will identify the recurring embedded compound as a commonality of these processing events through the perceptual and semantic similarity between the compounds. Furthermore, they will recognize the analogy between the variable heads or modifiers. The similarity between the different heads or modifiers will be recognized more easily, if they stem from the same semantic area and are thus paradigmatically connected. It is (i) the set of syntagmatic associations between the compound and its variable outer nouns together with (ii) the paradigmatic associations that connect these outer nouns, which incorporate a speaker's tacit knowledge of the use of a pattern. The more strongly developed these associations are, the easier it will be to process and produce new complex compounds based on this pattern.

I will illustrate this idea exemplarily with the highly productive pattern '*health care* + N'. Figure 28 is an extract of the paradigm of head nouns that *health care* combines with. The head nouns are given in decreasing order of the absolute frequency of the respective combination of *health care* and the particular head. The thickness of the arrows is intended to represent the strength of the syntagmatic association that holds between *health care* and each of the head nouns.

When speakers are exposed to concrete instantiations of this pattern, they recognize the formal and perceptual similarities of the different tripartite compounds. They recognize the recurrent function of *health care* as a modifier, the analogy between the outer nouns that act as heads, as well as the analogical relation between *health care* and the variable heads. The fact that the arrow that connects *health care* with *reform* is much thicker than that connecting it with *personnel* mirrors the expectation that the syntagmatic association is stronger in the former case than in the latter, based on the fact that *health care reform* has been more frequently

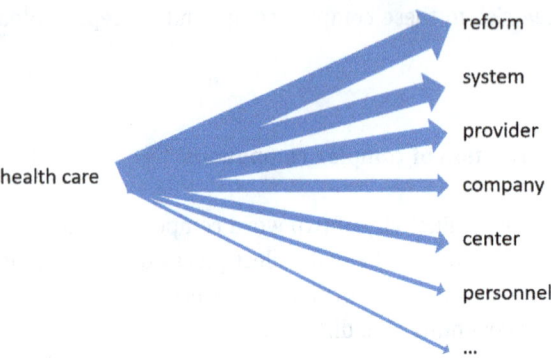

**Figure 28:** Different strengths of syntagmatic associations for *'health care* + N'.

processed by an average speaker than *health care personnel*. What is not illustrated in Figure 28 are the paradigmatic associations that hold between the head nouns. These nouns form semantic clusters in the sense illustrated in Section 8.4, with those nouns that are semantically similar showing stronger paradigmatic associations between each other than those that come from different semantic areas. It is the differently routinized syntagmatic and paradigmatic associations together which incorporate a speaker's tacit knowledge of the use of the pattern *'health care* + N'; namely that the compound *health care* is commonly followed by further nouns that it modifies, some of which, namely *reform* or *system*, are more likely to occur than others.

This constellation of associations equals the concept of a schema in its predictions about the processing and formation of instantiations based on the pattern *'health care* + N'. However, as opposed to schema-based approaches, this proposal does not find itself in the dilemma of having to determine which instances of the pattern might have been formed by analogy and which ones by means of a schema. Furthermore, it can also account for the knowledge that some head nouns are more likely to occur in the variable position, namely those whose syntagmatic associations are more strongly developed.

Based on these explanations, I intend to illustrate the concept of differently routinized associations in the process of schematization. For this purpose, Figures 29 (a)–(f) on the following three pages provide profiles of exemplary patterns that give rise to three-noun compounds, similar to those given in Section 8.2 for particular compounds, but now specified for compounds in a particular function. The concrete instances of three-noun compounds produced with a particular pattern (maximally 20) are displayed on the horizontal axis, while the corresponding token frequencies for each complex compound are displayed on the vertical axis. The exemplary patterns *'football* + N' and 'N + *network*' represent extremely productive

8.7 How is knowledge of compound productivity stored cognitively? — 221

(a)

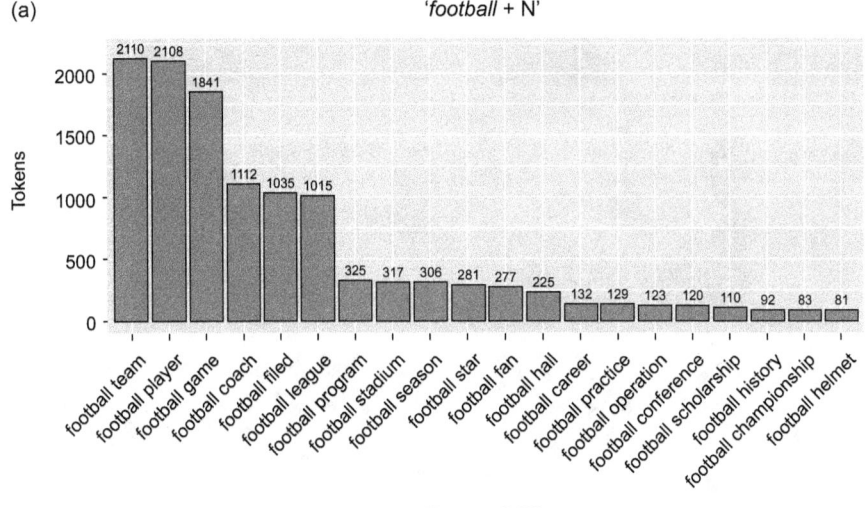

(b)

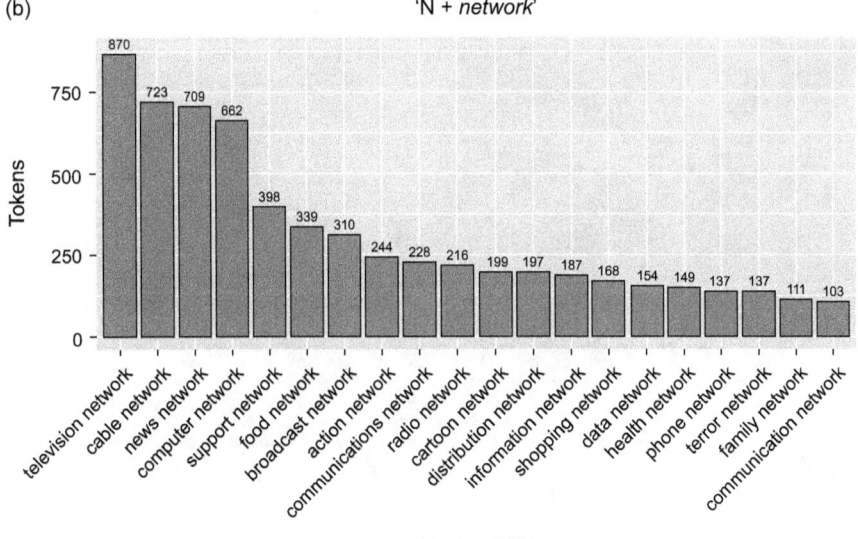

**Figure 29:** Use of exemplary patterns.

**222** — 8 Productivity in complex compounding

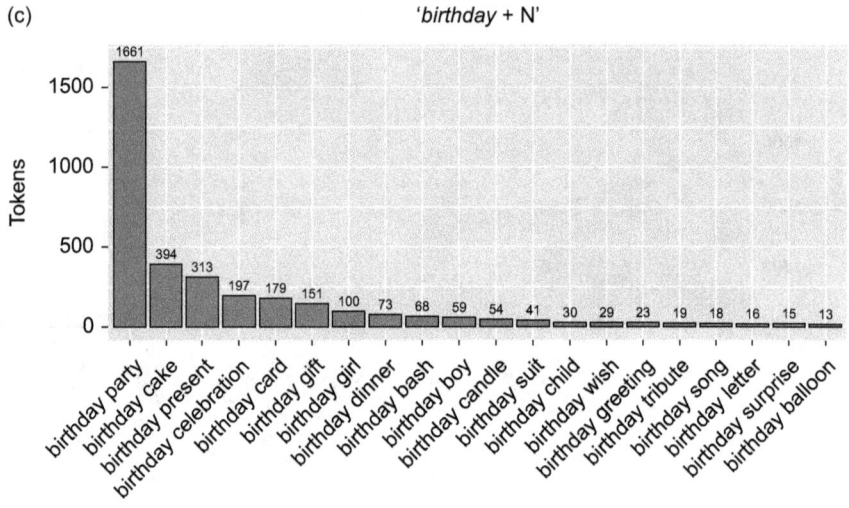

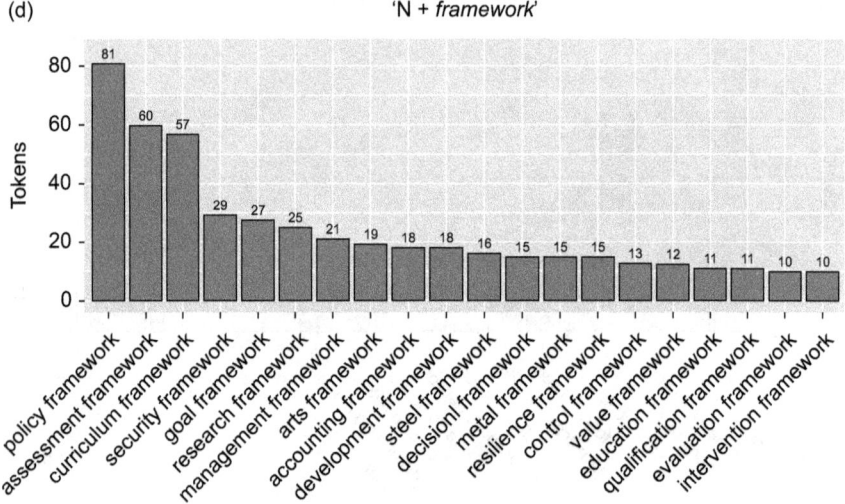

**Figure 29** (continued)

8.7 How is knowledge of compound productivity stored cognitively? — 223

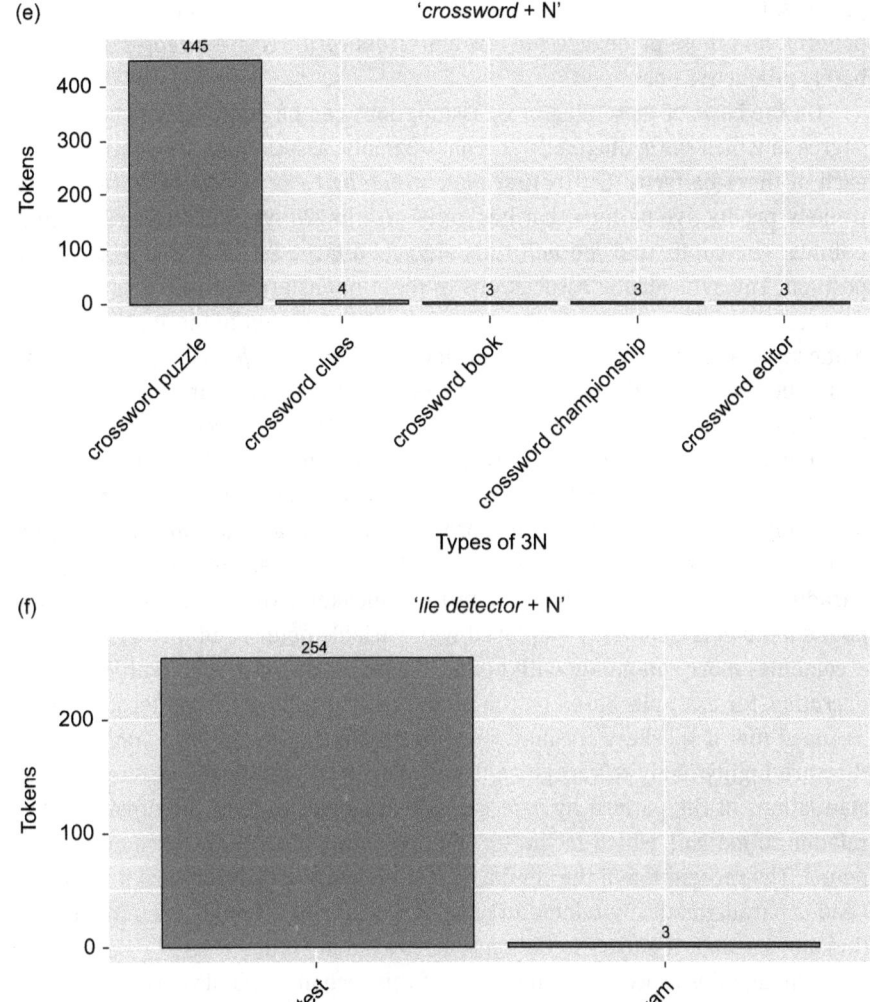

**Figure 29** (continued)

patterns, those of '*birthday* + N' and 'N +*framework*' represent highly productive patterns, and those of '*lie detector* + N' and '*crossword* + N' are a representation of barely productive ones.

On the basis of these diagrams, assumptions can be made with regard to the degree to which the syntagmatic and paradigmatic associations are routinized for each of these patterns. Let us first look at '*football* + N' in Figure 29 (a), an extremely productive pattern that has given rise to 238 types of three-noun compounds. The compound *football* thus attracts a large set of nouns in the head position. The syntagmatic associations to these nouns are routinized to different degrees, depending on the frequency of the relevant combination: the syntagmatic association will be very strongly developed between *football* and *coach*, but less so between *football* and *helmet*, for example. The outer nouns themselves are paradigmatically connected to each other with different degrees of strength, depending on their semantic similarity. It was shown in Section 8.4 that the semantic frame opened by *football* holds semantic clusters in the areas denoting agents or clothing, which suggests that the paradigmatic associations among these nouns will be comparatively strong. It is these differently entrenched syntagmatic and paradigmatic associations that constitute a speaker's knowledge that the compound *football* is commonly employed with variable nouns, and furthermore that it combines more commonly with nouns like *player* or *coach* than with *history* or *operation*, for example. Based on the productivity profile of this pattern, it can be assumed that if speakers encounter new formations of the pattern '*football* + N', they are highly likely to recognize the similarity to previously encountered instantiations of the pattern by detecting the analogical role of the novel head in relation to *football*, which facilitates the processing of the new three-noun compound. The recognition of the similarity is even more straightforward if the novel head is paradigmatically related to existing items with a similar meaning, i.e. fitting into a semantic cluster in the sense portrayed in Section 8.4.

Although this aspect is not the focus of this section, I will also briefly consider the whole three-noun compounds formed with the pattern '*football* + N'. Based on their high frequencies, instances such as *football team, football player, football game, football coach, football field* and *football league* can be assumed to be strongly entrenched concepts in the minds of average speakers. This means they are not just prominent attractors in the associative network, but their syntagmatic associations are presumably routinized to such a degree that they constitute units of processing that have developed a relatively strong symbolic association with its own set of syntagmatic, paradigmatic and pragmatic associations. However, the large number of paradigmatic competitors for the head slot and the fairly high degree of compositionality of these formations might somewhat weaken the syntagmatic strengthening of these complex compounds.

On a similar level of productivity, the pattern 'N + *network*' in Figure 29 (b) has produced 360 types of three-noun compounds, which means there is a great range of competing nouns in the modifier position. Accordingly, *network* holds a large number of syntagmatic associations with the various modifier nouns it combines with. Some of these associations are highly routinized, for example those between *network* and *television, cable* or *news*, respectively. In comparison, the syntagmatic associations between *network* and *family* or *communications* are developed comparatively weakly. The different modifier nouns are paradigmatically related to a stronger or lesser degree. *Television*, for example, can be assumed to be quite strongly connected to *computer, radio* and *phone*. These differently entrenched syntagmatic and paradigmatic associations constitute a speaker's knowledge that *network* can be employed quite extensively in more complex compounds with varying modifiers, some of which (namely those that describe electronic mediums) are more likely to occur than others.

Two slightly less productive patterns are exemplified by '*birthday* + N' and 'N + *framework*' in Figures 29 (c) and (d). They have formed 71 and 75 types of three-noun compounds respectively. For the pattern '*birthday* + N', *party* is a very prominent candidate in the competition among the outer nouns used as heads. Accordingly, the syntagmatic association between *birthday* and *party* is remarkably strong in comparison to the association with alternative nouns that are used in this position, such as *dinner, boy* or *wish*. The significant difference between the strength with which *birthday* is connected with *party* and the strength with which it is connected with the other heads suggests that in a context in which *birthday* is expected to be followed by a further noun, the word *party* will be strongly triggered. Based on the semantic map given in Section 8.4 for the nouns employed in the pattern '*birthday* + N', some of the competing nouns can be imagined to show stronger paradigmatic associations between each other than others, e.g. *girl* will be more strongly connected with *boy* and *child* than with *letter*. These associations capture the knowledge that *birthday* is commonly followed by different kinds of nouns, most prominently by *party*, but also by nouns denoting the people who are being celebrated on that day.

The pattern 'N + *framework*' is similarly productive as '*birthday* + N' regarding the number of types of three-noun compounds it has formed. However, comparing the token frequencies of the most frequent three-noun compounds for these two patterns (*policy framework*: 81 tokens; *birthday party* 1,661 tokens) indicates that the strength with which *framework* is connected with its most prominent modifier differs greatly in quality from the syntagmatic association with which *birthday* and *party* are connected. Competition between the nouns that can be used as modifiers with *framework* is more balanced than in the variable slot of '*birthday* + N', as the most frequent instantiations of the pattern 'N + *framework*' (i.e. *policy framework, assessment framework, curriculum framework*) show quite similar token frequencies. Thus, the syntagmatic associations between *framework* and the modifiers *policy, assessment* and *curriculum* can be expected to have a similar quality. These modifiers, however, are partly highly abstract, which might entail that paradigmatic associations between them might be less strongly developed, as semantic similarities between them are harder to detect. Accordingly, the knowledge that speakers have about the usage of the pattern 'N + *framework*' might be less distinctive than in the case of '*birthday* + N'.

Finally, I will look at the patterns '*lie detector* + N' and '*crossword* + N'. Both are barely used for the formation of tripartite compounds and thus do not show much variability for the slot in the head position. In the case of '*lie detector* + N', the only heads used are *test* and *exam*. While *test* is a very frequent slot-filler, the semantic competitor *exam* is a very infrequent alternative. Based on the relatively high token frequency of *lie detector test* and the fact that there are basically no competing heads, it can be assumed that there is a relatively strongly developed syntagmatic association between *lie detector* and *test*. The synonymous formation *lie detector exam* is evidence of the paradigmatic extension of the pattern '*lie detector* + N', based on the semantic similarity between the two nouns. The low token frequency of *lie detector exam* suggests that the syntagmatic association between *lie detector* and *exam* is only weakly developed. Accordingly, the implicit knowledge stored by speakers about the use of the pattern '*lie detector* + N' will be that *lie detector* is commonly followed by *test*.

A similar picture is found for '*crossword* + N'. Only 5 types of three-noun compounds have been formed with this pattern, the only salient of which is *crossword puzzle*, with all the other complex compounds being sporadic low-frequency occurrences. Based on the relatively high frequency of *crossword puzzle* on the one hand, and the lack of prominent competitors for the head slot on the other hand, there is presumably quite a strong syntagmatic association between *crossword* and *puzzle*. By contrast, the syntagmatic associations between *crossword* and *clues, book, championship* or *editor* must be assumed to be only very weakly developed. The paradigmatic associations between the variable head nouns can be expected to be rather low, as they are semantically quite distinctive. Accordingly, the tacit knowledge that speakers can be assumed to have about the usage of the pattern '*crossword* + N' is expressed through the fact that they are quite likely to expect the word *puzzle* upon encountering *crossword*.

To conclude, this section has attempted to model the knowledge that speakers have about the use of patterns that give rise to three-noun compounds. The different degrees to which the syntagmatic and partly also the paradigmatic associations can be routinized have been illustrated by means of a quantitative and qualitative insight into exemplary patterns. The knowledge that has been gained about the cognitive representation of the elements involved in the formation of tri-constituent compounds has some non-trivial implications for the future formation of complex compounds. Before I can proceed to these implications in Section 8.8, there is a point to be made, to which the next section will be devoted.

### 8.7.3 What about more abstract types of representation?

The previous section has argued that the knowledge of productive patterns in the formation of three-noun compounds is mainly derived from the strength of the associations that hold between specific compounds and the lexically anchored outer nouns they have been used with. Readers who are acquainted with conventional schema-based approaches to the cognitive representation of productive patterns might at this point wonder about more abstract kind of knowledge involving higher level generalizations. As has been explained in Section 8.7.1, in proposals that employ schemata, different levels of representation are assumed along a scale of schematicity, from lexically specific representations through semi-abstract ones to fully abstract schemata. Figure 30 sketches the schemata that conventional approaches might propose for the kinds of representations that underlie three-noun compounding. The figure displays four levels of representation, from higher level variable representations to lexically specific ones. The levels have been numbered from (1) to (4) not to suggest a consecutive order but merely to make reference to them easier.

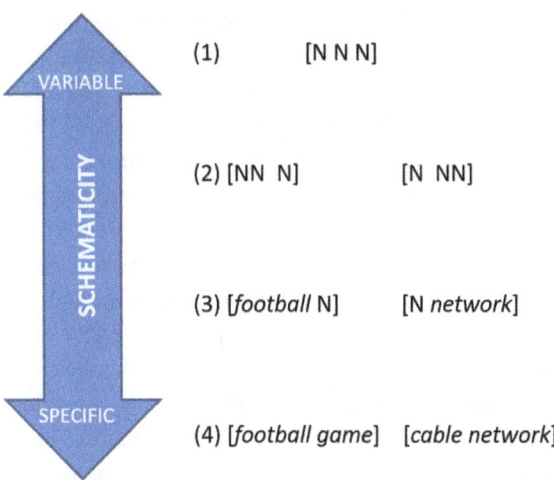

**Figure 30:** Potential degrees of schematicity for three-noun compounds.

On the highest level of schematicity (1), there is a maximally abstract schematic representation that consists of unspecific placeholders for nouns only and is not specified with regards to internal structure. On the next level of schematicity (2), there is another fully abstract representation with unspecific placeholders, but more specific than the former in that it is specified with regards to branching pattern, resulting in one schematic representation for left-branching items ([NN N]) and one for right-branching ones ([N NN]). The third level of schematicity (3) contains a semi-abstract lower-level schema in which a concrete compound in a particular function is combined with a variable noun. The most specific level of representation (4) is that of the lexically filled symbolic unit. In the proposal presented in this work, do speakers not have any knowledge about the productivity of compounds on more abstract levels of representation that would equate to a schema [NN N], [N NN], or even [N N N]? In order to engage with this idea, I will briefly contemplate these abstract schemata, which are potentially cognitively available in the hierarchical network of three-noun compounds.

For this purpose, Figure 31 specifies what these schemata on the four idealized levels of representation could look like, derived from Schmid's depiction for *un*-prefixation (Schmid 2016: 230). The boxes represent more or less strongly developed attractors in the cognitive network in the form of a symbolic association of form and meaning, with forms being displayed in the first line of each box and meanings in the second one. The thickness of the boxes is supposed to illustrate the different degrees to which the relevant representations might be assumed to be entrenched. The notion of *thing-concept* in the semantic description is used in the sense established by Langacker (1987b), describing concepts that are expressed by nouns. The two lowest levels of representation at the bottom of the figure display lexically specific items (e.g. *football game*) and ones which in schema-based approaches would be categorized as semi-schematic, partially filled representations (e.g. *football* N). These levels have merely been added for the sake of completeness and are not in the focus of interest here, as the focus is on the two abstract kinds of representation in the top half of the figure.

I will first consider the representations of [NN N] and [N NN], which reflect which type of three-noun compound is encountered with regard to the location and function of the embedded compound. Schema-based approaches might argue that these patterns are activated and strengthened if a new instantiation of a three-noun compound is formed or produced that contains an unproductive embedded compound and thus does not have a head or modifier family of formations. Based on the extreme number of three-noun compounds that are not productive and have low token frequencies (cf. Section 8.3), it could thus be assumed that these two general schemata are entrenched to some degree. Considering there are more instances of left-branching than right-branching compounds, it could be argued

8.7 How is knowledge of compound productivity stored cognitively? — 229

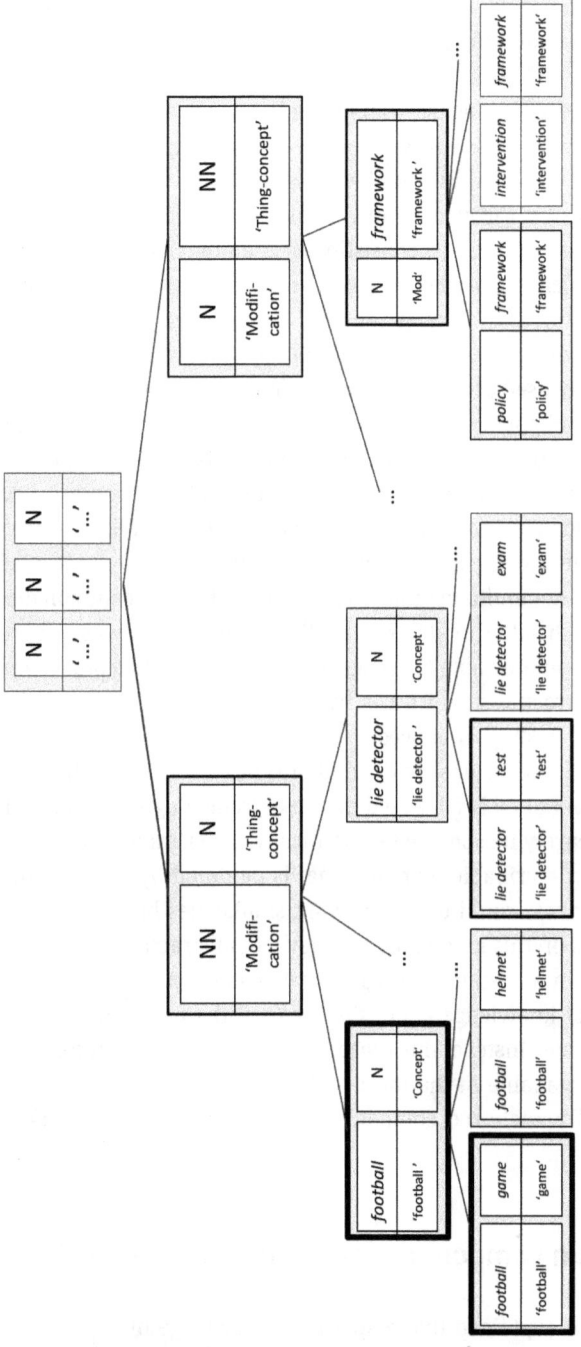

**Figure 31:** Potential levels of representations in three-noun compounding.

that the schema [NN N] is more strongly entrenched than that of [N NN], which is why the thickness of these boxes differs slightly.

However, based on the high degree of variability found in these patterns, both the formal and semantic specifications that can be made are extremely vague. The illustration shows that the schema [NN N] can merely be described as instances in which a compound in some way modifies another noun, both of which express any concept that can be expressed through nouns. Similarly, the description of the schema [N NN] can only be specified as consisting of a noun-concept that is expressed by a compound which is modified by a noun-concept. A situation in which speakers need to draw on these similarities can only be imagined if a new three-noun compound is encountered that contains a fully unproductive compound and a noun that is not commonly used as head or modifier in tripartite compounds and thus does not have any paradigmatic associations to other items. This might be the case, for example, when encountering the complex compounds *snack food personality* or *specialty gourmet shop*. Both have a token frequency of 3, and there are no other three-noun compounds with *gourmet shop* or *snack food* as modifier or head respectively. Accordingly, in the search for similarities with previously processed items, the lowest common denominator that could be found is the commonality that a compound acted as a head or modifier of another noun. It is, however, hard to imagine that speakers should be able to recognize relational or conceptual similarities on this level of abstractness, which is why a representation of knowledge on this level could only be weakly pronounced.

This is even truer for the more unspecific kind of representation on the most abstract and unspecific level of [N N N]. Based on the extreme degree of variability in this pattern, it can barely be specified semantically, other than that what is referred to is any concept describable by nouns that is modified by other nouns. It seems unlikely that speakers could detect relevant similarities between different three-noun compounds on this maximally high level of abstractness.

These explanations aim at demonstrating why it is not sensible to assume any more abstract kinds of knowledge about the usage of the patterns that give rise to three-noun compounds. Instead, this reasoning supports the claim that this knowledge is exclusively available in the form of differently routinized patterns of associations for lexically anchored compounds and the competing heads or modifiers they are used with.

## 8.8 Which three-noun compounds are likely to be formed?

The previous sections have explained that a speaker's knowledge of the productivity of a pattern builds on previous encounters with the relevant items. It is this knowledge which also governs the formation of new instances. As Dal and Namer (2016: 76) point out, "productivity deals not with the actual lexicon but with a future lexicon based on observation of the existing one". As a consequence, the analysis of existing forms has a predictive power for potential future formations. Accordingly, integrating all the information that has been gained about the behaviour of two-noun compounds in forming tri-constituent ones will permit predictions about the complex compounds that can be expected to be formed.

To do so, I will summarize the information that has been collected so far: Firstly, it has been shown to what degree particular compounds are productive in the formation of more complex compounds, as well as to what degree they are productive in the function of head or modifier. Based on the explanations given in the previous sections, the extent to which a pattern has been used to form three-noun compounds corresponds to the ease with which speakers can produce and process new instances, as productive patterns translate into strongly entrenched associations, which license new formations more easily. These findings allow us to claim that it is more likely that speakers will form new three-noun compounds with the pattern '*football* + N' than with 'N + *football*' or '*body mass* + N'. Importantly, the findings of this work do not just permit a prediction of which patterns are more likely to be used to form new instances of complex compounds, but also which kinds of instances are likely to be formed. Section 8.4 gave an insight into the semantic productivity of exemplary patterns, i.e. the range of meanings found among the slot-fillers of a pattern. This section will outline in what way this knowledge can be used to make even more specific predictions about potential new formations.

Goldberg (2016) argues that the productivity of a linguistic element in forming new items is conditioned by how well attested the relevant category is through similar exemplars. She explains that the way in which a pattern is extended for new formations depends on the coverage of that pattern across the semantic space with regard to two specifications. The first important factor is the semantic distribution of the types that have been formed so far with a pattern. There can be high coverage across the semantic space if the slot-fillers are evenly spread, or rather low coverage, with the semantic space being covered unevenly or large parts of the semantic space remaining empty. Goldberg suggests that coinages in a semantic space that shows high coverage can be expected to have a higher degree of acceptability than those in less densely covered areas (2016: 373–377). The second aspect that is important is the position of a new formation in the semantic space covered by a pattern. If it is similar to attested exemplars and thus located in an area with high coverage by other types, it is more likely to be accepted than coinages in sparsely covered semantic space.

This reasoning is based on the results of a study performed by Suttle and Goldberg (2011), in which the degree to which speakers rated new formations as acceptable was influenced by the coverage of the existing types in the semantic space. This phenomenon leads to what Hilpert (2018: 103) describes as the "Matthäus-Effekt": a high concentration of types in one semantic area will attract further formations. This claim is supported by the results of a diachronic study performed by Perek (2016), who reports that the coverage of a pattern correlates with the number of coinages it attracts. Further empirical support can be found in Lamberty and Schmid (2013), who show at the example of verbal compounds that the existence of an extensive word-family has an influence on the success of a new compound, as the association to the established items provides help in the assignment of meaning.

A theoretical explanation for the observation that the extension of a pattern to new formations is guided by semantic similarity to existing items is delivered by Schmid (2020: 288). He claims that new formations "are likely to be paradigmatically related to existing attractors", arguing that this phenomenon is an effect of paradigmatic associations. Accordingly, if speakers use a pattern to form a new instance, the variable slot-filler is more likely to be one that is paradigmatically related to existing ones and thus to be semantically similar, than to be completely different. On these grounds, Schmid claims that "paradigmatic associations constrain innovations" (2020: 288). I fully agree with his reasoning but would formulate this claim more carefully into "paradigmatic associations *guide* innovations", as speakers are still able to form new instances that are semantically unrelated to existing ones, they are just less likely to do so.

This theoretical background permits educated predictions about the kinds of three-noun compounds that are likely to be formed. The maps created in Section 8.4 showed the coverage of the semantic space that is taken by the concrete instances of a particular pattern. I will illustrate the benefit of this tool with the example of the pattern *'football* + N'. The illustration on page 169 shows firstly that there is a high degree of coverage of the space in the semantic frame opened by *football*. Accordingly, it can be reasoned that the pattern *'football* + N' is comparatively welcoming to new slot-fillers in the first place. Secondly, the outer nouns used in this pattern are quite diverse, semantically limited only by what kinds of instances can be modified within the frame of *football*. Still, some of these nouns form smaller or larger clusters. It is the densely populated areas which are most likely to be paradigmatically extended. Thus, in the formation of new items with the pattern *'football* + N', speakers will prefer to employ nouns from these semantic areas, as these are the ones that are most likely to be understood and accepted by other speakers. Accordingly, the potential formations *football dress* or *football bra* are more likely than a formation *football bucket*, as in the first cases the outer nouns stem from the semantic area of clothing, which is already covered by similar instances such as *football shoes, football shorts*, etc. In the case of *football bucket*, by contrast, there are no prominent outer nouns that are similar. In the same vein, if a speaker encounters a new item *football bra*, it is presumably processed with less effort than a potential coinage *football bucket*, whose processing might be comparatively less fluent.

By contrast, a look at the semantic map of the pattern '*roadside* + N' on page 175 shows that there is less coverage of the semantic space. This suggests that this pattern is less welcoming to new formations in the first place. Furthermore, the slot-fillers show a higher degree of semantic homogeneity, mainly referring to the concepts of bombing, accidents and accommodation/alimentation. Obviously, the paradigmatic associations between the heads with which *roadside* combines has guided the formations of further instances with semantically similar heads. New formations are more likely to be accepted if they denote a concept in the area of gastronomy, car maintenance or accident/road support, such as *roadside hotdog*, *roadside burger* or *roadside garage*, for example (of course given that the relevant concepts exist in the first place) than if they denote concepts in semantic areas that are not covered in the map.

The findings of this section go beyond conventional approaches to productivity which are limited to showing which patterns are likely to be used to create new forms. The investigation of the semantic area covered by the slot-fillers of a pattern in addition permits the semantic specification of potential new formations. As was pointed out above, speakers can of course form other instances than those suggested, which might deviate from the kinds of items predicted in that they use unproductive compounds to form new instances of tripartite compounds or use a productive pattern with a slot-filler that is semantically very distinct from others; however, they are definitely less likely to do so. These kinds of predictions are highly valuable since they sharpen the predictive apparatus when it comes to understanding the use of the patterns that give rise to complex compounds.

To conclude this section, I intend to present an assumption of how and why three-noun compounds are formed that are not produced through paradigmatic extension. It has been argued that an "organic", natural way of forming a new three-noun compound is through the usage of an entrenched two-noun compound that denotes a salient concept in the extra-linguistic world and thus opens a range of roles to be filled in the frame denoted by this compound (in the case of left-branching compounds). Accordingly, it shares syntagmatic relations of different strength with a larger or smaller set of nouns that can be used in the function of head. If a new concept in the semantic frame of this compound is to be named, the relevant pattern is paradigmatically extended to a new instantiation. Why, however, are there three-noun compounds that are based on a two-noun compound that is not strongly entrenched and not productive, such as *victims compensation coordination* or *mosquito repellent spray*? I claim that these constructions have not come to existence in a natural – in the sense of subconscious – way. I suggest calling these instances "drawing-board compounds", as they seem to have been designed consciously. The underlying assumption is that the speaker who has coined such complex compound is likely to have done so quite deliberately, contemplating which words could be combined to express the relevant concept. What these compounds have in common is their origin in bureaucratic areas, often governmental, or in marketing-related areas, naming trend-concepts, or denoting titles e.g. *transportation safety board, security council resolution, county district attorney, ice bucket challenge* or *body mass index*. In these cases, the three nouns seem to have been combined consciously to denote the relevant concepts. The respective tripartite compounds enter the language as complex terms, without the embedded compound having been entrenched as such beforehand. Accordingly, in the formation – and processing – of these compounds, there is no intermediate step over an entrenched two-noun compound, which makes these word-formation products less beneficial from a cognitive perspective. This does, however, not mean, that these three-noun compound as a whole cannot become established in the speech community, as some of the examples are fairly frequent. They can become entrenched as a whole if they are used extensively. Nevertheless, these kinds of compounds are comparatively rare, as the majority of tripartite compounds is based on an entrenched two-word compound such as *football, weekend* or *network*.

## 8.9 Summary and conclusions

Chapter 8 aimed to grasp the different behaviour of two-noun compounds when it comes to producing polylexemic compounds. It was proven that some compounds are significantly more productive than others, lending themselves extensively to complex compound formation, with the most productive ones accounting for hundreds of different three-noun compounds. It was also found that a compound's productivity depends on the function in which it is used, since compounds do not occur as heads and modifiers to the same degree. Productivity in tripartite compounding can thus be stated to be not just lexeme-based but also function-based. This finding indicates that it is little insightful to try and evaluate the general productivity of the abstract word-formation process in which three nouns are combined. Instead, it is much more informative to investigate the productivity of concrete patterns within this word-formation process, as it has been demonstrated that there are crucial differences among the patterns that employ particular items in a particular function. This observation is in line with construction grammarian approaches to productivity, which proclaim sub-patterns within one word-formation pattern to be more important sources of productivity than highly abstract patterns (cf. Hilpert 2018).

These insights show why it is reasonable to distinguish different types among the patterns that give rise to three-noun compounds, which are instantiated in the examples of *football game* and *night football*. These two types are not used for the formation of complex compounds to the same degree. Accordingly, the concept of productivity in complex compounding was defined as the different degrees to which patterns in the form of '*football* + N' or 'N + *football*' are used for the formation of three-noun compounds. It must be acknowledged at this point that the productivity of the different patterns that give rise to complex compounds as calculated in this work – just as well as in other corpus-based approaches – is of course a generalization. It must not be forgotten that the productivity of a pattern will always depend on the medium, register and subject (cf. Baayen 2009; Schmid 2016: 114). Productivity can, for example, vary considerably between spoken and written language, as Stumpf (2021) illustrates for German passe-partout compounds, which are highly productive in spoken language but barely used in other categories. Accordingly, when a pattern is said to be used productively, this does not take into account whether it is used by numerous individual speakers or only a few speakers who make excessive use of this pattern. Thus, the claims about the productivity of particular patterns in this work are a generalization of all speakers in a speech community that shows the maximal usage of a pattern.

In order to not just take into account quantitative aspects of productivity, I have also added a semantic facet to the concept of productivity. With the help of word embeddings, the range of meanings of the slot-fillers in exemplary patterns were investigated. It was shown that it is possible to recognize semantic clusters among the outer nouns that are used in a particular pattern. This insight adds to purely quantitative investigations of productivity, as it permits a more detailed description of the productivity of the different patterns that produce complex compounds.

To explain the differences in productivity, a variety of linguistic variables were explored. The frequency of a compound and its degree of internal association strength were shown to correlate with its tendency to be used for the formation of more complex compounds. These two variables can thus be claimed to be strong predictors for a compound's productivity. The relevance of these linguistic factors was explained by outlining the cognitive foundations of productivity. It was argued that the different usage intensities of compounds correspond to differing cognitive representations. Compounds with a high usage intensity display a strong degree of entrenchment, which means that they show strongly routinized associations in the cognitive network. This results in a cognitive advantage in processing and activation, which licenses the use of entrenched compounds for further word-formation processes. Accordingly, more strongly entrenched compounds are more likely to be used as input for further word-formation than weakly entrenched ones, as the latter require more cognitive work both for activation and for assembling and then for further combination. As a corollary, entrenched compounds are also more likely to be embraced by the speech community and hence to become conventionalized and thus re-used. A crucial implication that was drawn from these results is that three-noun compounds which are based on a strongly entrenched two-noun compound are actually pseudo-tri-constituent.

After explaining how the usage intensity of compounds translates into associations that are routinized to different degrees with a focus on individual compounds, I broadened the view and exposed the organization of the cognitive network of which these items are a part. I argued that more and less productive patterns find entrance to the cognitive network in the form of differently routinized syntagmatic and paradigmatic associations that are based on the recognition of commonalities and variability in different usage events. I also presented the implications of the insights gained throughout Chapter 8, demonstrating how the knowledge of compound productivity can be used to make predictions about the future use of the patterns that are used to form polylexemic compounds. I argued that the density of the semantic space covered by the nouns used in a pattern permits assumptions about the types of three-noun compounds that are most likely to be produced and thus demonstrated the predictive power of the information gathered in this work.

## Part V: **Synopsis**

# 9 A portrait of three-noun compounds

The analysis of various formal and functional features of three-noun compounds in Chapters 6 and 7 has led to a clearer image of what characterizes these complex compounds. The tracing of their formation process through the investigation of their embedded compounds in Chapter 8 has furthermore enlightened the nature of three-noun compounds by revealing what their components typically look like. The present chapter will summarize the pieces of information that have been collected in the course of this work with the aim to create a profile of three-noun compounds that illustrates their typical and less typical features.

Regarding their functional characteristics, three-noun compounds are typically determinative, endocentric compounds. They are used in a variety of genres and stem from various semantic areas. Tripartite nominal compounds are typically partly compositional, which means that their meaning can be derived from the meaning of the mostly lexicalized embedded compound and that of the outer noun. Three-noun compounds generally tend to not show alternation with alternative phrasal expressions.

Regarding their formal features, three-noun compounds can have a length from three to eleven syllables; on average, however, they do not exceed six syllables. Frequently used items tend to consist of three to five syllables only. When it comes to their morphological complexity, three-noun compounds have shown to consist of a maximum of six morphemes; the majority, however, consists of four morphemes only. They are mostly based on an embedded compound whose components are morphologically simple, and a simple or affixed outer noun. The embedded compound tends to be a strongly established compound that represents an entrenched concept and produces a whole range of complex compounds. Regarding their spelling, three-noun compounds occur mostly in the formats N N N, and NN N/N NN, less often in the format N-N N, and almost never in the remaining orthographic formats. The stress pattern can be specified in that three-noun compounds are stressed on the first element; further stress points could not be conclusively determined at this stage.

Besides these general characteristics, it was observed that three-noun compounding encompasses a heterogeneous set of instances. The most important variable in this context is their internal structure. There are more instances of left-branching than of right-branching, and, additionally, left-branching items tend to be used more frequently than right-branching ones. Left-branching compounds can be said to be slightly shorter than right-branching ones. They furthermore occur in the spelling format N-N N, the equivalent of which is not reported for right-branching ones. From a theoretical perspective, the instantiations of the two

**240** — 9 A portrait of three-noun compounds

branching patterns also differ regarding the quality of their non-primary stress points. Left- and right-branching compounds do not only differ from each other with regard to their formal characteristics, but also from a semantic perspective, as there are right-branching compounds which employ particular modifiers that give them an appearance of syntactic constructions, marking the fuzzy boundary between compounding in a narrow sense and syntax.

Figure 32 is an attempt to summarize the formal characteristics of three-noun compounds. It is supposed to illustrate what three-noun compounds typically look like and in what aspects less typical instantiations deviate from more typical ones. The prototypical core of three-noun compounds is displayed in the centre of the figure in the form of the pentagon. The attributes of this core are specified through the five aspects of LENGTH, MORPHEMES, BRANCHING PATTERN, SPELLING and EMBEDDED COMPOUND. The aspect of stress has been excluded in the figure, as the results of this work are not conclusive. The features that are portrayed as typical are those that are shared by the majority of three-noun compounds and which

**Figure 32:** More and less typical instances of three-noun compounding.

characterize the most frequent instances. Less typical compounds differ from the prototypical core in that they deviate in one or more of these five aspects, each of which is specified in a different area outside the pentagon. The areas are not to be seen as discrete categories; instead, each of them presents an attribute that can render a tripartite compound less typical. Within each category, there are further gradations regarding the typicality of the items. For example, in the category of right-branching compounds, short instances are still more typical than longer ones, while those with an adjectival modifier are again even less typical instances. Accordingly, the examples given are not categorical but most of them fit several areas at the same time (e.g. *law enforcement organization* is a less typical member of the category of three-noun compounds not just with regard to its morphological complexity, but also regarding its length).

The figure shows that the prime instances that form the core of the category of three-noun compounds are left-branching items that are based on a strongly established compound. Formally, these items have a length of 3–4 syllables and maximally consist of one morphologically complex noun. They occur in the spelling N N N or NN N. Accordingly, forms like *football game, health care center* or *birthday cake* exemplify highly typical instantiations of this word-formation pattern.

Less central instances of the category of three-noun compounding are those in which the embedded compound is located in the head position, i.e. right-branching items, such as *guest bedroom* or *terror network*. Among the group of right-branching compounds, less typical instances of complex compounding are those which use adjectival modifiers that lend them the air of a syntactic construction (e.g. *summer roadtrip, university law professor*).

Other rather peripheral members are tripartite compounds whose constituents are much longer than the average, having five syllables and more, and/or which are highly complex from a morphological perspective, containing several instances of derivation. The length and complexity that is instantiated in formations like *law enforcement official* or *information technology security*, for example, is rather exceptional.

Regarding their spelling, three-noun compounds most typically occur in the formats N N N and N NN in the case of left-branching compounds; a less typical orthographical format found is N-N N. Right-branching compounds occur most commonly in the formats NN N and N N N. Highly uncommon formats are the remaining formats of N N-N, N-N-N, N-NN NN-N and NNN. Compounds that are found in one of the latter spellings (e.g. *body-mass-index, home-health-care, gingerbread-house, aircraft-carrier*) are never established in this spelling format but will always be more frequently encountered in one of the first four formats.

Further less typical instances of three-noun compounding are those which are based on a less strongly established compound, e.g. *mosquito repellent spray* or *body mass index*. In this category, the least typical instantiations are such which are based on an embedded compound that is barely established, which is mostly true for "drawing-board compounds", e.g. *transportation safety board* or *victims compensation coordination*.

With this portrait of three-noun compounds, I intend to, on the one hand, highlight the heterogeneity that is found among the word-formation products of three-noun compounding. On the other hand, its aim is to demonstrate that typical instances of this word-formation process are far away from examples of the type *law enforcement authority* or *arctic cat observer* cited in other works on polymorphemic compounding. Instead, typical three-noun compounds are much more natural and discreet instances of the type *football game* and *airport hotel*.

This characterization can be assumed to hold true for even more complex compounds. Among four-constituent compounds, for example, as well, it is very likely that the most typical instances are such in which the embedded compound(s) is/are strongly established and the lexemes combined are rather simple when it comes to their morphological complexity and their number of syllables. Quite certainly, there will also be more and less typical realizations among the new options that come into play regarding morphological structure and spelling.

# 10 Summary and conclusions

This work has demonstrated at the example of three-noun compounds that the field of polylexemic compounding deserves more extensive study. Firstly, it provides highly interesting material for investigation. Obviously, the features that have been extensively discussed for simple compounds are even more intriguing for multi-word compounds, creating new options when it comes to spelling, orthography, stress and internal structure. Secondly, the systematic analysis of three-word compounds has demonstrated that the study of complex word-formation products can yield valuable insights into the process of word-formation itself.

One aspect that is crucial in polylexemic compounds is the internal morphological structure of these word-formation products. It was demonstrated that tripartite compounding comprises two fundamentally different types, which are instantiated in the examples of *football game* and *night football*. Thus, on a structural level, word-formation products consisting of three nouns should not be thought of as N+N+N, but rather NN+N or N+NN. These two patterns do not only differ in the extent to which they are used but also have their own formal characteristics regarding length, stress and orthography and show differences when it comes to semantic aspects. Therefore, three-noun compounding cannot be viewed as a homogeneous phenomenon but its examination needs to distinguish between these two different types of tripartite compounds. In this context, I highlighted the intricacies in determining the branching pattern of complex word-formation products and challenged established criteria. It can be seen as a major contribution of this work to have elaborated precise criteria that allow determining the internal structure of polylexemic word-formation products, firstly, and secondly, to present an automated tagging system that shows great potential for further application, as it can also be used to identify the morphological structure of other complex word-formation products.

I have furthermore demonstrated that tri-constituent compounds are not as infrequent as tends to be assumed, with almost 60,000 different types in COCA. The fact that the majority of these complex compounds are found in the lower frequency range does not deprive the word-formation process in which three nouns are combined of its importance, even if this process mainly creates temporary instances instead of contributing to extending the word stock of English in the long term. The low-frequency items are proof of the availability and effectivity of this word-formation process, as speakers obviously consider it a useful tool to address the need for denotation. Accordingly, three-noun compounding can generally be assessed as a productive word-formation process in English.

In the context of productivity, this book has added to the literature by elaborating an understanding of productivity in the area of compounding. It has demonstrated that instead of analysing the productivity of the general word-formation pattern that combines three nouns, it is more insightful to look into more concrete sub-patterns, namely the usage of a particular compound in a particular function. These results support construction grammarians' proposals concerning productivity, which allow a fine-grained view on productivity by looking into particular patterns within a morphological category instead of investigating it for general word-formation patterns or processes. Accordingly, productivity in three-noun compounding must be specified in terms of patterns that use a particular compound in a particular function, i.e. either as head or modifier, such as *'football* + N' or 'N + *network'*. Empirical data has supported this claim, reporting that these patterns show measurable differences in the extent to which they produce complex compounds. This approach has enabled a fine-grained description of the different degrees of productivity in three-noun compounding, which has singled out the role of simple compounds in the formation of more complex compounds. I have also introduced a semantic facet to the concept of productivity that permits making qualified predictions about the items that are likely to be formed by speakers. Thus, this proposal is a valuable asset to quantitatively oriented accounts of productivity, as is not limited to predicting which patterns are more likely to be used to form new words than others, but it can even specify which kinds of items can be expected to be formed.

The central finding of this project is the following: the decisive condition for a two-noun compound to be used productively to form tri-constituent compounds is its degree of entrenchment. Only compounds that are entrenched to a certain degree tend to be productively available for the formation of more complex compounds. These results are considered crucial as they reveal why only particular compounds repeatedly serve as a basis for more complex compounds and thus permit retracing the step from simple compounds to multi-word compounds. These insights demonstrate that polylexemic compounding is not separate from simple compounding but that the two are intertwined. This is furthermore supported by the fact that there are two-noun compounds that are so strongly entrenched that native speakers might not even realize they consist of two words (e.g. *football, network, birthday*).

Considering that a high number of tripartite compounds contain a relatively strongly entrenched embedded compound, this insight explains why three-word compounding is an effective means to create new words. Obviously, the same reasons apply as for simple compounds: they help condense the wealth of information contained in a particular concept in relatively little space and still remain informative by capturing the most important aspects in their form. Three-noun compounds have also been shown to be fairly transparent, which is another reason why they are successful in forming new words. Moreover, it was reasoned that productive (and thus entrenched) compounds can be assumed to use a limited set of semantic relations, which facilitates the interpretation of new formations. As it was additionally shown that new formations tend to employ outer nouns that are similar to established instances, it is understandable why the formation and processing of new three-word compounds that are based on an entrenched two-word compound are comparatively effortless – a further factor that promotes the use of this word-formation process.

In line with usage-based cognitive perspectives to word-formation, I have explained that the processing and formation of three-noun compounds is based on general cognitive abilities, such as schematization, categorization and generalization. In these explanations, I have taken a step away from mainstream construction grammarian approaches to a more dynamic cognitive representation of linguistic knowledge. I have argued that the representation of the knowledge that speakers have about the usage of compounds is provided in the form of associations, as this conception permits a dynamic account of the cognitive network. In order to explain what guides speakers in forming complex compounds, the knowledge that speakers have about the more and less productive use of different patterns was conceptualized in the form of differently routinized patterns of associations. It was demonstrated with the example of concrete patterns in how far this approach offers a plausible explanation for the formation of new items through the idea of paradigmatic extension. This reasoning delivered the explanation for the fact that (i) some patterns are more likely to produce new complex compounds than others and that (ii) they are more likely to produce new instances from particular semantic areas. These results have deepened our understanding of the formation and development of complex structures and of the working mechanisms of the brain regarding the storing and processing of polylexemic linguistic units.

In addition to the aspects that have focused on the phenomenon of multiword compounds, this book has made an effort to address the technical hurdles in working with large data. It has demonstrated that even for English, a language that boasts highly encompassing and professional corpora, the material provided is not fully reliable but needs improvement when it comes to tagging and orthographic conventions. The automatized searches in corpora have been shown to provide a relatively poor performance in terms of both precision and recall. Tagging in corpora is quite obviously still prone to errors and requires much more training and precision to reduce noise in the data. Furthermore, semantic and morphological information needs to be added to corpora in order to enable researchers to conduct more precise searches. Thus, it is desirable (and quite probable) for progress in these areas to be made to guarantee a higher quality for corpus-based research.

This work furthermore serves as a base for illustrating that computer-linguistic work cannot dispense with the intuition of a linguist. It was demonstrated that the operationalization of linguistic concepts through automated scripts must be complemented by additional filtering and manual post-processing. Sometimes even simple searches and frequency counts require labour-intensive manual refinement by a linguist to do justice to the differences between similar looking constructions. This is especially true for the operationalization of cognitive concepts, where research must be especially precise. These observations emphasize the importance of the interaction between computer-linguistic work and refinement through introspection in linguistic research, confirming Fillmore's claim that a good linguist is one who makes use of corpus data but does not go without their introspection.

Lastly, this work has highlighted the intricacies of working with compound data by presenting the limits and drawbacks of automated and technology-based research in the identification and distributional analysis of English compounds. It has introduced computer-linguistic proposals by means of which such hurdles can at least partly be overcome. In this context, I have not only introduced a technique to find compounds in allegedly simple words but have also presented the procedure that was undertaken to create a database of compounds. I have furthermore developed an automated method to determine the morphological structure in complex compounds, as well as a tool to study semantic productivity. These technical contributions are seen as a major achievement of this work, as they enable pursuing further research questions in the field of polylexemic compounding.

## 11 Outlook

All of the methods and technical applications that have been developed and presented in this book have room for further optimization. In the relevant sections, their deficits and problems were pointed out to permit suggestions for improvement. A deeper knowledge of computational linguistics would certainly be helpful in refining these methodological approaches. Moreover, the 3N database would definitely benefit from further deletion of noise and the correction of wrongly assigned branching patterns. This refinement could be performed in the form of a public crowd correction, in which all scholars who work with the database are also entitled to editing rights.

This work was necessarily selective in the research questions it answered. Nevertheless, it has hopefully managed to demonstrate that multi-word compounding is a phenomenon interesting enough to justify more extensive research. There are various questions that remain open when it comes to polylexemic compounds. This work has, for example, not been able to review semantic aspects to the extent necessary. This is merely due to space limitations, not because I deem these aspects to be uninteresting or unimportant, quite the contrary. It will certainly be fruitful to investigate whether the semantic relations found in three-word compounds are the same ones as those that are prevalent in two-word compounds, as well as to compare the semantic relations of left-branching and right-branching compounds. Furthermore, an investigation that contrasts the semantic differences in the use of a particular compound as a head and as a modifier can be expected to be insightful, analogously to what Bauer et al. (2019) have done for simple words. It can be expected that compounds like *football* feature distinctive semantic qualities in the function of head and modifier, each of which will foreground different semantic nuances. Semantic aspects will also be relevant when it comes to investigating why a particular compound is more productive in the head or modifier position.

As far as the data coverage is concerned, I was exclusively concerned with tripartite English noun compounds. While compounds consisting of three nouns can be assumed to be the most common form of polylexemic compounds in English, other kinds of tri-constituent compounds, as well as noun compounds with four constituents might be worth researching. In the data collection process, there were many instances of supposed three-word compounds in which both the head and modifier were complex, such as *newspaper headline* or *broadcast network*, i.e. instances that actually consist of four lexemes. It can be assumed that four-constituent compounds also mostly employ embedded compounds that are strongly established and entrenched. It will certainly be insightful to investigate the morphological structures found among these complex compounds, as theoretically the combination of four items would result in five possible options for hierarchical structures (cf. Section 5.1.5). A quantitative examination of the patterns that can give rise to four-constituent compounds – the most prevalent of which is presumably [[NN] [NN]] – as well as a qualitative analysis of these different patterns promises to be insightful. Another aspect that becomes potentially even more intriguing in compounds with more than three constituents is that of stress: Does a compound with the structure [[NN] [NN]] have a different stress pattern than one with the structure [[[NN]N]N]? Or does the stress pattern remain the same, no matter how complex a compound becomes?

Throughout this work I have explicitly pointed out aspects that deserve more extensive research that could not be provided in the framework of this book. I have performed a range of small-scale projects that can be seen as starting points for further exploration. The stress pattern in three-noun compounds, for example, requires more research with appropriate empirical testing equipment. Furthermore, the relationship between compounds and semantically equivalent syntactic phrases needs further research with a larger database. Moreover, the different aspects examined could not always be investigated separately for left- and right-branching compounds, as was the case in the analysis of compositionality, for example. Based on the observations shared in Section 7.4, however, it is conceivable that these two types of tripartite compounds show differences when it comes to their compositionality.

Many observations made in this book would benefit from further testing with more advanced methodology. The predictions made in Section 8.8 about the future formation of new three-noun compounds based on their presumed acceptability could be supported through an assessment by native speakers. An acceptability rating would provide a suitable methodology to verify whether novel formations from particular semantic areas will find higher degrees of acceptability. It would furthermore be beneficial to validate the different degrees of entrenchment through psycholinguistic testing. Moreover, contrasting the processing of left- and right-branching compounds is considered highly interesting, as well as the processing of those items whose branching pattern is unclear from a theoretical perspective.

Another aspect that I consider compelling is coordination in polylexemic structures, which is, however, probably more fruitful in the German language. Compare, for example, the formations *Behinderten- und Krankenfahrdienst* ('transport service for disabled people and patients') vs. *Kranken- und Pflegepersonenfahrt* ('ride for patients and care givers'). In both cases, the formal structure is identical; however, in the first case the omission expressed by the hyphen stands for the N2N3 word pair of the second compound (i.e. *Fahrdienst*), whereas in the second word pair the suspended hyphen replaces only the N3 of the second compound (i.e. *Fahrt*). It would be interesting to see how native speakers rate the acceptability of these two instances of coordination and whether the processing of such sequences shows any effects similar to those of garden-path sentences.

# References

Abbot-Smith, Kirsten & Michael Tomasello. 2006. Exemplar-learning and schematization in a usage-based account of syntactic acquisition. *The Linguistic Review* 23(3). 275–290.
Adams, Valerie. 2001. *Complex words in English*. Harlow: Longman.
Arnon, Inbal & Neal Snider. 2010. More than words: Frequency effects for multi-word phrases. *Journal of Memory and Language* 62(1). 67–82.
Augst, Gerhard. 1975. *Untersuchungen zum Morpheminventar der deutschen Gegenwartssprache*. Tübingen: Narr.
Baayen, Harald R. & Rochelle Lieber. 1991. Productivity and English derivation: A corpus-based study. *Linguistics* 29(5). 801–843.
Baayen, Harald R. 1992. Quantitative aspects of morphological productivity. In Geert Booij & Jaap van Marle (eds.), *Yearbook of Morphology (1991)*, 109–149. Dordrecht: Springer.
Baayen, Harald R. 1993. On frequency, transparency and productivity. In Geert Booij & Jaap van Marle (eds.), *Yearbook of Morphology (1992)*, 181–208. Dordrecht: Springer.
Baayen, Harald R. 2005. Morphological productivity. In Reinhard Köhler, Gabriel Altmann & Rajmund G. Piotrowski (eds.), *Quantitative Linguistics: An international handbook*, 243–255. Berlin: De Gruyter.
Baayen, Harald R. 2009. Corpus linguistics in morphology: Morphological productivity. In Anke Lüdeling (ed.), *Corpus linguistics. An international handbook*. Berlin: De Gruyter.
Baayen, Harald R. 2010. The directed compound graph of English: An exploration of lexical connectivity and its processing consequences. In Susan Olsen (ed.), *New Impulses in Word-Formation*, 383–402. Hamburg: Helmut Buske Verlag.
Baayen, R. H., Victor Kuperman & Raymond Bertram. 2010. Frequency effects in compound processing. In Sergio Scalise & Irene Vogel (eds.), *Cross-disciplinary issues in compounding*, 257–270. Amsterdam: John Benjamins.
Ball, Alice M. 1938. Uncle Sam and the compounding of words. *American Speech* 13(3). 169–174.
Ball, Alice M. 1941. *Compounding in the English language: A comparative review of variant authorities with a rational system for general use and a comprehensive alphabetic list of compound words*. New York: Wilson.
Ball, Alice M. 1951. *The compounding and hyphenation of English words*. New York: Funk & Wagnalls.
Barðdal, Jóhanna. 2008. *Productivity*. Amsterdam: John Benjamins.
Barlow, Michael & Suzanne Kemmer (eds.). 2000. *Usage-based models of language*. Stanford, California: CSLI Publications.
Bauer, Laurie. 1983a. *English word-formation*. Cambridge: Cambridge University Press.
Bauer, Laurie. 1983b. Stress in compounds: a rejoinder. *English Studies* 64(1). 47–53.
Bauer, Laurie. 1998. When is a sequence of two nouns a compound in English? *English Language and Linguistics* 2(1). 65–86.
Bauer, Laurie. 2001. *Morphological productivity*. Cambridge: Cambridge University Press.
Bauer, Laurie. 2005. Productivity: Theories. In Pavol Štekauer & Rochelle Lieber (eds.), *Handbook of word-formation*, 315–334. Netherlands: Springer.
Bauer, Laurie. 2017. *Compounds and compounding*. Cambridge: Cambridge University Press.
Bauer, Laurie & Rodney Huddleston. 2017. Lexical word-formation. In Rodney Huddleston & Geoffrey K. Pullum (eds.), *The Cambridge Grammar of the English Language*, 1621–1722. Cambridge: Cambridge University Press.

Bauer, Laurie, Natalia Beliaeva & Elizaveta Tarasova. 2019. Recalibrating productivity: Factors involved. *Zeitschrift für Wortbildung / Journal of Word Formation* 3(1). 44–80.

Bell, Melanie J. Martin Schäfer. 2013. Semantic transparency: challenges for distributional semantics. In Aurelie Herbelot, Roberto Zamparelli & Gemma Boleda (eds.), *Proceedings of the IWCS 2013 workshop: Towards a formal distributional semantics*, 1–10.

Bell, Melanie J. 2015. Basic relations and stereotype relations in the semantics of compound nouns. *Journal of Cognitive Science* 16(3). 224–260.

Benczes, Réka. 2006. *Creative compounding in English: The semantics of metaphorical and metonymical noun-noun combinations*. Amsterdam: John Benjamins.

Bertram, Raymond, Harald R. Baayen & Robert Schreuder. 2000. Effects of family size for complex words. *Journal of Memory and Language* 42(3). 390–405.

Bloomfield, Leonard. 1933. *Language*. New York: Holt.

Blumenthal-Dramé, Alice. 2012. *Entrenchment in usage-based theories*. Berlin: De Gruyter Mouton.

Blumenthal-Dramé, Alice. 2017. Entrenchment from a psycholinguistic and neurolinguistic perspective. In Hans-Jörg Schmid (ed.), *Entrenchment and the psychology of language learning: How we reorganize and adapt linguistic knowledge*, 129–152. Berlin: De Gruyter Mouton.

Booij, Geert E. 2010. *Construction morphology*. Oxford: Oxford University Press.

Bybee, Joan L. 1987. The evolution of future meaning. *Papers from the 7th International Conference on Historical Linguistics*. 109–122.

Bybee, Joan L. 2006. From usage to grammar: The mind's response to repetition. *Language* 82(4). 711–733.

Bybee, Joan L. 2007. *Frequency of use and the organization of language*. Oxford: Oxford University Press.

Bybee, Joan L. 2010. *Language, usage and cognition*. Cambridge: Cambridge University Press.

Carstairs-McCarthy, Andrew. 2018. *An introduction to English morphology: Words and their structure*. Edinburgh: Edinburgh University Press.

Chomsky, Noam & Morris Halle. 1968. *The sound pattern of English*. New York: Harper & Row.

Coolen, Riet, Henk J. van Jaarsveld & Robert Schreuder. 1991. The interpretation of isolated novel nominal compounds. *Memory and Cognition* 19(4). 341–352.

Croft, William. 2001. *Radical construction grammar: Syntactic theory in typological perspective*. Oxford: Oxford University Press.

Croft, William & Alan D. Cruse. 2004. *Cognitive Linguistics*. Cambridge: Cambridge University Press.

Dal, Georgette & Fiammetta Namer. 2016. Productivity. In Andrew Hippisley & Gregory Stump (eds.), *The Cambridge Handbook of Morphology*, 70–90. Cambridge: Cambridge University Press.

Davies, Mark. 2008. The Corpus of Contemporary American English: 520 million words, 1990–present. http://corpus.byu.edu/coca. (June 2021.)

Dell, Gary S. 1990. Effects of frequency and vocabulary type on phonological speech errors. *Language and Cognitive Processes* 5(4). 313–349.

Di Sciullo, Anna-Maria & Edwin Williams. 1990. *On the definition of word*. Cambridge: MIT Press.

Donalies, Elke. 2003. Hochzeitstorte, laskaparasol, elmas küpe, cow's milk, casa de campo, cigarette-filtre, ricasduenas . . . : Was ist eigentlich ein Kompositum? *Deutsche Sprache: Zeitschrift für Theorie, Praxis, Dokumentation* 31(1). 76–93.

Downing, Pamela. 1977. On the creation and use of English compound nouns. *Language* 53(4). 810–842.

Evert, Stephanie. 2005. *The statistics of word cooccurrences: Word pairs and collocations*. Stuttgart: Universität Stuttgart PhD dissertation.

Faiß, Klaus. 1981. Compound, pseudo-compound, and syntactic group especially in English. In Peter Kunsmann & Ortwin Kuhn (eds.), *Weltsprache Englisch in Forschung und Lehre: Festschrift für Kurt Wächtler*, 132–150. Berlin: Schmidt.

Foley, Louis. 1943. The how of the hyphen. *The Modern Language Journal* 27(6). 443–446.

Forster, Kenneth I. & Susan M. Chambers. 1973. Lexical access and naming time. *Journal of Verbal Learning and Verbal Behavior* 12(6). 627–635.

Gaeta, Livio & Davide Ricca. 2015. Productivity. In Peter O. Müller, Ingeborg Ohnheiser, Susan Olsen & Franz Rainer (eds.), *Word-formation: An international handbook of the languages of Europe*, 842–858. Berlin: De Gruyter.

Gagné, Christina L. & Edward J. Shoben. 1997. Influence of thematic relations on the comprehension of modifier–noun combinations. *Journal of Experimental Psychology: Learning, Memory, and Cognition* 23(1). 71–87.

Gagné, Christina L. & Thomas L. Spalding. 2006. Conceptual combination: Implications for the mental lexicon. In Gary Libben & Gonia Jarema (eds.), *The representation and processing of compound words*, 145–168. Oxford: Oxford University Press.

Giegerich, Heinz. 2009. The English compound stress myth. *Word Structure* 2(1). 1–17.

Giegerich, Heinz. 2015. *Lexical Structures*. Edinburgh: Edinburgh University Press.

Gobet, Fernand. 2017. Entrenchment, gestalt formation, and chunking. In Hans-Jörg Schmid (ed.), *Entrenchment and the psychology of language learning: How we reorganize and adapt linguistic knowledge*, 245–268. Berlin: De Gruyter Mouton.

Goldberg, Adele E. 2003. *Constructions: A construction grammar approach to argument structure*. Chicago: University of Chicago Press.

Goldberg, Adele E. 2006. *Constructions at work: The nature of generalization in language*. Oxford: Oxford University Press.

Goldberg, Adele E. 2016. Partial productivity of linguistic constructions: Dynamic categorization and statistical preemption. *Language and Cognition* 8(3). 369–390.

Hartsuiker, Robert J. & Agnes Moors. 2017. On the automaticity of language processing. In Hans-Jörg Schmid (ed.), *Entrenchment and the psychology of language learning: How we reorganize and adapt linguistic knowledge*, 201–226. Berlin: De Gruyter Mouton.

Haspelmath, Martin. 2010. *Understanding morphology*. London: Hodder Education.

Hauk, Olaf & Friedemann Pulvermüller. 2004. Effects of word length and frequency on the human event-related potential. *Clinical Neurophysiology* 115(5). 1090–1103.

Hay, Jennifer. 2001. Lexical frequency in morphology: Is everything relative?. *Linguistics* 39(6). 1041–1070.

Hein, Katrin & Stefan Engelberg. 2018. Morphological variation: The case of productivity in German compound formation. 36–50.

Hein, Katrin & Annelen Brunner. 2019. Why do some lexemes combine more frequently than others? An empirical approach to productivity in German compound formation. *Mediterranean Morphology Meetings* 12(1). 28–41.

Herbst, Thomas. 2010. *English linguistics: A coursebook for students of English*. Berlin: De Gruyter.

Heyvaert, Liesbet. 2011. Compounding in Cognitive Linguistics. In Rochelle Lieber & Pavol Štekauer (eds.), *The Oxford Handbook of Compounding*, 233–254. Oxford: Oxford University Press.

Hilpert, Martin. 2015. From hand-carved to computer-based: Noun-participle compounding and the upward-strengthening hypothesis. *Cognitive Linguistics* 26(1). 1–36.

Hilpert, Martin. 2018. Wie viele Konstruktionen stecken in einem Wortbildungsmuster? Eine Problematisierung des Produktivitätsbegriffs aus konstruktionsgrammatischer Sicht. In Stefan

Engelberg, Henning Lobin, Kathrin Steyer & Sascha Wolfer (eds.), *Wortschätze*, 91–106. Berlin: De Gruyter.

Huddleston, Rodney & Geoffrey K. Pullum (eds.). 2017. *The Cambridge Grammar of the English Language*. Cambridge: Cambridge University Press.

Jespersen, Otto. 1942. *A modern English grammar on historical principles: Morphology*. Copenhagen: Munksgard.

Ji, Hongbo, Christina L. Gagné & Thomas L. Spalding. 2011. Benefits and costs of lexical decomposition and semantic integration during the processing of transparent and opaque English compounds. *Journal of Memory and Language* 65(4). 406–430.

Jong, Nivja H. de, Robert Schreuder & R. Harald Baayen. 2000. The morphological family size effect and morphology. *Language and Cognitive Processes* 15(4–5). 329–365.

Juhasz, Barbara. 2007. The influence of semantic transparency on eye movements during English compound word recognition. In Roger P. G. van Gompel (ed.), *Eye movements: A window on mind and brain*, 373–390. Amsterdam: Elsevier Science.

Jurafsky, Daniel, Alan Bell, Michelle Gregory & William D. Raymond. 2001. Probabilistic relations between words. In Joan L. Bybee & Paul J. Hopper (eds.), *Frequency and the emergence of linguistic structure*, 229–254. Amsterdam: John Benjamins.

Kim, Su N. & Timothy Baldwin. 2006. Interpreting semantic relations in noun compounds via verb semantics. In Association for Computational Linguistics (ed.), *Proceedings of the COLING/ACL 2006 Main conference poster sessions*, 491–498.

Kopf, Kristin. 2018. The role of syntax in the productivity of German N+N comounds. A diachronic corpus study. *Zeitschrift für Wortbildung / Journal of Word Formation* 2(1). 61–92.

Krott, A., R. H. Baayen & R. Schreuder. 1999. Complex words in complex words. *Linguistics* 37(5). 905–926.

Krott, Andrea, Harald R. Baayen & Robert Schreuder. 2001. Analogy in morphology: Modeling the choice of linking morphemes in Dutch. *Linguistics* 39(1). 51–93.

Krott, Andrea, Robert Schreuder, Harald R. Baayen & Wolfgang U. Dressler. 2007. Analogical effects on linking elements in German compound words. *Language and Cognitive Processes* 22(1). 25–57.

Krott, Andrea. 2009. The role of analogy for compound words. In James P. Blevins & Juliette Blevins (eds.), *Analogy in Grammar*, 118–136. Oxford: Oxford University Press.

Kunter, Gero. 2011. *Compound stress in English. The phonetics and phonology of prosodic prominence*. Berlin: De Gruyter.

Lamberty, Angela & Hans-Jörg Schmid. 2013. Verbal compounding in English: A challenge for usage-based models of word-formation? *Anglia* 131(4). 591–626.

Langacker, Ronald W. 1987a. *Foundations of cognitive grammar: Vol. 1. Theoretical prerequisites*. Stanford, California: Stanford University Press.

Langacker, Ronald W. 1987b. Nouns and verbs. *Language* 63(1). 53–94.

Langacker, Ronald W. 1991. *Foundations of cognitive grammar: Vol. 2. Descriptive application*. Stanford, California: Stanford University Press.

Langacker, Ronald W. 2008. *Cognitive grammar: A basic introduction*. Oxford: Oxford University Press.

Langacker, Ronald W. 2009. *Investigations in Cognitive Grammar*. New York: De Gruyter.

Langacker, Ronald W. 2017. Entrenchment in Cognitive Grammar. In Hans-Jörg Schmid (ed.), *Entrenchment and the psychology of language learning: How we reorganize and adapt linguistic knowledge*, 39–56. Berlin: De Gruyter Mouton.

Lees, Robert B. 1968. *The grammar of English nominalizations*. The Hague: Mouton.

Levi, Judith N. 1978. *The syntax and semantics of complex nominals*. New York: Academic Press.

Levshina, Natalia. 2015. *How to do linguistics with R: Data exploration and statistical analysis.* Amsterdam: John Benjamins.

Libben, Gary, Martha Gibson, Yeo B. Yoon & Dominiek Sandra. 2003. Compound fracture: the role of semantic transparency and morphological headedness. *Brain and Language* 84(1). 50–64.

Libben, Gary & Gonia Jarema (eds.). 2006. *The representation and processing of compound words.* Oxford: Oxford University Press.

Lieber, Rochelle. 2010. *Introducing morphology.* Cambridge: Cambridge University Press.

Lieber, Rochelle & Pavol Štekauer. 2011a. Introduction: Status and definition of compounding. In Rochelle Lieber & Pavol Štekauer (eds.), *The Oxford Handbook of Compounding*, 3–18. Oxford: Oxford University Press.

Lieber, Rochelle & Pavol Štekauer (eds.). 2011b. *The Oxford Handbook of Compounding.* Oxford: Oxford University Press.

Lieber, Rochelle, Ingo Plag & Laurie Bauer. 2015. *The Oxford reference guide to English morphology.* Oxford: Oxford University Press.

Maaten, Laurens van der & Geoffrey Hinton. 2008. Visualizing data using t-SNE. *Journal of Machine Learning Research* 9. 2579–2605.

Marchand, Hans. 1960. *The categories and types of present-day English word-formation: A synchronic-diachronic approach.* Wiesbaden: Otto Harrassowitz.

Marchand, Hans. 1969. *The categories and types of present-day English word-formation.* Munich: Beck.

Olsen, Susan. 2000. Composition. In G. E. Booij, Christian Lehmann & Joachim Mugdan (eds.), *Morphologie: Ein internationales Handbuch zur Flexion und Wortbildung*, 897–916. Berlin: De Gruyter.

Ortner, Lorelies & Hanspeter Ortner (eds.). 1984. *Zur Theorie und Praxis der Kompositaforschung: Mit einer ausführlichen Bibliographie.* Tübingen: Narr.

Perek, Florent. 2016. Using distributional semantics to study syntactic productivity in diachrony: A case study. *Linguistics* 54(1). 149–188.

Plag, Ingo. 2003. *Word-formation in English.* Cambridge: Cambridge University Press.

Plag, Ingo. 2006a. Productivity. In Bas Aarts & April McMahon (eds.), *The Handbook of English Linguistics*, 537–556. Malden, MA, USA: Blackwell Publishing.

Plag, Ingo. 2006b. The variability of compound stress in English: Structural, semantic, and analogic factors. *English Language and Linguistics* 10(1). 143–172.

Plag, Ingo, Gero Kunter & Sabine Lappe. 2007. Testing hypotheses about compound stress assignment in English. A corpus-based investigation. *Corpus Linguistics and Linguistic Theory* 3(2). 199–232.

Plag, Ingo, G. Kunter, S. Lappe & M. Braun. 2008. The role of semantics, argument structure, and lexicalization in compound stress assignment in English. *Language* 84(4). 760–794.

Plag, Ingo. 2010. Compound stress assignment by analogy: The constituent family bias. *Zeitschrift für Sprachwissenschaft* 29(2). 243–282.

Plag, Ingo & Melanie J. Bell. 2012. Informativeness is a determinant of compound stress in English. *Journal of Linguistics* 48(3). 485–520.

Plag, Ingo, Sabine Arndt-Lappe, Maria Braun & Mareile Schramm. 2015. *Introduction to English Linguistics.* Berlin: De Gruyter.

Quirk, Randolph, Sidney Greenbaum & Geoffrey Leech (eds.). 1985. *A comprehensive grammar of the English language.* London: Longman.

Ryder, Mary E. 1994. *Ordered chaos: The interpretation of English noun-noun compounds.* Berkeley: University of California Press.

Sanchez-Stockhammer, Christina. 2018. *English compounds and their spelling*. Cambridge: Cambridge University Press.
Sandra, Dominiek. 1994. *Morphology in the reader's mental lexicon*. Frankfurt am Main: Lang.
Scalise, Sergio & Irene Vogel (eds.). 2010. *Cross-disciplinary issues in compounding*. Amsterdam: John Benjamins.
Scalise, Sergio & Antonietta Bisetto. 2011. The classification of compounds. In Rochelle Lieber & Pavol Štekauer (eds.), *The Oxford Handbook of Compounding*, 34–53. Oxford: Oxford University Press.
Schäfer, Martin. 2018. *The semantic transparency of English compound nouns*. Berlin: Language Science Press.
Schäfer, Martin & Melanie J. Bell. 2020. Constituent polysemy and interpretational diversity in attested English novel compounds. *The Mental Lexicon* 15(1). 42–61.
Schmid, Hans-Jörg. 2000. *English abstract nouns as conceptual shells. From corpus to cognition*. Berlin: De Gruyter.
Schmid, Hans-Jörg. 2007. Entrenchment, Salience, and Basic Levels. In Dirk Geeraerts & Hubert Cuyckens (eds.), *The Oxford Handbook of Cognitive Linguistics*, 117–138. Oxford: Oxford University Press.
Schmid, Hans-Jörg. 2008. New words in the mind: Concept-formation and entrenchment of neologisms. *Anglia* 126(1). 1–36.
Schmid, Hans-Jörg. 2010. Does frequency in text really instantiate entrenchment in the cognitive system? In Dylan Glynn & Kerstin Fischer (eds.), *Quantitative methods in cognitive semantics: Corpus-driven approaches*, 101–133. Berlin: De Gruyter Mouton.
Schmid, Hans-Jörg & Helmut Küchenhoff. 2013. Collostructional analysis and other ways of measuring lexicogrammatical attraction: Theoretical premises, practical problems and cognitive underpinnings. *Cognitive Linguistics* 24. 531–577.
Schmid, Hans-Jörg. 2014. Lexico-grammatical patterns, pragmatic associations and discourse frequency. In Thomas Herbst, Hans-Jörg Schmid & Susen Faulhaber (eds.), *Constructions Collocations Patterns*, 239–293. Berlin: De Gruyter.
Schmid, Hans-Jörg. 2015. A blueprint of the Entrenchment-and- Conventionalization Model. *Yearbook of the German Cognitive Linguistics Association* 3(1). 3–25.
Schmid, Hans-Jörg. 2016. *English morphology and word-formation: An introduction*. Berlin: Erich Schmidt Verlag.
Schmid, Hans-Jörg. 2017a. A framework for understanding linguistic entrenchment and its psychological foundations. In Hans-Jörg Schmid (ed.), *Entrenchment and the psychology of language learning: How we reorganize and adapt linguistic knowledge*, 9–35. Berlin: De Gruyter Mouton.
Schmid, Hans-Jörg (ed.). 2017b. *Entrenchment and the psychology of language learning: How we reorganize and adapt linguistic knowledge*. Berlin: De Gruyter Mouton.
Schmid, Hans-Jörg. 2017c. Linguistic entrenchment and its psychological foundations. In Hans-Jörg Schmid (ed.), *Entrenchment and the psychology of language learning: How we reorganize and adapt linguistic knowledge*, 435–452. Berlin: De Gruyter Mouton.
Schmid, Hans-Jörg. 2020. *The dynamics of the linguistic system: Usage, conventionalization, and entrenchment*. Oxford: Oxford University Press.
Smet, Hendrik de & Hubert Cuyckens. 2007. Diachronic aspects of complementation: Constructions, entrenchment, and the matching problem. In Christopher M. Cain & Geoffrey Russom (eds.), *Shaking the tree: Fresh perspectives on the genealogy of English*, 187–213. Berlin: De Gruyter.

Stefanowitsch, Anatol & Susanne Flach. 2017. The corpus-based perspective on entrenchment. In Hans-Jörg Schmid (ed.), *Entrenchment and the psychology of language learning: How we reorganize and adapt linguistic knowledge*, 101–128. Berlin: De Gruyter Mouton.
Štekauer, Pavol. 2000. *English word-formation. A history of research (1960–1995)*. Tübingen: Gunter Narr.
Stumpf, Sören. 2021. Passe-partout-Komposita im gesprochenen Deutsch. Konstruktionsgrammatische und interaktionslinguistische Zugänge im Rahmen einer pragmatischen Wortbildung. *Zeitschrift für germanistische Linguistik* 49. 1–51.
Suttle, Laura & Adele E. Goldberg. 2011. The partial productivity of constructions as induction. *Linguistics* 49(6). 1237–1269.
Tarasova, Elizaveta. 2013. *Some new insights into the semantics of English N+N compounds*. Wellington: Victoria University PhD dissertation.
Tarasova, Elizaveta. 2019. Productivity of form and productivity of meaning in N+N compounds. *SKASE Journal of Theoretical Linguistics* 16(1). 49–69.
Taylor, John R. 2002. *Cognitive Grammar*. Oxford: Oxford University Press.
Turney, Peter D. & Patrick Pantel. 2010. From frequency to meaning: Vector space models of semantics. *Journal of Artificial Intelligence Research* 37. 141–188.
Ungerer, Friedrich & Hans-Jörg Schmid. 1998. Englische Komposita und Kategorisierung: Eine empirische Untersuchung. *Rostocker Beiträge zur Sprachwissenschaft* 5. 77–99.
Ungerer, Friedrich & Hans-Jörg Schmid. 2013. *An introduction to cognitive linguistics*. Harlow: Pearson Longman.
Vaan, Laura de, Robert Schreuder & R. H. Baayen. 2007. Regular morphologically complex neologisms leave detectable traces in the mental lexicon. *The Mental Lexicon* 2(1). 1–23.
Warren, Beatrice. 1978. Semantic patterns of noun-noun compounds. Göteborg: Acta Universitatis Gothoburgensis.
Zipf, George K. 1935. *The psycho-biology of language*. Boston: Houghton Miflin.
Zwitserlood, Pinie. 1994. The role of semantic transparency in the processing and representation of Dutch compounds. *Language and Cognitive Processes* 9(3). 341–368.

# Subject index

3N database  32, 35, 47, 50, 59–60, 67, 77, 79, 93, 95, 97, 99, 101, 105, 107, 109, 111, 114, 121

affix  13, 15, 36–37, 65, 70, 146–147
association strength  178, 183, 185, 189–190

BNC  19, 96
branching patterns  13, 35–37, 40, 47, 50, 70, 79, 88, 101–102, 107, 239

chunking  193, 204–205
COCA  19, 21, 23, 27, 31, 39, 51, 76, 80, 105, 111, 114, 126, 131, 135, 178
cognitive network  193, 195, 202, 215, 228
compositionality  11, 118–119, 138
Compound Stress Rule  8, 86–87
conventionalization  75, 197–198, 200
corpus  19–21, 197
corpus-as-input view  200, 202
corpus-as-output view  200, 202
corpus-to-cognition-principle  197, 200

EC-Model  198
embedded compound  16, 21, 23, 35, 51, 69, 76, 85, 94, 104, 120, 123, 126, 145, 148, 178, 212, 239
entrenchment  193–195, 197, 199–200, 203, 205, 207, 209–210

fake compounds  25
frequency  51, 95, 181, 190

genre  110–112, 135, 239

head  6, 9–10, 13, 65, 94, 104

lexicalization  10, 118–119, 121, 140, 184

modifier  6, 9–10, 13, 69, 85, 88, 94, 106
morphological complexity  63, 70, 178
morphological structure  13, 36, 38, 40, 44, 49, 51, 73, 78, 88, 92, 102

OALD  100
OED  27, 64, 100, 188

paradigmatic associations  195–196, 206, 208, 211, 218–220, 225, 230, 232–233
paraphrasing  36, 40–42
pattern  167
pragmatic associations  195–196, 206–207
productivity  145, 147–148, 157, 167, 177, 193, 215

realized productivity  148
recursivity  12, 15
routinization  194–195, 197, 206, 217

salience  183, 199, 208
schematization  194, 216–217, 219–220, 227–228
semantic productivity  167, 231
semantic relations  9, 176
simple compounds  7, 15, 85–86, 120, 148
spelling  7, 20, 72–73, 76, 79, 239
stress  8, 10–11, 14, 45, 85, 88, 239–240
syllables  60, 68, 179
symbolic associations  195–196, 206–208, 214, 218, 228
syntactic phrases  10, 97, 125–127, 131, 137
syntagmatic associations  195, 203–206, 208–211, 218–219, 224
syntagmatic-strengthening principle  205, 207

transparency  119, 121

www.ingramcontent.com/pod-product-compliance
Lightning Source LLC
Chambersburg PA
CBHW050520170426
43201CB00013B/2022